Goddess of the Americas
La Diosa de las Américas

Goddess of the Americas
La Diosa de las Américas

WRITINGS ON
THE VIRGIN OF GUADALUPE

edited by Ana Castillo

Riverhead Books New York 1996

Riverhead Books
a division of G. P. Putnam's Sons
Publishers Since 1838
200 Madison Avenue
New York, NY 10016

A list of permissions can be found on page 229.

Library of Congress Cataloging-in-Publication Data

Goddess of the Americas/La diosa de las Américas:
Writings on the Virgin of Guadalupe / edited by
    Ana Castillo.
        p.   cm.
    English and Spanish.
    ISBN 1-57322-029-9
    1. Guadalupe, Our Lady of.   I. Castillo, Ana.
    BT660.G8G59   1996   96-25860 CIP
    232.91'7'097253—dc20

Printed in the United States of America
10   9   8   7   6   5   4   3   2   1

This book is printed on acid-free paper. ∞

Book design by Iris Weinstein

A Note on Italics

*T*raditional usage requires that languages other than English in a predominantly English text be set in italics. Some of the authors in this anthology adhere to this practice in their fiction and poetry; others have chosen not to differentiate between the two languages. This anthology respects the different style each author prefers to use in their work.

Acknowledgments

*F*irst, we give Her thanks, Our Mother. Out of Her boundless love for us grow all things magnificent, big and small—including this book which we offer to all those who love Her.

I would like to thank Riverhead's Julie Grau and her assistants, Nicky Weinstock and Nicole Wan. Julie Grau is the editor behind the scenes of this book and I am completely indebted to her for helping to bring it to fruition. I thank her and Riverhead for the opportunity to pay homage to Our Mother by way of this collection. Also, Susan Bergholz, my agent and the agent of a number of the contributors here, deserves special recognition. Among the many new agnostic devotees of Guadalupe, she brought this project to me and has generously given herself to its development and completion.

I thank the National Endowment for the Arts for a second writers' fellowship. I pray that funding will continue to help our writers and artists to breathe life into the soul of this country.

I would like to thank all the writers here, past and present, who have contemplated Her name and lent their own names to this book. My personal thanks to Elsa Saeta for her research assistance, her constant support, and for the blessing of her unconditional friendship. Special thanks go to dear Clarissa Pinkola Estés for her support, her friendship, her contribution, but especially for her *don* of storytelling, which helped me complete my own essay included here.

In my life, there are many whose love gives me strength and encouragement. They know who they are and they are remembered every day in my thoughts and meditations.

In Her name,

Ana Castillo
May 12, 1996, *día de las madres*
Chicago

In Her name—
Whose Love is Endless,
Who has never abandoned us.
On the contrary, we have
left Her too long.
These humble words are offered to
Her, a simple knock on Her door:
Mother, we have returned.
Forgive our absence, neglect,
and ingratitude please.

Contents

Introduction

We call Her the Virgin of Guadalupe or Our Lady of Guadalupe. The Spaniards christened her Nuestra Señora Santa María de Guadalupe, the Virgin Mary imported from Guadalupe, Extremadura, the province in Spain where many of the conquistadors, including Cortés, originated. The name Guadalupe is a corruption of Arabic meaning *río de amor, río de luz* river of love, river of light. Let us recall that the year the Spaniards set sail to the New World was the year of the Reconquest of Spain, when Spain regained its independence after more than seven centuries of Islamic domination. Their Catholicism was fervent and indomitable during that point in their own volatile history. Santa María de Guadalupe is the name she was dubbed by the colonists, just as Tenochtitlan became simply Mexico, just as every stretch of land, desert, forest, shore, island in the New World was renamed, as if a name did not exist before; and with the new name a new belief, a firm and tangible idea thick as a vine, was given over to sustain the lives and the souls of those who were here before the European conquest.

We know Her as the Virgin of Guadalupe, but She was known by many other names, before and after the Conquest of Mexico, as She is known throughout the world by other names today. According to information given in the *Nican Mopohua*—a post-Conquest Nahuatl account of the Virgin of Guadalupe's five visitations in 1531—when officials asked Juan Diego's *tío* Juan Bernardino, he may have responded that She had called Herself Tequatlasupe. Effective translation of language only works when you have similar symbols in both languages and, to be sure, a sense of the culture from which the other language derives. The Church officials, therefore, proceeded not to translate at all, but to make Castilian sense of the Nahuatl; and this is how, according to many scholars throughout the ages, they came up with Guadalupe, patroness of Extremadura, Spain. Whereas we don't find the consonants *b, d, f, g, r, y, s* in Nahuatl but an abundance of *l, x, t, z, tl, tz,* the name She imparted to Juan Diego and his uncle may have been Tequatlanopeuh: She Whose Origins Were in the Rocky Summit.

Most Mexicans and Mexic-Amerindians recognize Her as Tonantzin, "Our Mother." Our Mother was every mountain, every summit, sometimes hand-built, on which one could climb and pray to Mother Earth. But there was, in fact, one particular summit, the one of Tepeyac, where She appeared to the recently converted Aztec, Juan Diego—Our Lady of Tepeyac—and where She insisted Her temple be built. Four times She appeared, four being a sacred number of completion for indigenous peoples everywhere. It is the total number of the four cardinal points—the elements, air, fire, water, land. And there is one more number, one to make it complete, the center. She appeared, a fifth time, to Juan Diego's uncle, who lay on his petate, gravely ill, and who recovered after the visitation.

When the Spanish Church officials went to Juan Diego's home—home meaning un jacal, a humble shack with a dirt floor, as modest as any inhabited by an impoverished being of the indigenous race ten years after the Conquest and still today—to question his uncle, some sources claim Juan Bernardino answered: "She calls herself Tlecuauhtlacupeuh." Tlecuauhtlacupeuh does not translate as the Christian Mary. Tlecuauhtlacupeuh means She Who Comes Flying from the Light Like an Eagle of Fire. The region of light, one might readily say, was and is the Christian's heaven. But the region of light in Aztec religion was also where the gods resided. And, as most any Mexican knows, the eagle as a symbol was always seen as a sign from the gods. She may have identified herself or Juan Diego may have identified her to the Spanish officials, as some scholars speculate, as Tequantlaxopeuh: She Who Banishes Those That Ate Us. And yet one more Nahuatl alternative offers us a similar suggestion—Coatlaxopeuh: She Who Crushed the Serpent's Head.

If we look to our past in order to help explain why we are here, the Conquered Mexic-Amerindians may have turned to the Mother—and it was She who responded—to bring comfort, assurance, hope, when their mighty male gods became silent. As heirs to a militant imperialist patriarchy, the Supreme God was imaged as Father made manifest by the sun, too great to descend upon the earth and explain the terrible downfall of the empire. So it is the gentle nurturing mother archetype that appears and speaks with such melodic tenderness that it was compared to the singing of birds, flor y canto—that is, beauty and truth. It sounded like music never heard before. She identified herself to Juan Diego in the following ways, all immediately recognizable in the Aztec religion, as they are the five names given to the Supreme God of the Nahua people:

Inninantzin in huelneli Teotl Dios: Mother of the True God.
Inninantzin inipalnemohuani: Mother of the Giver of Life.
Inninantzin in Teyocoyani: Mother of the Inventor of Humanity.
Inninantzin in Tloque Nahuaque: Mother of the Lord of Near and Far (this in fact is the name of the omnipotent, invisible Supreme Creator known to the pre-Conquest Mexicans).
Inninantzin in Ilhicahua in Tlalticpaque: Mother of (the Lord of) Heaven and Earth.

For ages men everywhere have shown themselves to have great power over laws and man. Men and women alike, therefore, were forced by the nature of our society and those societies from which we descend to keep their distance and pay revenue and reverence to the male figure(s) in power. What we are left in need of, then, is something—an idea, an image—to comfort us when law and regulations are imposed without mercy on our personal needs. This is what She assures Juan Diego when he expresses his concerns about his uncle, gravely ill with smallpox, a new and deadly disease to the Indian people. She asks five questions, five times assuring him of her unconditional, ever-present maternal love—again, five being beyond the number of completion but also the center, the sum of totality:

> Am I not here, your Mother?
> Are you not under my shadow and protection?
> Am I not your foundation of life?
> Are you not in the folds of my mantle, in the crossing of
>   my arms?
> Is there anything else you need?

Men in pursuit of power, conquest, battles to be won, would see a goddess as their divine protectress. Our Lady of Guadalupe led the battle for independence from Spain by way of the banner held by Father Hidalgo. In the United States, in recent times, the late leader of the United Farmworkers Union, César Chávez, carried Her banner forth in his relentless struggle for economic justice for the farmworkers.

Like all mythistory there is no one version, one meaning, handed down to subsequent generations. The image, infused as much with the legend as with mystery and endless meaning, is a fusion of Byzantine artform and Native American naturalism. But it is not an image painted in the tradition of native iconography. Therefore, neither scholar of the subject nor theologian, I remain— like all heirs of Mexican sentiments, students of the theme, Catholics and lapsed Catholics alike—mystified.

Myths are the stories that explain a people's beliefs about their purpose for living and their reason for dying. The stories are often told through allegory and parable to facilitate a cultural understanding of what is by its nature perhaps too complex for the general populace to grasp. The Mexican indigenous account of the apparitions of the Mother Goddess is rich with Nahua symbolism and meaning. To ignore the meaning the account of Her apparitions may have had for the Nahua people, merely ten years after the violent conquest and destruction of their world, and despite their recent (imposed) conversion to Catholicism, would be a travesty.

The Aztecs maintained a hierarchical caste system of their own which was demolished and rendered ineffective by the Conquest when all indigenous people became slaves and servants. The first version of the account of the apparitions is that of the Virgin Mary appearing to a representative of the newest converts of the Catholic Church, a servant and subject of the queen, Juan Diego. However, the indigenous interpretation, not commonly known, reveals layers of sophisticated and noble understanding of Our Mother. According to the *Nican Mopohua*, Juan Diego's Nahuatl name before he was baptized was Cuauhtlatóhuac. In English this would translate to He Who Speaks Like an Eagle. In Nahuatl, an intrinsically symbolic language, the eagle represented the sun, and the sun was a god. There existed an order of nobility of elders who were of the eagle. Such a name suggests that Juan Diego, although among the humblest of the new society created by New Spain, may have been considered an elder speaker of his people. He was on his way to Mass and to Catholic instruction when She appeared to him. When he explained that he was on his way to Her house, She insisted that he ask the Church officials to build Her temple there, on the mount of Tepeyac, the same where the Mexica goddess had been worshiped. Their conversations are filled with moving expressions of mutual tenderness and respect. If she calls him "the smallest of my children," he calls her "my little girl." Today, a close listener of Mexic-Amerindian speakers will note the tendency to make diminutive everyone and everything by way of showing affection and care.

Unlike the Virgin Mary's apparitions in Europe—where language, faith, and custom were already in place—in Mexico we have a confrontation of beliefs that serve opposing social and cultural interests, and yet, within a theological context, uncannily fit like a Chinese puzzle and do not contradict each other. Tonantzin is a mother of a god; Holy Mary is the mother of Jesus; both are referred to as the Mother of God.

La Virgen wears the fertility sash, She is *en cinta*, pregnant, but the little symbol of the forthcoming child that dangles below it is the nagvioli flower, which represented Huitzilopochtli, the great, ferocious sun god of the Aztecs. Guadalupe is Coatlicue, mother of Huitzilopochtli.

Every detail of Her image defies comfortable explanations of any kind. The *tilma*[1] is of a coarse fabric woven from the maguey (the same succulent cactus from which tequila is made). Despite the rough fiber, there is depth to the painting not found in pre-Conquest iconography. She is supremely sublime, a sacred version of Da Vinci's Mona Lisa, the same mysterious smile, skin not pale but not the coffee bean color of the full-blood Nahua. Perhaps She wasn't "olive-skinned" at all, as has been vastly claimed, but Her translucent face was gold, a woman bathed in gold. In the Nahua belief, a person's face, like a personality, tells who the person is; She was bathed in gold, a metal reserved for nobility and for the sacred. Her mantle, which covers Her head, is not a queenly crown but similar to the rebozo used by Indian women; it is the color of the quetzal—a highland bird whose feathers also were quite valuable and used only to connote nobility and that which is holy. And while it is only a matter of personal opinion, those eyes, eyebrows, and nose are more reminiscent of Her supposed Basque origins than suggestive of any kinship to Juan Diego. It is even speculated, as a result of close examination, that Her delicate hands were once long-fingered but shortened to resemble more closely those of an Indian.

And returning to those mesmerizing downcast eyes, the eyes of a Madonna without question, thought for centuries to be the green ones of a mestiza—they are peopled, not pupiled! In recent years, through the process of digitalization, a number of unidentified figures have been discovered in each eye. Easy to dismiss as inkblots except that exactly the same image appears in each eye. Simply the reflection of Juan Diego, but Gandhi-style, mostly bare and in the lotus prayer position? No, there is also a friar, and a black woman lamenting. A woman all in black or a black woman, like the servant of the bishop who is said to have been witness to the event? What is really going on in there? Even for a skeptic, it's enough to lose sleep over. This is indeed one of the great mysteries that no expert, ophthalmologist or computer engineer, has been able to explain aptly. Indeed, that the painting has been tampered with is easy to detect now that the little cherub at Her feet is peeling. The crown

---

[1] This is the coarse fabric worn by Juan Diego on which the Virgin of Guadalupe's image is said to have miraculously appeared.

over Her head is also fading. Though the composition of the pigment is not yet known and the fabric is not a fine, durable linen like those on which European masterpieces are preserved, but a coarse fibrous cloth akin to burlap, which usually wears out in a dozen years or so, Her image of nearly five hundred years remains immaculately preserved with no indications of human interference.

In homage to Our Mother, at the end of this century and the end of a millennium of migrations, miscegenation, conquests, and endless hope and prayer, these writings and contemplations on Guadalupe-Tonantzin have been gathered. They are as diverse as each individual, as individual as the shape of a nose. But if they don't all share the faith of the throngs who journey to Her temple every December 12 in Mexico City, they all have in common respect for Her and Her power over the social and spiritual lives of millions.

The feminist writers place emphasis on recapturing Our Mother's omnipotence, retrieving the feminine face of God. "What message does Our Lady of Guadalupe offer to the spiritual orphans of the twentieth century through the metaphor of mother? That we are lovable and capable, that we belong, that we can grow and be transformed, and that there is a reason to live and a reason to hope," the scholar Jeanette Rodriguez writes. "She gives them not the will to suffer under injustice, but the will to continue *la lucha* (the struggle)." The poet Pat Mora gives a sassy rendition of the Aztec's astronomical account of Coatlicue giving birth in the cosmos, giving birth to the cosmos.

Men, too, have come to the controversial fold. Dr. F. Gonzalez-Crussi offers a delectable, informative piece on the evolution of the goddess since the Conquest. The performance artist Guillermo Gómez-Peña states in his essay that although he acknowledged it as "irrational," he once believed that the Virgin of Guadalupe was the sole domain of the feminists. The call to contribute an essay for this project served as a personal challenge, which he discusses here in his recognizable invigorating style.

Guadalupe, Our Mother by any other name, is the domain of no one save those who love Her. Luisah Teish, native daughter of New Orleans and devotee of the Orishas, practitioner of her

African ancestors' beliefs, evokes Guadalupe as "Oya, the Wind Mother, the Warrior Queen, a freedom fighter." The descendant of slaves brought, as we know, under horrendous conditions to these shores, she thanks Guadalupe for receiving her people, for Her embrace, protection, and love in their struggle for freedom.

"Jews must be everywhere," writes Miriam Sagan, a poet who resides in New Mexico and whose poems here reflect a fascination and deep connection between all that is Mexican Catholic and her own traditions. Denise Chávez, the New Mexican writer and playwright, has devoted a one-woman show, the narrative given in its entirety here, to contemporary women of her own culture, each linked by her devotion to Our Lady of Guadalupe. Had Nancy Mairs, another contributor to this volume, not moved to Tucson from New England, where her inherited Protestant religion offered her neither the Virgin Mary nor "any feminine figure, for that matter," she thinks she never would have discovered the mestiza María. "Thanks perhaps to a persistent Protestant intractability, I have an uneasy relationship with the miraculous," she states. But as a peace activist, she finds the story of Guadalupe infused with real and vital sociopolitical meaning.

Such testimonies recur here: from Richard Rodriguez, Margaret Randall, and the Jewish Mexican cultural critic Felipe Ehrenberg, among others. But political activism and faith are not mutually exclusive; nor does skepticism or lapsed Catholicism exclude complete devotion to Our Mother. Luis Rodríguez, known best perhaps for his work with gang youth and his own related experiences as recounted in his book *Always Running*, states here, "I've learned that the Creator has many faces, many languages, and that all religions worship the same transcendent reality, but give it a different name." Journalist-writers Rubén Martínez and Francisco Goldman also combine love of the Mother with the complexities of Latino masculine identities, and their political assessments of the United States, Mexico, and Central America. In a spirited essay on current issues that directly relate the United States and Mexico today, Martínez says of Guadalupe, "It's no coincidence that she's been appearing more often lately. In times of crisis, she's always there. Today, the crisis is on both sides of the border." Goldman, who also recalls the painful recent events in Guatemala involving massacres of innocent indigenous peoples, places Guadalupe alongside a male Mayan god–cum–pseudo Catholic saint, Maximón–San Simón, "whom the times do seem to have been calling out for." The poet Francisco X. Alarcón, having attended numerous funerals for friends who died of AIDS, wrote as an elegy the moving poem "Tlazolteotl," which evokes one of the many faces of the Mexica Mother Goddess. And yet we may still set our sights on the future of such conviction in the tender call from the unshakably faithful in Clarissa Pinkola Estés's essay, "The Path of the Broken Heart," in which she instructs young devotees of Our Lady of Guadalupe on how to serve Her through acts and deeds.

The experience of Guadalupe is not necessarily a somber one, even if it is always transcendental. There are lighter, extremely personal accounts of Guadalupe's meaning, which may place a frown on the conservative guadalupanos, but we make no claim to represent the Catholic Church here, thank goddess. The only claim we make is our right to love Her. Elena Poniatowska, premier Mexican writer, makes this point in her near-surrealist story of a visit to a men's prison with the late Spanish director Luis Buñuel, in her jewel of an essay " 'Don't Go Away, I'm Going to Bring You Something.' " The tale does not involve Guadalupe right away, as most of the narratives here do, but don't go away; Poniatowska's promise is not a shallow one.

They are all humble offerings, the poems, essays, stories, and dramatic writings gathered here, an unorthodox rosary, worn worry beads on which to meditate. Many of the contributors, for all their renown, were very hesitant, even nervous about discussing their love of Our Mother and what She means to them, which is always and foremost as private to each person as a prayer. These writings also all serve as impassioned testimony of the need for recognition of Mother in a world that is hanging by a thin thread of hope. I offer this collection to the reader in Her name. The thread is a golden cable; let's grab for it, catch it fast. Her love is waiting.

Ana Castillo
May 12, 1996, Mother's Day
Chicago

Conocí a la Virgen de Guadalupe en Extremadura, España, y la nuestra la mexicana, es más guapa. Creo estar enamorado de la imagen de la Virgen de Guadalupe.

I saw the Virgin of Guadalupe in Extremadura, Spain, and our Mexican one is better-looking. I think I am in love with the image of the Virgin of Guadalupe.

—JUAN GABRIEL
Contemporary Mexican composer

The Anatomy of a Virgin

F. GONZALEZ-CRUSSI

Strange to tell, my memories of Our Lady of Guadalupe are largely olfactory. Perhaps it is no coincidence that a religious symbol should abide in the perceptions of the most subtle, most ethereal, and least intellectual of the senses. Above all, I remember the aroma of *gorditas*, the disc-shaped small cakes made of a maize-based dough, baked by humble vendors on rustic braziers outside the church, and sold in cylindrical stacks wrapped in brightly colored cellophane paper twisted at each end. Next, the smell of burnt copal, the fossil resin that from time immemorial has been used as incense in Mexico. And lastly, the strong smell of the unkempt crowds, the all-pervading, animal emanations of the sweating, pressing, eddying multitudes that throng in the ample esplanade of the basilica of Guadalupe, mercilessly devoid of shelter under a vertical sun.

So what if all these scents were incidental, alien to the religious ideas and inimical to the respect and quiet contrition that the place was supposed to inspire? To me, they are still powerful, elemental memories. They are the threads that hold my past history together and ensure its integrity. I am convinced that I shall remain able to recollect their pungency, their unctuous, visceral, indescribable character, until the day I die. Still more, their disappearance will be the best proof that I have died. For the dead are those who have forgotten, those in whom the core memories—sights, sounds, or scents—have dissolved, washed out by the stream of forgetfulness. Apollonius of Rhodes wrote (*Argonauts* I, 463) that Hermes, in order to render immortal his half-human son, began by giving him an unchanging memory, that despite traversing the Acheron, and commuting between the reign of shadows and the kingdom of light, "he should always remember what he had seen." Just so, while alive, I must remember those scents.

Almost all else I have forgotten. I could not tell, for instance, the reason for our visit to the shrine. I vaguely recall that a conflict's tension had suddenly relaxed; that a problem had vanished when its unyielding crush was at its most painful. It could have been the unexpected recovery of a sum of money long given up for lost, precisely in time to avert the landlord's eviction order, or just as the bank was about to close in on us and repossess its property. Or it could have been the normal results of laboratory tests when all seemed to indicate the onset of a serious illness. Adversity takes so many forms to torment an unskilled, uneducated young widow who struggles to raise two children alone! The fact is, Providence extended to us a magnanimous hand in the nick of time. And this happened—my mother had not the slightest doubt about that—through the intercession of the swarthy Madonna, whose succor she had assiduously beseeched. Which is why she declared, with a peremptory tone calculated to undo my childish resistance: "I promised *Her* that we would go." Even a child could understand that one does not default on a promise to the deity.

With no little astonishment, I watched the simple directness with which my mother addressed her earnest thanks to the celestial queen for her magnanimous dispensation. I was then told that her image, displayed on the main altar, was not the product of human hands, but the handiwork of supernatural powers. Later that day, I saw the anonymous eighteenth-century painting kept in the basilica's treasury that represents the actual performance of the portent. God the Father is depicted here with the usual ingenuous and somewhat childish anthropomorphism then fashionable. He seems to be the same old gentleman that Michelangelo portrayed on the ceiling of the Sistine Chapel extending his right forefinger in the procreative gesture that brought forth Adam from his inchoate condition. Same rich mane of hair, dignified white beard and white robe; same left-sided manly profile; but all this, of course, in mediocre technique, sadly lacking the power of the Italian master. The Almighty appears here in the guise of a painter, sitting on an artist's chair, palette and brushes in his left hand while with the right he delivers the finishing brushstrokes to the Virgin's portrait. God is performing this work on a piece of coarse cloth: it is the cloak of Juan Diego, a humble Indian to whom the Virgin appeared, and presumably the selfsame fabric that is shown on the main altar today. The cloth is not resting on an easel, but is borne on the hands of adipose little angels who watch the execution of the portrait with visible contentment on their faces, as do two pairs of disembodied, winged cherubim. Behind the divine portraitist stands a blue-robed Jesus Christ with outstretched arms, in a gesture of elation. With the right hand, between his index finger and thumb, he holds a rose. In front of him, at chest level, flies the white dove of the Holy Spirit. At the bottom of the painting, two angels extend a flowing, horizontal tape on which is inscribed *Non fecit taliter omni nationi*—She has not done so with any other nation—words taken from Psalms 147:20, and reportedly uttered in amazement by Pope Benedict XIV when he was first shown a copy of the miraculous portrait.

No Mexican can ignore the powerful, simple faith manifested by her worshipers. Some deplore it as obscurantism and superstition; others admire it as token of a precious spiritual resource ever more scant in the world. In any case, the Queen of Heaven in her Mexican version is a powerful, living presence. Not a remote, awe-inspiring or intimidating empress, but a majestic being who is not above hearing the daily concerns of her vassals, and is always ready to grant them a sympathetic ear. And the Mexican people, heirs to the Latin culture, express their concerns and frustrations in a style that is familiar and simple; a manner of address that can be most touching in its unadorned directness. I recall a Spanish anecdote recounted by Juan de Valera, as an example of this moving sense of immediacy. A spinster comes daily to church, to pray to a statue of a Virgin with Child that she may find a husband. A mischievous altar boy, aware of her routine, hides behind the chapel's drapes and waits for her arrival. Upon hearing her entreaties, the boy fakes a supernatural voice and exclaims: "You shall remain a spinster! You shall die a spinster!" Utterly absorbed in her address to the Virgin, the woman rejoins, irate: "You be quiet, brat. I am talking to your mother."

How did this queen come to reign over her present domains? Cosmic objects have a history and deities, if they are of the sort that can speak to us—and we to them—must have, like us, a genealogy. If we lack knowledge of their origin, the gods become unintelligible: mighty but opaque entities that are altogether unreachable and preclude all possibilities of communion. Communication is easier when those who engage in dialogue share much in common, and the brunette Virgin's past strikingly resembles that of her children. Like today's Mexicans, whose origins are traced to a race that was nearly exterminated, then reinvigorated by genetic admixture—death, then rebirth under a different guise— Our Lady of Guadalupe represents the last point in a theogony characterized by successive reincarnations.

When the Spaniards first arrived at the sacred hill of Tepeyacac (today Tepeyac), Mexico was a city of lake-dwellers. The Europeans came on barges through the northern causeway that ran, marvelously straight and spanned by many wooden bridges, all the way from Tlatelolco. Upon disembarking they encountered, on top of a low hill, the temple to the goddess Tonantzin, meaning "Our Mother." Her semblance was not likely to please the fanatical friars who came with the invaders. Scandalized, they urged the immediate demolition of the idol. So that when Fray Bernardino de Sahagún (1512–1590), the compulsive chronicler, finally arrived, the imposing image had been reduced to rubble, and in its place stood a cross. This was regular procedure, made official in 1552 by a decree[1] that also commanded, "if the place were decent," the erection of a shrine dedicated to an object of worship sanctioned by the Holy, Roman and Apostolic Catholic religion, the faith for whose preservation and furtherance Spain had shed, with multisecular, unwavering zeal, the blood of her most cherished sons.

Sahagún would have liked nothing better than to portray the dying Tonantzin. Not that he felt any genuine sympathy for what he probably deemed heretical idolatry and spiritual barbarism. But he was, constitutionally, the chronicler: the need to witness, then to record, suffused the very marrow of his bones. And he was not a zealous fanatic. The urge to describe for posterity the things that aliens value never exists without a certain openness to the idea that all men, regardless of race, share a fundamental kinship; and

---

[1] Fray Juan de Torquemada (OFM): *Monarquia Indiana*, vol. 2, bk. 10. Mexico, 1943 (facsimile of Madrid 1723 edition). Pp. 245b, 246a.

that precisely because they relate equally to a common source, everywhere they create things worthy of being preserved. Yet, how to describe the destroyed goddess? Her likeness, even at the heyday of her reign, had been seen by very few, almost exclusively priests and sacrificial victims, who alone were admitted into her sanctuary. Now, she lay comminuted into a heap of dust.

To reconstruct her, it was pointless to question the subdued Mexicans who—bewildered, tearful, and confused, their cities and temples made waste as a wilderness—answered only what the questioner wanted to hear. Their answers, if melancholy wails may be so called, were little more than the babbling of terror, interrupted here and there by a silent hiatus of morose resentment. Hence the ambiguity of her depiction. Sahagún affirmed that Tonantzin was also the goddess Cihuacoatl, "the Snake-Woman," attired in white skirt, white blouse, and white mantle, and carrying on her back a cradle with a child in it. But other historians disagreed. The Jesuit Clavijero, for instance, asserted that she was Centeotl, another dark figure of the dark Aztec pantheon. Thus the Aztec goddess died a violent death. Killed by men, her cadaver was promptly buried under a newly erected temple, and her stark features slowly rotted, melted away, became indistinct, until they seemed no more than a blur, a barely discernible outline behind the image of Our Lady.

But can men assassinate a goddess whose roots sink deep into the Neolithic period in complete impunity and leaving no trace? The conquistadors thought so. Above the ruinous temple of Tonantzin they installed their own venerated Virgin, the *morenita* or "little brunette," of Villuercas, in the district of Guadalupe, in Extremadura, Spain. Her history was resplendent, and her tradition as rich in legend and miraculous accomplishment as that annexed to the highest of holy images in Christendom. Cardinal Cisneros, Cortés, Pizarro, Andrea Doria: an impressive number of the grandees that made the undying glory of Spain had knelt before her. In the treasury of her temple may be admired, to our day, a scorpion made of solid gold bullion that Cortés offered her, as an *ex voto*, in thanks for having healed him of a scorpion bite. The first American Indians to be transported to Spain were baptized in her temple, under the proud auspices of royal godparents. Thus, to the

Spaniards the new shrine of Tepeyac could be no more than a pale reflection of the original temple, and the sacred image a familiar symbol transplanted from its indigenous soil to the New Continent.

Tonantzin, however, was not quite dead, and did not take kindly to the humiliation. Chthonic force that she was, she drew strength from being buried in the earth, and from her burial place began a silent, obstinate resistance. The first thing she did was to take advantage of the colonists' greed, their most notorious weakness. As long as the new Lady of Guadalupe was only a representative or a substitute of a loftier and absent majesty residing elsewhere, all tributes, alms, offerings, and donations heaped upon her could be whisked away on short notice, transferred to the principal figure of which she was only a deputy. This the priests at her service found unbearable. Only by bestowing a new personality on the native Virgin, an identity sufficiently different from that of her Iberian homologue, could those riches—the amazing treasures of the fabled, relentlessly exploited New World—be retained. Thus, at the origin of Guadalupe's process of differentiation, of her naturalization as Latin American citizen and protectress, there is a rather sordid affair of monies, an unconfessable yearning after cold cash in greedy, wrangling ecclesiastics—a squalid note that hagiographers prefer to ignore. Un-Christian sentiments that Our Indian Mother, the Snake-Woman, she of the white attire and the cradle with child on her back, must have been pleased to fan from her subterranean enclave, with barely the intimation of a vengeful smile on her obsidian face.

Her subversive, covert acts do not end here. Shortly after the Conquest is complete, an anonymous Indian painter transfers the features of the celestial woman onto a fabric made of agave fibers. For the notion of divine pictorial authorship is not accepted by historians, except those who are deeply religious doctrinaires. But the painter does not copy the exalted features of the Spanish model, in spite of its attribution to the hand of Saint Luke, who, it was said, had expertly wielded a sculptor's chisel under divine inspiration. Tonantzin guides the limner's hand, and so drives it as to produce important discrepancies. The Iberian Lady holds the Holy Child; the new one stands alone and brings her delicate palms together in prayer. That one wears a queen's crown on her head; this one covers it with a mantle that might pass for a *rebozo*, the local shawl. Twelve scintillating stars hover above the celestial Spanish queen; the Mexican is framed by a refulgent sun, while her feet, light as feathers, rest upon a black crescent moon. That one flaunts the fair skin that Castilian bards never tire of comparing to alabaster and snow tinged by the blush of dawn. This one's complexion is brown, the distinct copper brown of Indian skin, a feature that the painter generously extends to the angel who, at the Virgin's feet, opens her mantle with outstretched arms, joyous at the supreme honor of Our Lady's propinquity.

Tonantzin's resistance movement did not fail to evoke a counterinsurgency. This was first organized by Franciscan friars who, steeped in the ideas of Erasmus of Rotterdam, wished to put a stop to a spreading cult which, they said, contained disturbing elements of idolatry. Imagine! A competition between Tonantzin—a cosmic, elemental, chthonic being—and Erasmus, the vacillating, irony-prone intellectual who timorously disclaimed the paternity of his own ideas as soon as he realized what their terrible consequences could be in the time of religious wars: *Erasmo o la cobardia*—Erasmus, or cowardice—reads the suggestive title of an essay by the Spanish writer Guillermo Díaz-Plaja. The outcome was as predictable as the ocean's tides, and just as inevitable: Tonantzin, now in the guise of a brunette Christian deity, emerged the uncontested winner. The cult of the Mexican Virgin rapidly spread throughout the country, eventually to spill beyond its borders; her therapeutic miracles multiplied; and even her prodigies were cast in a distinct local style. The Spanish Virgin, a resident of the dusty and desolate Castilian plains, could make water drop down from the vault of heaven toward a thirsty, parched earth, sown with salt like Sodom's turf; her Mexican counterpart, born in a city founded on a lake, was uniquely efficacious in forestalling floods. More than once her sacred image left the basilica in solemn procession, in order to save the city from a flood or to stop the progress of an epidemic.

All these portents, however, were not enough. For Our Lady to kindle a universal fervor, it was necessary that she materialize and that she leave a patent proof of her existence—a mark of her concrete, *corporeal* reality. For it is a curious fact, worthy of the most detailed attention, that for some peoples a concrete object must at all events sustain their loves, even at their most spiritual and exalted. Middle Eastern religions barred the representation of the human figure, but the human body remained a disturbingly prominent feature, at times shockingly so, of the mysticism of Caterina of Siena and Teresa of Ávila. André Gide was perhaps thinking of this when he entered in his diary, on July 14, 1940: " 'The resurrection of the flesh,' says the Church, knowing that the soul needs the body to grow fond, and that, had the Verb not been "made flesh," It would have few worshipers. Can you imagine these ones prostrated before a triangle?"[2]

Indeed. There are Spanish Virgins that approach the hypothetical geometry-worshiping model. The Lady of the Seven Pains, paraded in processions all over the Iberian Peninsula, is in fact a triangle: her basic anatomy consists of a doll's head surmounted by a rich imperial crown and resting on a stick. Taking off from the base of the head, where one would expect the neck, begins a dark dress that gradually widens in diameter as it descends toward the feet. But there are no feet. The dress is very taut and flattened, so that no part of the anatomy is even remotely hinted at. At chest level, she is pierced by seven silver daggers. But there is no chest. She is pure abstraction: a head—"the seat of counsel," as Plato called it—and a tense, triangular or conical dress that bears the emblem of pain. Mexicans did not create this semi-incorporeal image. They might feel inclined to agree with Gide: "We are ineluctably steeped in matter, and even our most mystical loves cannot do without material representations. We need symbols, monuments, statues, flags, to furnish our sentiment with some hold: a perch on which that which flies out of our hearts, but could not sustain its flight too long, may come back to roost."[3]

Hence the success of the "apparitionist" tradition, according to which the Virgin appeared several times to a humble aborigine, an adult man of pure Indian stock, Cuautlatóhuac, known since his baptism in 1524 by the more easily pronounceable name Juan Diego. The miracle was recounted by an Indian chronicler, Anto-

---

[2]André Gide: *Journal 1939–1949. Souvenirs.* Gallimard, Collection Pléiade, 1954. Pp. 38–39. Author's translation.

[3]André Gide: *loc. cit.*

nio Valeriano (1520–1605) in the *Nican Mopohua* ("Here it is told"), the earliest document that narrates the apparitions of the Virgin, written in the ancient language of the Aztecs, but using the phonetic European, Romanic characters instead of the primitive hieroglyphs.[4] By manifesting herself atop the hill of Tepeyac, former lee for idolatry and abode of the goddess Tonantzin, her Mexicanization was well under way; it became fully consolidated when her miraculous appearance was recounted in the native pre-Columbian language. It has since been argued that her name was not the Spanish Guadalupe, but Tequalasupe or Tlecuauhtlacupe, "she who comes from the light, like a fire-eagle," since the sounds of the letters *g* and *d* do not exist in the language of the ancient Aztecs, being most likely an Arabic importation into Spanish. In due course, the likeness of the thoroughly nationalized Virgin of Guadalupe would be conspicuous in the banners raised by Mexican insurgents fighting for independence from the colonial rule of Spain.

What is more striking yet is that the celestial Lady left an abiding mark of her passage through the Valley of Mexico: no less than her true portrait, miraculously imprinted on Juan Diego's *tilma* (a calf-length cloak styled by the Indians, worn over the front of the body and fastened with a knot over the left shoulder), when he obeyed her instructions to gather roses in a barren winter's landscape. The flowers, as is well known, were the objective evidence needed to convince an incredulous Bishop Zumárraga of the reality of the apparitions. The Church officially sanctions the miracle, and the Latin American peoples have since possessed, in this piece of preternatural handiwork, the concrete image endowed with the tangible corporeal attributes that their sensibilities yearned for.

Her image being concrete and distinct, it admits of prolix description. Consequently, a sort of "descriptive anatomy" of the sacred likeness has been cultivated for generations. Some of the chief points uncovered by this discipline are as follows:

The fabric on which it is painted measures 170 by 104 centimeters and is made of woven agave fibers. It is actually made of

---

[4] Antonio Valeriano: *Nican Mopohua, Narraciones de las Apariciones de la Virgen de Guadalupe.* Transl. Mario Rojas. Librería Parroquial de Clavería, Mexico, undated.

two rectangular pieces joined by their long sides in the middle with a coarse suture of the same material. The fabric is hard and rough on its obverse, but soft and pliant on its reverse, "which is," says a Church brochure, "unexplainable by natural causes." In the mid-seventeenth century, prominent local scientists analyzed the image and concluded, on March 28, 1666, "that the Nitre carried in the air should spoil the image, as it does the stones from the local quarry or the silver in the chapel, which turns black; therefore the incorruptibility of the Image surpasses all human understanding." For 116 years, the sacred image was exposed without protection, and so placed that the faithful could easily touch it. During the first 150 years it was taken out six times, in solemn processions aiming to prevent calamity, or because of renovations to the temple. The cloth was exposed to all sorts of untoward influences and undesirable contacts that can wear off bronze and marble, as may be seen at St. Peter's church in Rome, and wherever sacred images are left within reach of the faithful. Nevertheless the painting has remained unaltered. In 1791, silversmiths repairing the gilt frame accidentally spilled nitric acid in the upper left corner of the fabric (right of the observer), and the spill spread two thirds of the way down the length of the cloth. Traces of the damage may still be seen, but they become fainter as time goes by. Intoned Bustamante, the chronicler of the accidental spill: "Where is the corrosive strength of *aqua fortis*, which even spilled over the cloth by negligence of the silversmiths respected the weak tissue, leaving only a faint vestige as testimony of this prodigy for all times?"[5]

On November 14, 1921, an anticlerical fanatic placed a bomb inside a vase with a floral offering. The bomb went off, shattering the flower vases, destroying the altar's steps, bending a metallic crucifix, and breaking the windowpanes of the neighboring houses. The sacred image remained intact.

"In 1936, Dr. Richard Kuhn, Nobel laureate in chemistry and researcher from the Emperor Wilhelm Institute in Heidelberg, Germany, subjected two fibers of the cloth to chemical analysis. He reported that in the examined fibers there were neither chemical,

---

[5]Quoted by Guadalupe Pimentel M.: *Mi Niña, Dueña de mi Corazón*. Editorial Progreso, Mexico City, 1991.

nor animal, nor mineral dyes. It is a painting . . . without paint! Two American scientists . . . Dr. Phillip S. Callahan and Jody Brand Smith, having performed a series of studies by means of infrared photography, concluded [. . .] that it is a scientifically unexplained painting, and thus not made by human hands."[6]

The Virgin is represented as framed by the sun, whose rays surround her and appear to emanate from her. There are sixty-two rays on her right side, and seventy-seven on her left; the sunbeams are either straight and narrow or wide and curved, each form succeeding the other, in alternation. The Majestic Lady stands in front of the sun: she is more powerful than the sun, foremost deity of the Aztecs. Although her skin is dark, her facial features are not those of an Indian, but of a mestizo woman, the product of racial mixture between European and Mesoamerican Indian: her physiognomy is prophetic, announcing the foundation of a new race.

She is no disembodied, abstract triangle; although celestial, she is a woman. Her left lower limb is flexed, giving us distinct reference points on the position of her thigh and knee. She walks: she is a missionary coming to evangelize. And she is pregnant: she wears a black sash around her waist, as did the pregnant Indian and mestizo women of colonial Mexico, and wears it above the waist to indicate that she is with child, fastening it with a large bow that protrudes below her joined hands.

She is, as it was once said of an Aztec deity, "a beehive of symbols." By means of imaginary lines traced over the sacred image according to various fanciful principles, some contend that the central figure of the painting is not the Virgin at all, but Jesus Christ, inside the maternal womb, about to come to deliver his salvific message. Under her feet is a crescent black moon, symbol of the ancient, cruel deities of the Aztecs, now trampled by the power of the new queen.

The study of her descriptive anatomy is, of course, symbol-oriented. Take, for instance, the stars that adorn her mantle. Upon casual inspection, it may be concluded that they are merely ornamental. But anatomists know that seeing is a difficult art, and that we are bound to see only that for which we are mentally prepared.

[6]Guadalupe Pimentel, M.: *loc. cit.*, p. 104.

Therefore, look again: trace certain lines that join the different stars, and your tracings will reveal the pattern of specific constellations. A book printed under the auspices of the Catholic Church contains a transparent overlay with line tracings that can be superimposed to a printed copy of the painting on the next page, thereby revealing the unsuspected constellations: Scorpio, Lupus, and so on.[7] Thus the reader is made to realize that the relative position of the stars in the Virgin's mantle is not random or purely ornamental, but indicative of the position of certain constellations at a specific point in time. The reader is then informed that, on the authority of scientific calculations by astronomers of the National University, the position of the constellations shown in the Virgin's mantle is the position they held, as seen from the Valley of Mexico, at precisely the time of the miraculous apparition, December 12, 1531, at 10:40 hours.

The most striking features of her anatomy are the eyes. On December 11, 1955, on the eve of the Virgin's most solemn festivity, Archbishop Luis María Martínez stirred a commotion when he announced on the radio that he had appointed a commission for the scientific study of the Virgin's eyes. Years before, an artist, studying close-up photos of the painting, had discovered certain reflections in the corneas that to his own artist's eyes suggested a human shape. In the area of the ocular iris, the reflection suggested a human being, perhaps none other than Juan Diego kneeling in adoration before the Queen of Heaven! There followed claims and counterclaims. Need we say that no consensus is yet reached? Ophthalmologists have attempted to reproduce a comparable effect in the eyes of living persons, by photographing volunteers who gaze upon other subjects under different lighting conditions and variable distances. Computer-generated, digitized, and highly magnified images of the Virgin's eyes have been prepared. However, as might have been predicted, the higher the magnification, the more confusing the images. There are some who see nothing but an amorphous blur where others are certain to detect a kneeling Juan Diego, or the profile of Bishop Zumárraga, or the outline of the man

---

[7]Carmen y Bernarda Aparicio: *Un Caminar de María Santísima en la Iglesia.* Libería Parroquial de Clavería, Mexico, 1992.

who acted as translator for Juan Diego, or an entire group of persons. Up to seventeen different persons have been spotted in the pupils of Our Lady.

Superstition? Contemptible credulity? I am no theologian, nor would I dream of disputing the claims of the faithful. But as one concerned with the problems of anatomy, I must say that questions concerning structure are much more difficult to settle than most people surmise. Seeing, as a German anatomist aptly put it in the heyday of pathologic anatomy, is *eine schwere Kunst*, a difficult art. Gross observation suffices to decide on gross matters and gross queries. After all, these call only for gross answers. But the more delicate problems call for techniques that invariably distort the subject of inquiry and hide its real nature: no one knows in detail the real structure of living tissues, since these are always studied after fixation, freezing, staining, and other lethal manipulations. Thus, to expect that the most subtle and ethereal problem of the intimate structure of the Holy Virgin's eyes will be settled to everyone's satisfaction is, I suspect, the extreme of optimism. Observers will continue to see what they want to see, not excluding those who pride themselves on scientific objectivity.

Fifty years after my first visit to the shrine, I visit my mother in Mexico City. She is now elderly, and has just been transported to a hospital for an abdominal operation. The sight of her fatigued, mortified body covered by extensive bruises and emerging catheters makes me despondent. In her apartment, conspicuously displayed, is an image of the Virgin of Guadalupe. "The sunrays are not just painted," observes my sister, "but they are hollowed out. If you place the picture against the light it seems as if the sun were resplendent, and she in the center." True, the image is a quaint production of folk artisans, painted on wood; where the sunbeams are represented the wood has been carved out, so the light can shine through. My sister then returns to the hospital, to offer her company to my mother. In Mexico, provisions exist that make it possible for the relatives to stay with the patient overnight.

Alone in the deserted apartment, unable to fall asleep, I read until the early hours of the morning. I lift my eyes from the book, and I encounter the sacred image. I cannot suppress the thought of addressing a plea to her, in the same familiar style that my mother might have used. Inwardly, I say: "Listen: Give her a break, please. I beg of you. I may be undeserving, praying for help when in need, and never when untroubled. But I ask in her behalf. She has been sincere in her belief and unvarying in her loyalty. You know how harsh her life has been. Please do not allow that she should suffer much, or for very long. Protect her. Do not let her down."

Those who know me for a rationalist and agnostic might smile condescendingly when I confess that I really thought of this prayer. My mother, by the way, recovered from her illness. Do I believe this was owed to the supernatural intercession of the Empress of the Americas? I can think of no better answer than that of Niels Bohr, Nobel laureate and genial physicist. The cabin in which he was staying during a scientific meeting had a conspicuous good-luck charm affixed to the door, which he nailed in place when it wobbled. Teased by his colleagues for his superstitious concern, and asked if a pioneer in elementary particle physics and Nobel laureate such as himself really believed in the protective ability of a good-luck charm, Bohr replied: "I have heard that these charms work even for those of us who do not believe in them."

Just so. In these days of economic crisis, mounting social problems, disintegrating traditional values, rising crime, drug trafficking, environmental pollution, and threatening epidemics, many a Mexican will turn skeptic or cynic. But, as Octavio Paz once wrote, when Mexicans no longer believe in anything, they will still hold fast to their belief in two things: the National Lottery, and the Virgin of Guadalupe. In this, I think, they will do well. For both have been known to work, even for those of us who believe in neither.

Hotel Flora

MIRIAM SAGAN

I want to go to Mexico City and be mysterious and sad
I want a one-way ticket and a blank notebook
I want to stay at the Flora Hotel
Cheap, but very clean,
Hotel with an interior courtyard
Poinsettias that are taller than I am
I want to go to Mexico City and be mysterious and sad
Men, and women too, will look at me and ask
Who is that beautiful mysterious woman
And why is she sad?
Every day at five o'clock
I will walk through the Alameda Gardens
Give one American quarter to each of the first three beggars
Watch the man swallow fire
I will go to the lobby with the Diego Rivera mural
Death walking on a Sunday with Mrs. Death
I will order two shots of tequila
I will drink only one
I will lick the back of my hand
Sprinkle salt on it
Lick that off
Like a child who has stayed all day at the beach
I will drink a shot of tequila with a ghost
I want to go to Mexico City with a borrowed suitcase
All my bras will be black and my underpants white
I will wash them by hand in the little sink
Hang them on the balcony to dry slowly
Smelling of diesel fumes

I will build a shrine on my bureau top:
Red plastic comb, two pesos,
Postcard of Frida Kahlo
Sequined Virgin of Guadalupe
Piece of lava, and a key
To a room that is not mine.

India

RICHARD
RODRIGUEZ

We have hurled—like starlings, like Goths—through the castle of European memory. Our reflections have glanced upon the golden coach that carried the Emperor Maximilian through the streets of Mexico City, thence onward through the sludge of a hundred varnished paintings.

I have come at last to Mexico, the country of my parents' birth. I do not expect to find anything that pertains to me.

We have strained the rouge cordon at the thresholds of imperial apartments; seen chairs low enough for dwarfs, commodious enough for angels.

We have imagined the Empress Carlota standing in the shadows of an afternoon; we have followed her gaze down the Paseo de la Reforma toward the distant city. The Paseo was a nostalgic allusion to the Champs-Elysées, we learn, which Maximilian recreated for his tempestuous, crowlike bride.

Come this way, please. . . .

European memory is not to be the point of our excursion. Señor Fuentes, our tour director, is already beginning to descend the hill from Chapultepec Castle. What the American credit-card company calls our "orientation tour" of Mexico City had started late and so Señor Fuentes has been forced, regrettably,

". . . This way, please . . ."

to rush. Señor Fuentes is consumed with contrition for time wasted this morning. He intends to uphold his schedule, as a way of upholding Mexico, against our expectation.

We had gathered at the appointed time at the limousine entrance to our hotel, beneath the banner welcoming contestants to the Señorita Mexico pageant. We—Japanese, Germans, Americans—were waiting promptly at nine. There was no bus. And as we waited, the Señorita Mexico contestants arrived. Drivers leaned into their cabs to pull out long-legged señoritas. The drivers then balanced the señoritas onto stiletto heels (the driveway was cobbled) before they passed the señoritas, *en pointe*, to the waiting arms of officials.

Mexican men, meanwhile—doormen, bellhops, window washers, hotel guests—stopped dead in their tracks, wounded by the scent and spectacle of so many blond señoritas. The Mexican men assumed fierce expressions, nostrils flared, brows knit. Such expressions are masks—the men intend to convey their adoration of prey—as thoroughly ritualized as the smiles of beauty queens.

By now we can see the point of our excursion beyond the parched trees of Chapultepec Park—the Museo Nacional de Antropología—which is an air-conditioned repository for the artifacts of the Indian civilizations of Meso-America, the finest anthropological museum in the world.

"There will not be time to see everything," Señor Fuentes warns as he ushers us into the grand salon, our first experience of the suffocating debris of The Ancients. Señor Fuentes wants us in and out of here by noon.

Whereas the United States traditionally has rejoiced at the delivery of its landscape from "savagery," Mexico has taken its national identity only from the Indian, the mother. Mexico measures all cultural bastardy against the Indian; equates civilization with India—Indian kingdoms of a golden age; cities as fabulous as Alexandria or Benares or Constantinople; a court as hairless, as subtle as the Pekingese. Mexico equates barbarism with Europe—beardedness—with Spain.

It is curious, therefore, that both modern nations should similarly apostrophize the Indian, relegate the Indian to the past.

Come this way, please. Mrs. . . . Ah . . . this way, please.

Señor Fuentes wears an avocado-green sports coat with gold buttons. He is short. He is rather elegant, with a fine small head, small hands, small feet; with his two rows of fine small teeth like a nutcracker's teeth, with which he curtails consonants as cleanly as bitten thread. Señor Fuentes is brittle, he is watchful, he is ironic, he is metropolitan; his wit is quotational, literary, wasted on Mrs. Ah. He is not our equal. His demeanor says he is not our equal. We mistake his condescension for humility. He will not eat when we eat. He will not spend when we shop. He will not have done with Mexico when we have done with Mexico.

Señor Fuentes is impatient with us, for we have paused momentarily outside the museum to consider the misfortune of an adolescent mother who holds her crying baby out to us. Several of us confer among ourselves in an attempt to place a peso value on the woman's situation. We do not ask for the advice of Señor Fuentes.

For we, in turn, are impatient with Señor Fuentes. We are in a bad mood. The air conditioning on our "fully air-conditioned coach" is nonexistent. We have a headache. Nor is the city air any relief, but it is brown, fungal, farted.

Señor Fuentes is a mystery to us, for there is no American equivalent to him; for there is no American equivalent to the subtleties he is paid to describe to us.

Mexico will not raise a public monument to Hernán Cortés, for example, the father of Mexico—the rapist. In the Diego Rivera murals in the presidential palace, the Aztec city of Tenochtitlán is rendered—its blood temples and blood canals—as haughty as Troy, as vulnerable as Pompeii. Any suggestion of the complicity of other tribes of Indians in overthrowing the Aztec empire is painted over. Spaniards appear on the horizons of Arcadia as syphilitic brigands and demon-eyed priests.

The Spaniard entered the Indian by entering her city—the floating city—first as a suitor, ceremoniously; later by force. How should Mexico honor the rape?

In New England the European and the Indian drew apart to regard each other with suspicion over centuries. Miscegenation was a sin against Protestant individualism. In Mexico the European and the Indian consorted. The ravishment of fabulous Tenochtitlán ended in a marriage of blood—a "cosmic race," the Mexican philosopher José Vasconcelos has called it.

Mexico's tragedy is that she has no political idea of herself as rich as her blood.

The rhetoric of Señor Fuentes, like the murals of Diego Rivera, resorts often to the dream of India—to Tenochtitlán, the capital of the world before conquest. "Preconquest" in the Mexican political lexicon is tantamount to "prelapsarian" in the Judeo-Christian scheme, and hearkens to a time Mexico feels herself to have been whole, a time before the Indian was separated from India by the serpent Spain.

Three centuries after Cortés, Mexico declared herself independent of Spain. If Mexico would have no yoke, then Mexico would have no crown, then Mexico would have no father. The denial of Spain has persisted into our century.

The priest and the landowner yet serve Señor Fuentes as symbols of the hated Spanish order. Though, in private, Mexico is Catholic; Mexican mothers may wish for light-skinned children. Touch blond hair and good luck will be yours.

In private, in Mexican Spanish, *indio* is a seller of Chiclets, a sidewalk squatter. *Indio* means backward or lazy or lower-class. In the eyes of the world, Mexico raises a magnificent museum of anthropology—the finest in the world—to honor the Indian mother.

In the nave of the National Cathedral, we notice the floor slopes dramatically. "The cathedral is sinking," Señor Fuentes explains as a hooded figure approaches our group from behind a column. She is an Indian woman; she wears a blue stole; her hands are cupped, beseeching; tear marks ream her cheeks. In Spanish, Señor Fuentes forbids this apparition: "Go ask *padrecito* to pry some gold off the altar for you."

"Mexico City is built upon swamp," Señor Fuentes resumes in English. "Therefore, the cathedral is sinking." But it is clear that Señor Fuentes believes the sinkage is due to the oppressive weight of Spanish Catholicism, its masses of gold, its volumes of deluded suspiration.

Mexican political life can only seem Panglossian when you consider an anti-Catholic government of an overwhelmingly Catholic population. Mexico is famous for politicians descended from Masonic fathers and Catholic mothers. Señor Fuentes himself is less a Spaniard, less an Indian, perhaps, than an embittered eighteenth-century man, clinging to the witty knees of Voltaire against the chaos of twentieth-century Mexico.

Mexico blamed the ruin of the nineteenth century on the foreigner, and with reason. Once emptied of Spain, the palace of Mexico became the dollhouse of France. Mexico was overrun by imperial armies. The greed of Europe met the Manifest Destiny of the United States in Mexico. Austria sent an archduke to marry Mexico with full panoply of candles and bishops. The U.S. reached under Mexico's skirt every chance he got.

"Poor Mexico, so far from God, so close to the United States."

Señor Fuentes dutifully attributes the mot to Porfirio Díaz, the Mexican president who sold more of Mexico to foreign interests than any other president. It was against the regime of Porfirio Díaz that Mexicans rebelled in the early decades of this century. Mexico prefers to call its civil war a "revolution."

Mexico for Mexicans!

The Revolution did not accomplish a union of Mexicans. The Revolution did not accomplish a restoration of Mexicans to their landscape. The dust of the Revolution parted to reveal—not India—but Marx *ex machina*, the Institutional Revolutionary Party, the PRI—a political machine appropriate to the age of steam. The Institutional Revolutionary Party, as its name implies, was designed to reconcile institutional pragmatism with revolutionary rhetoric. And the PRI worked for a time, because it gave Mexico what Mexico most needed, the stability of compromise.

The PRI appears everywhere in Mexico—a slogan on the wall, the politician impersonating a journalist on the evening news, the professor at his podium. The PRI is in its way as much a Mexican institution as the Virgin of Guadalupe.

Now Mexicans speak of the government as something imposed upon them, and they are the victims of it. But the political failure of Mexico must be counted a failure of Mexicans. Whom now shall Señor Fuentes blame for a twentieth century that has become synonymous with corruption?

Well, as long as you stay out of the way of the police no one will bother you, is conventional Mexican wisdom, and Mexico continues to live her daily life. In the capital, the air is the color of the buildings of Siena. Telephone connections are an aspect of the will of God. Mexicans drive on the sidewalks. A man on the street corner seizes the opportunity of stalled traffic to earn his living as a fire-eater. His ten children pass among the cars and among the honking horns to collect small coins.

Thank you. Thank you very much. A pleasure, Mrs. . . . Ah. Thank you very much.

Señor Fuentes bids each farewell. He accepts tips within a handshake. He bows slightly. We have no complaint with Señor Fuentes, after all. The bus was not his fault. Mexico City is not his fault. And Señor Fuentes will return to his unimaginable Mexico and we will return to our rooms to take aspirin and to initiate long-distance telephone calls. Señor Fuentes will remove his avocado-green coat and, having divested, Señor Fuentes will in some fashion partake of what he has successfully kept from us all day, which is the life and the drinking water of Mexico.

The Virgin of Guadalupe symbolizes the entire coherence of Mexico, body and soul. You will not find the story of the Virgin within hidebound secular histories of Mexico—nor indeed within the credulous repertoire of Señor Fuentes—and the omission renders the history of Mexico incomprehensible.

One recent afternoon, within the winy bell jar of a very late lunch, I told the story of the Virgin of Guadalupe to Lynn, a sophisticated twentieth-century woman. The history of Mexico, I promised her, is neither mundane nor masculine, but it is a miracle play with trapdoors and sequins and jokes on the living.

In the sixteenth century, when Indians were demoralized by the routing of their gods, when millions of Indians were dying from the plague of Europe, the Virgin Mary appeared pacing on a hillside to an Indian peasant named Juan Diego—his Christian name, for Juan was a convert. It was December 1531.

Peering through the grille of her cigarette smoke, Lynn heard and she seemed to approve the story.

At the Virgin's behest, this Prufrock Indian must go several times to the bishop of Mexico City. He must ask that a chapel be built on Tepeyac where his discovered Lady may share in the sorrows of her people. Juan Diego's visits to the Spanish bishop parody the conversion of the Indians by the Spaniards. The bishop is skeptical.

The bishop wants proof.

The Virgin tells Juan Diego to climb the hill and gather a sheaf of roses as proof for the bishop—Castilian roses—impossible in Mexico in December of 1531. Juan carries the roses in the folds of his cloak, a pregnant messenger. Upon entering the bishop's presence, Juan parts his cloak, the roses tumble; the bishop falls to his knees.

In the end—with crumpled napkins, torn carbons, the bitter dregs of coffee—Lynn gave the story over to the Spaniards.

The legend concludes with a concession to humanity—proof more durable than roses—the imprint of the Virgin's image upon the cloak of Juan Diego . . .

A Spanish trick, Lynn said. A recruitment poster for the new religion, no more, she said (though sadly). An itinerant diva with a costume trunk. Birgit Nilsson as Aïda.

Why do we assume Spain made up the story?

The importance of the story is that Indians believed it. The jokes, the vaudeville, the relegation of the Spanish bishop to the role of comic adversary, the Virgin's chosen cavalier, and especially the brown-faced Mary—all elements spoke directly to Indians.

The result of the apparition and of the miraculous image of the Lady remaining upon the cloak of Juan Diego was a mass conversion of Indians to Catholicism.

The image of Our Lady of Guadalupe (privately, affectionately, Mexicans call her La Morenita—Little Darkling) has become the unofficial, the private flag of Mexicans. Unique possession of her image is a more wonderful election to Mexicans than any political call to nationhood. Perhaps Mexico's tragedy in our century, perhaps Mexico's abiding grace thus far, is that she has no political idea of herself as compelling as her icon.

The Virgin appears everywhere in Mexico. On dashboards and on calendars, on playing cards, on lampshades and cigar boxes; within the loneliness and tattooed upon the very skins of Mexicans.

Nor is the image of Guadalupe a diminishing mirage of the sixteenth century, but she has become more vivid with time, developing in her replication from earthy shades of melon and musk to bubble-gum pink, Windex blue, to achieve the hard, literal focus of holy cards or baseball cards; of Krishna or St. Jude or the Atlanta Braves.

Mexico City stands as the last living medieval capital of the world. Mexico is the creation of a Spanish Catholicism that attempted to draw continents together as one flesh. The success of Spanish Catholicism in Mexico resulted in a kind of proof—a profound concession to humanity: the *mestizaje.*

What joke on the living? Lynn said.

The joke is that Spain arrived with missionary zeal at the shores of contemplation. But Spain had no idea of the absorbent strength of Indian spirituality.

By the waters of baptism, the active European was entirely absorbed within the contemplation of the Indian. The faith that Europe imposed in the sixteenth century was, by virtue of the Guadalupe, embraced by the Indian. Catholicism has become an Indian religion. By the twenty-first century, the locus of the Catholic Church, by virtue of numbers, will be Latin America, by which time Catholicism itself will have assumed the aspect of the Virgin of Guadalupe.

Brown skin.

Guadalupe: The Feminine Face of God

JEANETTE
RODRIGUEZ

*T*he significance of Our Lady of Guadalupe in popular religiosity must assume a dialectic posture with contemporary Catholic theology, and so we look at the insights that feminist theology has given us in terms of the maternal or feminine face of God.

Hispanic colonial evangelization taught that the Christian God was more powerful than the indigenous gods. The proof was that those who fought under the banner of the Christian God became successful conquerors. The Christian God was, more likely than not, imaged by those in power to reflect themselves. There is thus a metaphor and a constellation of images surrounding the God brought by the conquistadors.

Christianity preached forgiveness, mercy, compassion, and reconciliation. The symbol used by the dominant Spanish culture to communicate these values was the Virgin Mary. Representing Christianity to the newly conquered, the missionaries did not connect these fundamental Christian elements with God in their catechisms; they did connect them with Mary. These traits at the time were held to be maternal and also may have reflected the way the Spanish might have wanted the Indians to feel toward their oppressors. All of these "maternal" qualities were attributed to God by the missionaries, but in the conquered population's mind the association of God with the powerful and victorious was primary. Mary, however, was presented as loving, comforting, and accepting; she was clearly the faithful and solidarious one (Espín 1991:99).

Even in the early history of Hispanic Christianity, there is a dichotomy of attributes: those that are powerful but somewhat alienating were attributed to the male white European Christian God, and the more affective, maternal reconciling ones to the Virgin Mary. Dr. Espín (1991:98) asks, "How do Hispanics experience God as faithfully solidarious with them?" He suggests that perhaps we need to remove from the word "God" all the dominant, conquering demons it evokes.

If, instead of looking for the explicit use of the term "God" or other God-related activities, we look at instances when Mexican Americans seem to be relating explicitly or implicitly to a divinity closer to the Gospel's real God, we will discover a very clear presence of faithful solidarity in their operative definition of that God. The surprise is that this faithfully solidarious one is Mary, the Virgin, says Espín (1991:100). There is historical evidence that these stereotypical attributes of the feminine have been presented through Marian symbols and thus have traditionally been ascribed to Mary as Our Lady of Guadalupe. It is easy to perceive Our Lady of Guadalupe as the maternal or female face of God, because she evokes an unconditional love, solidarity, and a never-failing presence at the affective level. But in doing so, we inaccurately remove these attributes from where they rightly belong: to God.

I myself struggle with this concept, because naturally I am drawn to the caring and nurturing presence of Our Lady of Guadalupe, but I am committed to retrieving the basic meaning of her message and placing it within a new context. I am in a relationship with her; when a relationship is expressed, it reveals something about both the person and (in my case) that person's relationship with God through Our Lady of Guadalupe. What does the metaphor of Our Lady of Guadalupe tell us about who God is?

A tremendous amount of scholarly work has been done on Mariology, less on Our Lady of Guadalupe. Because Our Lady of Guadalupe is a Marian image, Mariology can contribute to an understanding of the image of Our Lady of Guadalupe and the truth about God which she expresses. In this section I rely heavily upon the insightful scholarship of Elizabeth Johnson.

The Marian phenomenon throughout history has been powerful precisely because it is a female representation of the divine, bearing attributes otherwise excluded from mainline Christian perceptions of God as Father, Son, and Spirit. In official religiosity, the feminine face of God has been suppressed and excluded, and female images of God have migrated to the figure of Mary. Now some Catholics feel what Johnson calls a theological necessity: to express the mystery of a Christian God adequately, God must be envisioned in ways inclusive of the reality of women and other marginalized groups. Those elements in the Marian symbol which properly belong to divine reality must be retrieved (Johnson 1989:500–501).

Toward a more gender-inclusive theology of God, the Marian tradition offers its powerful maternal and other female images of the Divine. Through this process of integration, the figure of Mary no longer has to bear the burden of keeping alive female imagery of the Divine, and the figure of God becomes our loving Mother to whom we entrust our needs. Again, for some, it may be difficult to image the male face of God as a loving provider, but the Marian image is not meant to replace but to enhance the personhood of God.

There are many incidents of the split of divine attributes traditional in Christianity. In an influential work, theologian Edward Schillebeeckx (1964:101–128) argued that God's love is both paternal and maternal but that the mother aspect of God cannot be expressed through the historical figure of Jesus as a male. God selected Mary so that the "tender, mild, simple, generous, gentle and sweet" aspects of divine love could be made manifest: "Mary is the translation and effective expression in maternal terms of God's mercy, grace and redeeming love which manifested itself to us in a visible and tangible form in the person of Christ, our Redeemer."

Feminist theologian Elisabeth Schussler Fiorenza (1979) explains the split by a long process of patriarchalization, as a result of which the divine image became more remote and judgmental, while Mary became the beloved "other face" of God. Intellectually a distinction was maintained between adoration of God and veneration of Mary, but on the affective, imaginative level people experienced the love of God and the saving mystery of divine reality in the figure of Mary (Johnson 1989:513; Schussler Fiorenza (1983:130–140).

What accounts for Hispanics' massive and persistent devotion to Mary? Latin American and U.S. Hispanic theologians view Marian images from a liberationist theology point of view: Mary's cult appeals strongly to the oppressed because she gives dignity to downtrodden people and thus renews their energy to resist assimilation into the dominant culture. Further, as Virgil Elizondo points out, the cult not only liberates downtrodden peoples but also liberates us from a restrictive idea of God (Johnson 1989:514; Elizondo 1977:25–33, 1983b).

Within the Roman Catholic tradition Our Lady of Guadalupe is a Marian image, and within the Hispanic culture she is a mestiza, a mixture of both Spanish and Indian blood. The event and figure of Our Lady of Guadalupe combined the Nahuatl female expression of God with the Spanish male expression of God which had been incomprehensible to the Indians' duality—their belief that everything perfect has a male and female component. Each understanding of God was expanded by the other, yielding a new mestizo expression which enriches the understanding of the selfhood of God (Johnson 1989:515). "The results of the new expressions of God and the Mother of God are an amazing enrichment to the very understanding of the self-hood of God. There is no longer the European expression of God-Nahuatl, but a new mestizo expression which is mutually interpreted and enriching" (Elizondo 1983b:61).

"Even for those who do not find Mary a personally viable religious symbol, she nonetheless does represent the psychologically ultimate validity of the feminine, insuring a religious valuation of bodiliness, sensitivity, relationality, and nurturing qualities. . . . The symbol of Mary as feminine principle balances the masculine principle in the deity, which expresses itself in rationality, assertiveness, and independence" (Johnson 1989:517).

Within the Roman Catholic tradition Marian devotion and the study of Mary are sources of understanding the divinity in female language and symbols. Johnson identifies five female images for God: mother, divine compassion, divine power and might, divine presence (immanence), and a source of recreative energy. I take the same five images and apply them to Our Lady of Guadalupe.

Our Lady of Guadalupe manifests God as mother: Our Lady of Guadalupe identifies herself as Our Loving Mother and people see her as a mother, a maternal presence, consoling, nurturing, offering unconditional love, comforting—qualities which tell us that mother is an appropriate metaphor for God. "Transferring this maternal language back to God enables us to see that God has a maternal countenance. All that is creative and generative of life, all that nourishes and nurtures, all that is benign, cherishes, and sustains, all that is solicitous and sympathetic originates in God/Her" (Johnson 1989:520).

Madonna Kolbenschlag's work *Lost in the Land of Oz* (1988:9) addresses the importance and necessity of the maternal. She identifies orphanhood metaphorically as "the deepest, most fundamental reality: experiences of attachment and abandonment, of expectation and deprivation, of loss and failure, and of loneliness." What message does Our Lady of Guadalupe offer to the spiritual orphans of the twentieth century through the metaphor of mother? That we are lovable and capable, that we belong, that we can grow and be transformed, and that there is a reason to live and a reason to hope.

Our Lady of Guadalupe manifests God's compassion: Our Lady of Guadalupe came to show forth her love, compassion, help, defense, and her presence among the people. "Returning this language to God, to whom it properly belongs, enables us to name the holy mystery as essentially and unfathomably merciful. God is the Mother of mercy who has compassionate womb-love for all God's children. We need not be afraid to approach. She is brimming over with gentleness, loving kindness, and forgiveness" (Johnson 1989:521). In the interviews with the women in my study, we have seen how they take their troubles to Our Lady of Guadalupe because they experience her as being compassionate and responsive to their needs, in a way which, if present, nevertheless has not been identified in their relationship to God. She will understand them better than the male face of God because she too is female and a mother.

Our Lady of Guadalupe manifests divine power and might: The word "power" comes from the Latin *posse,* meaning to be able, yet often when we think of power it is in terms of having power *over* someone or something, rather than having power *with.* Again and again, the women in my study found that in encountering and being in the presence of Our Lady of Guadalupe they regained their sense of self in an accepting and empowering relationship.

Our Lady of Guadalupe images power *with,* in a dynamism centered around mutuality, trust, participation, and regard. The power accessed by these women in their dialogue with Our Lady of Guadalupe is the power of memory, which she continues to stand for, justice, solidarity with the oppressed, belonging, unconditional love, the power of expressed feelings and sharing (women come to her and share their immediate needs and they feel heard). The power of commitment, the power to endure suffering, the power of caring, the power of risk ("As long as she is beside me, I'm going to keep trying"), the power of naming their fears, the power of knowing that the way things are is not the way things are meant to be, and with her help they are encouraged and given hope. She gives them not the will to suffer under injustice, but the will to continue la lucha (the struggle).

Our Lady of Guadalupe manifests, symbolizes, and activates the power of the people, in this case the power of the poor people. In the Nican Mopohua, it is the poor Indian Juan Diego who evangelizes the bishop, whose conversion enables him to work with the poor, the marginalized, and the indigenous. Siller emphasizes the Nahuatl image of yollo (the heart), which moves us to action; if a devotion to Our Lady of Guadalupe does not bring us closer to action and to solidarity with the cause of the poor, then the devotion is not authentically Guadalupana. This heart, love, relationship, and consciousness emerging from the poor calls us to act on behalf of the poor.

Our Lady of Guadalupe manifests the presence of God: (I have addressed this in the previous section about Our Lady of Guadalupe as a symbol of God's unconditional love.)

Our Lady of Guadalupe manifests God as a source of recreating energy: "Attributing this imagery of plenty and new beginnings directly to God allows us to affirm that it is God's own self that is the source of transforming energy among all creatures. She initiates novelty, instigates change, transforms what is dead" (Johnson 1989:524). This is clearly seen in the timing of the apparition of Our Lady of Guadalupe. As argued [previously], she came at a time when the people were spiritually dead, abandoned by their gods, with no reason to live. Our Lady of Guadalupe's coming restored the people's reason to live and to hope. She identified herself using the familiar Nahuatl expressions of God, which showed the people that she came from the region of the gods.

In the Nahuatl culture the one supreme god, Ometeotl, was the god of duality, with both masculine and feminine principles. Because Ometeotl was invisible, there was no physical representation of this god, who was known by the titles of the Most True God, the God Who Gives Us Life, the Inventor and Creator of People, the Owner of What Is around Us and Very Close to Us, and the Owner and Lord of the Earth (Siller-Acuña 1989:48).

The Nahuatl names for God are not just dimensions but ultimate metaphors for who God is. And because they contain that which gave life to the people, those metaphors become a source of recreating energy.

Bibliography

Elizondo, Virgilio P. "Our Lady of Guadalupe as a Cultural Symbol: The Power of the Powerless," in *Liturgy and Cultural Religious Traditions*, ed. Herman Schmidt and David Power, 25–33, Concilium 102. New York: Seabury, 1977.

———. *La Morenita: Evangelizer of the Americas*. San Antonio: Mexican American Cultural Center, 1980.

Espín, Dr. Orlando. "The Vanquished, Faithful Solidarity and the Marian Symbol: A Hispanic Perspective on Providence," in *On Keeping Providence*, ed. J. Coultas and B. Doherty. Terre Haute, Ind.: St. Mary of the Woods Colleges Press, 1991.

Johnson, Elizabeth A., C.S.J. "The Incomprehensibility of God and the Image of God Male and Female," *Theological Studies* 45, no. 3 (1984): 441–80.

———. "The Marian Tradition and the Reality of Women," *Horizons: Journal of the College Theology Society*, 12, no. 1 (1985):116–35.

———. "Mary and the Female Face of God." *Theological Studies*, 50, no. 3 (1989), 501–26.

Kolbenschlag, Madonna. *Lost in the Land of Oz*. San Francisco: Harper and Row, 1988.

Schillebeeckx, Edward. *Mary, Mother of the Redemption*. New York: Sheed and Ward, 1964.

Schussler Fiorenza, Elizabeth. *In Memory of Her: A Feminist Theological Reconstruction of Christian Origins*. New York: Crossroads, 1983.

Siller-Acuña, Clodomiro L. *Flor y canto de Tepeyac: Historia de las apariciones de Santa Maria de Guadalupe; Texto y comentario*. Xalapa, Veracruz, Mexico: Servir, 1981.

———. "Para comprender el mensaje de María de Guadalupe," in *Editorial Guadalupe*, n.d.

Tonantzin

FRANCISCO X.
ALARCÓN

Madre	Mother
¿aquí estás	are you here
con nosotros?	with us?
enjuáganos	wipe up
el sudor	our sweat
las lágrimas	our tears
Coatlicue	Coatlicue
tú que reinas	you who rule
sobre las serpientes	over snakes
Chalchiuhcueye	Chalchiuhcueye
haznos	grant us
el favor	our request
Citlalcueye	Citlalcueye
que nos guíen	let your stars
tus estrellas	guide us

Guadalupe	*Guadalupe*
sé nuestra aurora	be our dawn
nuestra esperanza	our hope
¡bandera	the flag
y fuego de	and fire of
nuestra rebelión!	our rebellion!

Guadalupe: The Path of the Broken Heart

CLARISSA PINKOLA ESTÉS

Understand my life, thereby understand my work.
V. S. NAIPAUL

Listen young ones, you have written to me that you feel called as mystics. Some of you have had several visions or just one little one—which can be enough to last many a lifetime—or you have rightfully swooned in some other way for Nuestra Señora, Guadalupe, in one of Her many forms. And now you write to me because you have heard of our La Sociedad de Nuestra Señora, Guadalupe, our group of social activists dedicated to being contemplatives in the world. And you wish to know what to call the experiences you have been having. The old-fashioned words are *appearances* and *apparitions*. But I advise you to just call them by simple words. They are *visits*, as from a great and beloved sister-mother, who because of long-standing love and familiarity with you, comes through the door without knocking in order to deliver some sweet or strong dulces o carnes, sweet bread or meaty nourishments to you.

Now you have stated seriously that you have no access to caves where you can take up residence in order to pursue your love of Her in a solitary way. M'hijas y m'hijos, understand that wherever is your bed, that is the right cave for you. Your own cellar, your own table, your own street corner, your own bicycle, your own alley—these are all the right caves. It is true that some people teach that mystics live in out-of-the-way places, but many, many across the world live exactly as you do—in the most hidden way of all—as very extraordinary souls living in very ordinary circumstances.

This is right and proper, for although it is lovely to think of retiring to a faraway place of great beauty and serenity where the outer world hardly ever intrudes, She grows her strongest roses in the soil where they are most needed, among horns honking, ambulances running, children crying, all the people groaning and dancing and making love, the complete trochimochi of humanity whose singings, sounds, and cries are the exact basis for the harmonious music of the cosmos.

Some say that sudden knowledge of mystical matters is accomplished in complete quietude, or that God, in God's many forms, appears only in orderly ways that are beauteous and picturesque, or in completely silent ways, and for some, this is definitely true. For instance, the great mystic Jakob Boehme saw a sunbeam glint on the edge of a pewter plate and was transported into a lifelong religious ecstasy. Castiejo entered a convent. Others developed under what many would call privileged conditions. But the best, m'hijos y m'hijas, grow where they are seeded. Exactly.

You ask, since your visits from Her were not calm like those at Fatima or Lourdes, or even those of our dear relative now known in history by his colonized name only, Don Diego—are your experiences somehow wrong? No, no, my hearts, no they are not wrong. They are completely righteous. I assure you most definitively that The Beloved One comes in complete calmness to some. But, in my experience, more often, She appears in times that are not calm; in clouds of dust that are not particularly picturesque. She comes skidding to a sudden stop in dark cars on even darker gravel roads. She stands in the midst of broken glass at curbs. She walks in every street, stands at every street corner, even those where it seems that maybe even God Herself ought to be cautious.

To be a contemplative and a follower of Her, I believe it is likely that She will appear to you as much in the midst of noise, upheaval, and times when we feel the sky is falling, as when there is peace all around, at least in one's own little universe. She is often most present when there is most need for order, strength, fierceness, hope, and vitality.

Now, you write that all around you everything seems often in complete mayhem, and this causes you great sadness. I would agree completely. Our own sorrows seem heavy enough even when lifted by certain long-term joys. But watching others hurt and hurting is the breaker of most any heart. She is clearly with you, for the kinds of lives we have led would lead many to become thick with cynicism and biting. And so here are your hearts still unruined. This is a very good sign. Too, I would like to say to you that there is great power in the broken heart. Unlike many that close or hide when hurt, the heart broken open, stays open. The heart broken open can be a blessing beyond compare. It not only allows you to see others, it allows you to constantly see Her.

Just this last December, one more time, my heart broke again. How many times must a heart break in a single lifetime? When I ask this question, I always receive this answer—a thousand times a thousand for anything worth having.

Allow me to tell you about it and perhaps this can demonstrate to you two important things. First, that ministering in Her name is very, very simple. Second, that for many, the essence of God does not occur in silent and golden appearances, but more often in the midst of the mud and dirt, in the storms and thunder of daily life.

Last December, I spent an entire morning preparing to go on pilgrimage. This kind of pilgrimaging I have done many times, over thirty years' time. The pilgrimage I go on has no ending that I know of. I go to the shrine where most people never go, to a dark, dark hovel filled with the most imploring souls imaginable, the most brave, the most innocent of almost any, a place filled with people who have many, as Adrienne Rich puts it, courage bones. Although I have for part of my adult life looked longingly at the colorful brochures that are popular of late, those advertising group tours and exotic voyages to faraway sites — the Aegean Islands, the Temple Sites tour, the Stonehenge Gathering, the others—I have gotten to be fifty years old and I have not yet been away from North and South America. Perhaps someday. If I hear Her call me there.

For now, I am preparing to go to that place where no one is asking for much other than only to endure, and to one day be freed from all that oppresses. It is a place where no soap, no rag can wipe away the tears that have been shed on the floors there. It is a condensed world made from the distillation and packing together of many souls, all ready to either unfurl or run or pounce. Unlike most shrines—and it is a shrine to the profound humility of the wanderer—but instead of being filled with hope, this place is filled with misled hearts, with cruel twists of fate, with broken promises from coyotes, and worse.

I am a pilgrim to the immigration jail. All the people to be deported are being held there and cannot go back home to their Haitian, Mexican, or Puerto Rican families, for the Republicans in the 104th Congress have threatened and made good on a shutdown of the federal government. Many souls will be held in jail until late January, some longer. Their parents, loved ones, their novias and novios will not know their whereabouts for a long and chilling time. There are many frightened mothers and sisters and fathers and brothers praying at the iglesias in Mexico, Haiti, and Puerto Rico for the safe return of their loved ones. With extra charges placed on prison phone calls, calling collect to Mexico alone, with hook-up fee and all the rest, can cost more than five dollars a minute. Most here do not even have fifty cents. It is a joke among us all about who ought to be put in jail, our hermanos y hermanas, or los políticos, the politicians.

I pack my bolsita with various small treasures, holy cards, various tiny remedios that the guards will let me bring in, rosaries for those in greatest need. Lastly comes the tiny container with the much used cotton ball saturated with chrism. Before Father Melton, a giant black priest teaching a midwestern parish of astonished Euro-Americans his deeply ethnic form of Catholicism, graciously gave me his own personal container of healing oil, mine was made of a bullet shell casing that my great-aunt swore came from Emiliano Zapata's own rifle during the revolución.

There is something else I take with me on pilgrimage also, the most important something that has no object attached to its memory. I take a mandate from mi Guadalupe, one given to me long ago as a child. Every time I go on pilgrimage to prison or to the street or to my writing table, I think of events from long ago. And this is what I will now relate to you here. For why should I leave my warm bed to go to a cold jail in the midst of winter to see those whom I will never see again? You, already having your own visits from Her already know how She works. Let us see.

When I was seven years old, the grown-ups from my home and school life told me that I had at last reached "the age of reason."

Apparently, in spite of my many childhood jailbreaks, running away from the house to be in the massive cathedrals of the forest, or baptizing flowers and children smaller than I in the creek, or staying late in the forest at night to see the eerie swampfire, in spite of these semi-terrible transgressions, I, the little ecstatic child-wanderer, was now qualified to be "reason-able."

In our family, several of our old ones did their own blessings and ablutions after the more formal ones at the parish, whether baptism, first confession, holy communion. Back in those times, members of the family had three times more sacraments than the parish had, including the old ablutions for childbearing and child-bearing loss, for recovery from failed love, repair of the body's inner sight and hearing, repair from wars of many kinds, and pledges of loyalty and foreverness for the betrothed and blessings on many, many other matters of life and death and rebirth.

So it was not unusual that after this talk about having reached the age of reason one of my aunties, Kati, whom I loved the smell and sight and sound of, leaned near, and joked that this whole passage should really be called "the ache of reason." She was my cohort in little mischiefs, such as staying too long gazing at sunset over the fields, letting me take my grisly shoes off, which were heavy "corrective" ones that went in directions my feet and ankles did not. Those kindly sorts of things.

But now she gazed at me seriously and instructed that for two weeks after my consecration to Her, Our Lady, I might be able to know my future. That the curtain between the worlds would part for two weeks only. That I might be able to see across the void to the other world. That I should pay deep attention to what I would see, for what events, matters, comings and goings in particular would capture my heart. And that these special noticings could be understood as pointing the way toward my future life and work.

This whispering and rustling of my aunt, and of the wings around her, did not disturb me, for what is a Católica born to strive toward but the charisms, the gifts of the Holy Spirit? We try to take our spiritual understandings both seriously and with good humor. We know we sometimes appear to others as following odd rituals and requirements. But we nevertheless strive toward what we hold to be true—in my case and those all around me, our insights, intuitions, visions, prayers, dreams and prophecies that surround the intercession of The Great Holy Woman.

Now that I was old enough, sentient enough, I received my lifetime consecration to La Mujer Grande, the Great Woman. Ah, it was a ritual that I think Thoreau would have approved, even though he cautioned against occasions requiring new clothes. I had a new little shawl my aunt had crocheted for me. There was no pomp, but there were avid and earnest askings and blessings. The old women and nuns—all seemed to wear the same kind of black shoes with Cuban heels. There were fog banks of incense, chanting of the most vivid adorations and much swinging of black rosaries, some with beads made from the walnut tree, some made of seeds. All of this I loved from the very center of my being outward and back again.

With my arms outstretched to their fullest extent, and my eyes lifted to Her, I knelt for what seemed like hours on the coldest brick floor imaginable, until that terrible ache from cold, like a pneumonia in the knees, began. I was asked to repeat after the adults many things—and I remember also repeating words that pledged my virginity to Blessed Mother for all time. I said the holy words earnestly as I had been taught—"with thinking, but without blinking." I knew what a virgin was: Firstly, it was Guadalupe's first name. Like my own first two names, or like one of my friends, María Cecilia. Virgin Guadalupe. Secondly, to be "virgin" meant to try to be as She was—brilliantly colored, fierce, watchful, with the loyalty of a good dog.

My aunt having told me that in the next thirteen days I would see thirteen things that would affect me for life, "that will call for your help, your hands, your heart for the rest of your life," I now tried to keep my eyes truly open. She had said, "You are a little child and you can still see what most who are older no longer care to see, you can see what needs help."

In that week I saw many things. Most were not out of the ordinary for our lives and times; they were either arrestingly beautiful or arrestingly violent, but no more than usual, for I lived in a place where great beauty and great violence in the midwestern rural backwoods was unrelentingly normative. There, many feasted on the beauty and many, many had become inured to the violence in its many forms. In response and in efforts to repair themselves from the latter, some hardened, some fell, some bowed heads and went on, some escaped, others endured. Anyone who has lived through this knows exactly how it was.

So, many things did I see during those thirteen holy days that my aunt had prepared me for. But one of the most startling I saw as I wandered down a dirt road through the far woods. A little ways down the road a big sheriff's car, in an even bigger cloud of dust, skidded to a stop off to the side of the road where a little deeper in the woods was a stick-pole encampment of some of the hobo people who regularly jumped from the freight train uproad and stayed for periods of time in our neck of the woods.

I think there are times when you can smell mal-intention coming. I quickly jumped into the field at the roadside and lay down to hide, amongst the dry stalks there. The deputies jerked aside the canvas flap of the stick-pole tent and charged right in. Less than a minute later, amidst all hell breaking loose and with terrible sound of cook pots clanging and falling and scuffling sounds, and much crying out and epithets, one deputy dragged a half-naked man in manacles from out of the canvas hovel.

He was dressed like many who lived hidden in that part of the woods, many who came up from the hills, some of whom I had made best friends with. His torn strappy T-shirt was gray with oils, his trousers were stained with paint and dirt. He was unwashed, unshaven, uncombed, and, like a bull roped to the ground, his eyes were rolling, his mouth slobbering as he cried out what sounded to me like, "Milady! Milady!" The deputy shoved the disheveled man into the patrol car and slammed the door and ran back to the tent.

As I watched frightened and horror-stricken, I thought I heard in my head a calm and gentle voice asking, "Do you love me?"

"Love you? Love you?" I thought. My anguish over what I was seeing was so great I could hardly comprehend the words being spoken into the ear of my heart.

"If you love me, comfort them."

"What?" I thought, trying to understand. Before I could react, the deputies dragged a screaming woman from the tent. She struggled against their manhandling of her. She had a short lit cigarette between two fingers, and she wore only one shoe, a broken-down black flat, making me think of crickets and shiny beetles. The men had hold of her so-thin arms, like a corpse's almost, and right before my eyes they bent her arms backwards to angles not truly possible. And she was all flaming words and flailing limbs. She screamed and screamed and for one breathtaking moment I felt she looked directly at me, appealing directly to me, though surely she could not have seen me in the dense field across the road. "Help me, help me," she cried in the most pitiful manner.

One officer had pulled her head back by her long hair. Another was trying to pull her sweater up out of the back of her trousers to pull it up over her head like a hanging hood. "Help me, help me," she screamed again and again.

I heard a calm voice in my panicked heart ask:

"Do you love me?

"If you do, then help me."

I felt deeply confused, yet I shot up like a quail. I had sudden turbines in my legs, my arms reaching ten feet ahead of me, my lungs filling with a gigantic thundercloud. My head back, I ran like a crazy child the distance down and across the road. The deputies were pushing her into the car, they were slamming the door on the couple. The officers piled into the front seat and slammed their own doors. I could still hear the woman screaming:

"Help me, help me."

Completely panicked but somehow able, I thought, "Yes, I will help you." Agonized still, but in a new way, I thought, "But how? How?"

I came up alongside the back end of the big sedan just as the car began pulling away. I yelled out loudly—I hope I called out in a voice that could be heard from earth to the heavens, but I am afraid that I was so filled with fear that maybe I only croaked. Yet, I felt I pulled in the breath of windstorms and that I thundered out as strongly as I could, just as I had witnessed the old women do in the healing rituals, "In Her name and all that is holy, do these people no harm!"

The deputies startled and braked the car. I just had enough time to throw myself across the trunk where the faces of the two haggard and manacled souls gazed up at me with what seemed like excellent wonder. I just had enough time, one split second, to use three of my fingers at once to make the Sign of the Cross on the dusty back window and cry out, "These souls are under my protection." Now the car window was rolling down on the driver's side. I skidded off the car and fell to the road, seeing my own reflection in the mud-specked hubcap. Now the door was opening on the driver's side. I scrabbled to my feet, and ran as though a demon were chasing me. I ran and ran like a crazy thing far into the field.

The patrol car pulled away and kept going. Over my shoulder I could see the crosses on the back window of the car. I had made them big, all three of them, all intersecting, big and bold. Like Her. Igualmente. Like the hearts and souls of the man and the woman they took away. Igualmente. Like the true hearts and souls of the unawakened men who took them away. Igualmente.

I did not know what I enacted then or later. I am not ever certain yet these many years later. I only know I followed rather than led. After the sheriff's car was gone, I crashed deeper and deeper into the forest until I found my way to the creek, sat down, fell down really, and could not get up again for my legs shook so. My stomach was sick just like the time I once, in a childish experiment, mixed together milk and grapefruit juice and drank it. I finally rolled on my side and threw up. I crawled over into one of the hanging scrub oak warrens, lay facedown for a long time, breathing in the rich healing fragrance of the iron-filled earth of my home. I cried many tears about matters that I can hardly explain. Later, I walked into the river with my big awkward shoes on. I lay in the loving water, not as Ophelia, but as baptism, reburied into the life of the living once more.

I do not know what the man and woman did wrong. Likely nothing. Vagrant. Talking too loud, making love too loud, or just by their presence disturbing the gentry who had come to build big houses out in the woods and who we knew were made uncomfortable by us, the truly rustic. I only know that the sounds of thuds of fists on bone is a truly sickening sound and sight, and the sound and feel of these were not unfamiliar to me before or after. Life went on. But for me, not as before.

Though I could go on as before, pick self up for thousandth time, millionth time, and go on because there was nothing else to do, because it was a wrong time in the culture wherein there was no direct help, no aid, no looking to see what was wrong about the things I had witnessed that day and more—still, I could never forget. I had had a strange moment in time, what I someday would come to understand as the transformative moment, as when lightning strikes, and all vision and knowing is changed in an instant. On the road with the people in the woods, I thought I had seen the holy people being manhandled. Through the back of the car window, those poor imprisoned innocents, I thought I saw for a moment, both of them, man and woman, as mi Guadalupe. I thought I for a split second, saw in both of them mi Guadalupe suffering. I thought I saw Her being assaulted. This was the end of my life as I had known it to that time. "Do you love me? Then help me." This was one of my thirteen post-consecration callings.

When I told my aunt what had happened, she cried and took my hands. "You do not have to ask who says, 'They are under my protection,' " she said. "You already know."

I felt I did know.

Twelve years later, when I was nineteen, I heard this from Her:

"Do you love me, my sister?"

I answered, "Yes, my Dear One, I love you."

"How much do you love me?"

"With all my heart, my Beloved."

"Will you then visit me in prison?"

"In prison?"

I was afraid to go to prison. But I went, as I would go on pilgrimage in the ensuing years to other prisons, those made by government, and those many, many soul prisons, human-made, and to my own imprisonments, as well, some of choice, some by fate.

I promised then that if I kept hearing Her call, I would try to keep going where sent. As you can see, I am a fool for Her completely. I am still going. This time it is the immigration jail; other years, it has been pilgrimages several times a year to other places— the locked institution for boys aged eighteen to twenty-one, the locked institutions for girls and boys aged twelve to eighteen, the men's penitentiary, the women's federal prison, the city and the county jails, the state prisons, sometimes ministering to patients at city hospitals brought in chains for a needed surgery.

It goes on, as it always has.

Do you love me?

Yes, I love you.

Will you then come visit me in the home for unwed mothers?

I would—and there the next sword was run through my heart.

Do you love me?

Yes, I love you.

Will you help run a shelter for battered women? Will you lick the wounds of the wounded?

Yes. Another sword.

Do you love me?

Yes, I love you, my Dear.

Will you walk with me through skid row with alcohol swabs and wipe hands and feet teeming with bacteria, the cuts and hurts of the men and women who can hardly be told apart. Will you do that for me?

Yes. A big sword.

Do you love me?

With all that I am.

Will you stand in the cold of a Chicago night in the dead of the winter listening to me dressed as an old man telling his life's tale with the worst breath you could ever imagine?

Yes, this I can do.

Do you love me? Do you love me?

Yes, yes, a thousand times yes.

So, m'hijas y m'hijos, now I am at the end of this missive to you. You have asked me the way to continue and to deepen your devotion to Her. I have this great feeling in my bones that you already well know the way and just need a tiny little reminder. She comes in untidy ways mostly, often in very big and very bold form rather than demure. You will recognize Her on sight, for She is a woman who looks just like you and all that you love.

Mi Guadalupe is a girl gang leader in heaven.
She is unlike the pale blue serene woman.
She is serene, yes, like a great ocean is serene.
She is obedient, yes, like the sunrise
is obedient to the horizon line.
She is sweet, yes,
like a huge forest of sweet maple trees.
She has a great heart, vast holiness
and like any girl gang leader ought,
substantial hips.

Her lap is big enough
to hold every last one.
Her embrace
can hold us,
All . . .[1]

[1] Excerpt from epic 65-page poem, "Mi Guadalupe" by C. P. Estés © 1980.

Guadalupe the Sex Goddess

SANDRA CISNEROS

*I*n high school I marveled at how white women strutted around the locker room, nude as pearls, as unashamed of their brilliant bodies as the Nike of Samothrace. Maybe they were hiding terrible secrets like bulimia or anorexia, but to my naive eye then, I thought of them as women comfortable in their skin.

You could always tell us Latinas. We hid when we undressed, modestly facing a wall, or, in my case, dressing in a bathroom stall. We were the ones who still used bulky sanitary pads instead of tampons, thinking ourselves morally superior to our white classmates. *My mama said you can't use tampons till after you're married.* All Latina mamas said this, yet how come none of us thought to ask our mothers why they didn't use tampons *after* getting married?

Womanhood was full of mysteries. I was as ignorant about my own body as any female ancestor who hid behind a sheet with a hole in the center when husband or doctor called. Religion and our culture, our culture and religion, helped to create that blur, a vagueness about what went on "down there." (So ashamed was I about my own "down there" that until I was an adult I had no idea I had another orifice called the vagina; I thought my period would arrive via the urethra or perhaps through the walls of my skin.)

No wonder, then, it was too terrible to think about a doctor— a man!—looking at you down there when you could never bring yourself to look yourself. *¡Ay, nunca!* How could I acknowledge my sexuality, let alone enjoy sex, with so much guilt? In the guise of modesty my culture locked me in a double chastity belt of ignorance and *vergüenza*, shame.

I had never seen my mother nude. I had never taken a good look at myself either. Privacy for self-exploration belonged to the wealthy. In my home a private space was practically impossible; aside from the doors that opened to the street, the only room with a lock was the bathroom, and how could anyone who shared a bathroom with eight other people stay in there for more than a few minutes? Before college, no one in my family had a room of their own except me, a narrow closet just big enough for my twin bed and an oversized blond dresser we'd bought in the bargain basement of *el Sears*. The dresser was as long as a coffin and blocked the door from shutting completely. I had my own room, but I never had the luxury of shutting the door.

I didn't even see my own sex until a nurse at an Emma Goldman Clinic showed it to me—*Would you like to see your cervix? Your os is dilating. You must be ovulating. Here's a mirror, take a look.* When had anyone ever suggested I take a look or allowed me a speculum to take home and investigate myself at leisure!

I'd only been to one other birth control facility prior to the Emma Goldman Clinic, the university medical center in grad school. I was twenty-one, in a strange town far from home for the first time. I was afraid and I was ashamed to seek out a gynecologist, but I was more afraid of becoming pregnant. Still, I agonized about going for weeks. Perhaps the anonymity and distance from my family allowed me finally to take control of my life. I remember wanting to be fearless like the other women around me, to be able to have sex when I wanted, but I was too afraid to explain to a would-be lover how I'd only had one other man in my life and we'd practiced withdrawal. Would he laugh at me? How could I look anyone in the face and explain why I couldn't go see a gynecologist?

One night a classmate I liked too much took me home with him. I meant all along to say something about how I wasn't on anything, but I never quite found my voice, never the right moment to cry out—*Stop, this is dangerous to my brilliant career!* Too afraid to sound stupid, afraid to ask him to take responsibility too, I said nothing, and I let him take me like that with nothing protecting me from motherhood but luck. The days that followed were torture, but fortunately on Mother's Day my period arrived, and I celebrated my nonmaternity by making an appointment with the family-planning center.

When I see pregnant teens, I can't help but think that could've been me. In high school I would've thrown myself into love the way some warriors throw themselves into fighting. I was ready to sacrifice everything in the name of love, to do anything, even risk my own life, but thankfully there were no takers. I was enrolled at an all-girls' school. I think if I had met a boy who would have me, I would've had sex in a minute, convinced this was love. I have always had enough imagination to fall in love all by myself, then and now.

I tell you this story because I am overwhelmed by the silence regarding Latinas and our bodies. If I, as a graduate student, was shy about talking to anyone about my body and sex, imagine how difficult it must be for a young girl in middle school or high school living in a home with no lock on the bedroom door, perhaps with no door, or maybe with no bedroom, no information other than misinformation from the girlfriends and the boyfriend. So much guilt, so much silence, and such a yearning to be loved; no wonder young women find themselves having sex while they are still children, having sex without sexual protection, too ashamed to confide their feelings and fears to anyone.

What a culture of denial. Don't get pregnant! But no one tells you how not to. This is why I was angry for so many years every time I saw *la Virgen de Guadalupe*, my culture's role model for brown women like me. She was damn dangerous, an ideal so lofty and unrealistic it was laughable. Did boys have to aspire to be Jesus? I never saw any evidence of it. They were fornicating like rabbits while the Church ignored them and pointed us women toward our destiny— marriage and motherhood. The other alternative was *puta*hood.

In my neighborhood I knew only real women, neither saints nor whores, naive and vulnerable *huerquitas* like me who wanted desperately to fall in love, with the heart and soul. And yes, with the *panocha*, too.

As far as I could see, *la Lupe* was nothing but a goody two shoes meant to doom me to a life of unhappiness. Thanks but no thanks. Motherhood and/or marriage were anathema to my career. But being a bad girl, that was something I could use as a writer, a Molotov to toss at my papa and *el Papa* who had their own plans for me.

Discovering sex was like discovering writing. It was powerful in a way I couldn't explain. Like writing, you had to go beyond the guilt and shame to get to anything good. Like writing, it could take you to deep and mysterious subterranean levels. With each new depth I found out things about myself I didn't know I knew. And, like writing, for a slip of a moment it could be spiritual, the cosmos pivoting on a pin, could empty and fill you all at once like a Ganges, a Piazzolla tango, a tulip bending in the wind. I was no one, I was nothing, and I was everything in the universe little and large—twig, cloud, sky. How had this incredible energy been denied me!

When I look at *la Virgen de Guadalupe* now, she is not the Lupe of my childhood, no longer the one in my grandparents' house in Tepeyac, nor is she the one of the Roman Catholic Church, the one I bolted the door against in my teens and twenties. Like every woman who matters to me, I have had to search for her in the rubble of history. And I have found her. She is Guadalupe the sex goddess, a goddess who makes me feel good about my sexual power, my sexual energy, who reminds me I must, as Clarissa Pinkola Estés so aptly put it, "[speak] from the vulva . . . speak the most basic, honest truth," and write from my *panocha.*

In my research of Guadalupe's pre-Columbian antecedents, the she before the Church desexed her, I found Tonantzin, and inside Tonantzin a pantheon of other mother goddesses. I discovered Tlazolteotl, the goddess of fertility and sex, also referred to as Totzin, Our Beginnings, or Tzinteotl, goddess of the rump. *Putas,* nymphos, and other loose women were known as "women of the sex goddess." Tlazolteotl was the patron of sexual passion, and though she had the power to stir you to sin, she could also forgive you and cleanse you of your sexual transgressions via her priests who heard confession. In this aspect of confessor Tlazolteotl was known as Tlaelcuani, the filth eater. Maybe you've seen her; she's the one sold in the tourist markets even now, a statue of a woman squatting in childbirth, her face grimacing in pain. Tlazolteotl, then, is a duality of maternity *and* sexuality. In other words, she is a sexy mama.

To me *la Virgen de Guadalupe* is also Coatlicue, the creative/destructive goddess. When I think of the Coatlicue statue in the National Museum in Mexico City, so terrible it was unearthed and then reburied because it was too frightening to look at, I think of a woman enraged, a woman as tempest, a woman *bien berrinchuda,* and I like that. *La Lupe* as *cabrona.* Not silent and passive, but silently gathering force.

Most days I, too, feel like the creative/destructive goddess Coatlicue, especially the days I'm writing, capable of fabricating pretty tales with pretty words, as well as doing demolition work with a volley of *palabrotas* if I want to. I am the Coatlicue-Lupe whose square column of a body I see in so many Indian women, in my mother, and in myself each time I check out my thick-waisted, flat-assed torso in the mirror.

Coatlicue, Tlazolteotl, Tonantzin, *la Virgen de Guadalupe.* They are each telescoped one into the other, into who I am. And this is where *la Lupe* intrigues me—not the Lupe of 1531 who appeared to Juan Diego, but the one of the 1990s who has shaped who we are as Chicanas/*mexicanas* today, the one inside each Chicana and *mexicana.* Perhaps it's the Tlazolteotl-Lupe in me whose *malcriada* spirit inspires me to leap into the swimming pool naked or dance on a table with a skirt on my head. Maybe it's my Coatlicue-Lupe attitude that makes it possible for my mother to tell me, *No wonder men can't stand you.* Who knows? What I do know is this; I am obsessed with becoming a woman comfortable in her skin.

I can't attribute my religious conversion to a flash of lightning on the road to Laredo or anything like that. Instead, there have been several lessons learned subtly over a period of time. A grave depression and near suicide in my thirty-third year and its subsequent retrospection. Vietnamese Buddhist monk Thich Nhat Hanh's writing that has brought out the Buddha-Lupe in me. My weekly peace vigil for my friend Jasna in Sarajevo. The writings of Gloria Anzaldúa. A crucial trip back to Tepeyac in 1985 with Cherríe Moraga and Norma Alarcón. Drives across Texas talking with other Chicanas. And research for stories that would force me back inside the Church from which I'd fled.

My *Virgen de Guadalupe* is not the mother of God. She is God. She is a face for a god without a face, an *indígena* for a god without ethnicity, a female deity for a god who is genderless, but I also understand that for her to approach me, for me to finally open the door and accept her, she had to be a woman like me.

Once, watching a porn film, I saw a sight that terrified me. It was the film star's *panocha*—a tidy, elliptical opening, pink and shiny like a rabbit's ear. To make matters worse, it was shaved and looked especially childlike and unsexual. I think what startled me most was the realization that my own sex has no resemblance to this woman's. My sex, dark as an orchid, rubbery and blue purple as *pulpo*, an octopus, does not look nice and tidy, but otherworldly. I do not have little rosette nipples. My nipples are big and brown, like the Mexican coins of my childhood.

When I see *la Virgen de Guadalupe* I want to lift her dress as I did my dolls' and look to see if she comes with *chones*, and does her *panocha* look like mine, and does she have dark nipples too? Yes, I am certain she does. She is not neuter like Barbie. She gave birth. She has a womb. *Blessed art thou and blessed is the fruit of thy womb* . . . Blessed art thou, Lupe, and, therefore, blessed am I.

Coatlalopeuh, *She Who Has Dominion Over Serpents*

GLORIA ANZALDÚA

Mi mamagrande Ramona toda su vida mantuvo un altar pequeño en la esquina del comedor. Siempre tenía las velas prendidas. Allí hacía promesas a la Virgen de Guadalupe. My family, like most Chicanos, did not practice Roman Catholicism but a folk Catholicism with many pagan elements. *La Virgen de Guadalupe's* Indian name is *Coatlalopeuh.* She is the central deity connecting us to our Indian ancestry.

Coatlalopeuh is descended from, or is an aspect of, earlier Mesoamerican fertility and Earth goddesses. The earliest is *Coatlicue,* or "Serpent Skirt." She had a human skull or serpent for a head, a necklace of human hearts, a skirt of twisted serpents and taloned feet. As creator goddess, she was mother of the celestial deities, and of *Huitzilopochtli* and his sister, *Coyolxauhqui,* She With Golden Bells, Goddess of the Moon, who was decapitated by her brother. Another aspect of *Coatlicue* is *Tonantsi.* The Totonacs, tired of the Aztec human sacrifices to the male god, *Huitzilopochtli,* renewed their reverence for *Tonantsi,* who preferred the sacrifice of birds and small animals.

The male-dominated Azteca-Mexica culture drove the powerful female deities underground by giving them monstrous attributes and by substituting male deities in their place, thus splitting the female Self and the female deities. They divided her who had been complete, who possessed both upper (light) and underworld (dark) aspects. *Coatlicue,* the Serpent goddess, and her more sinister aspects, *Tlazolteotl* and *Cihuacoatl,* were "darkened" and disempowered much in the same manner as the Indian *Kali.*

Tonantsi—split from her dark guises, *Coatlicue, Tlazolteotl,* and *Cihuacoatl*—became the good mother. The Nahuas, through ritual and prayer, sought to oblige *Tonantsi* to ensure their health and the growth of their crops. It was she who gave *México* the cactus plant to provide her people with milk and pulque. It was she who defended her children against the wrath of the Christian God by challenging God, her son, to produce mother's milk (as she had done) to prove that his benevolence equaled his disciplinary harshness.

After the Conquest, the Spaniards and their Church continued to split *Tonantsi/Guadalupe.* They desexed *Guadalupe,* taking *Coatlalopeuh,* the serpent/sexuality, out of her. They completed the split begun by the Nahuas by making *la Virgen de Guadalupe/Virgen Maria* into chaste virgins and *Tlazolteotl/Coatlicue/la Chingada* into *putas;* into the Beauties and the Beasts. They went even further; they made all Indian deities and religious practices the work of the devil.

Thus *Tonantsi* became *Guadalupe,* the chaste protective mother, the defender of the Mexican people.

In 1660 the Roman Catholic Church named *Guadalupe* Mother of God, considering her synonymous with *la Virgen María;* she became *la Santa Patrona de los mexicanos.* The role of defender (or patron) has traditionally been assigned to male gods. During the Mexican Revolution, Emiliano Zapata and Miguel Hidalgo used her image to move *el pueblo mexicano* toward freedom. During the 1965 grape strike in Delano, California, and in subsequent Chicano farmworkers' marches in Texas and other parts of the Southwest, her image on banners heralded and united the farmworkers. *Pachucos* (zoot suiters) tattoo her image on their bodies. Today, in Texas and Mexico she is more venerated than Jesus or God the Father. In the Lower Rio Grande Valley of south Texas it is *la Virgen de San Juan de los Lagos* (an aspect of *Guadalupe*) that is worshipped by thousands every day at her shrine in San Juan. In Texas she is considered the patron saint of Chicanos. *Cuando Carito, mi hermanito,* was missing in action and, later, wounded in Vietnam, *mi mamá* got on her knees *y le prometío a Ella que si su hijito volvía vivo* she would crawl on her knees and light novenas in her honor.

Today, *la Virgen de Guadalupe* is the single most potent religious, political and cultural image of the Chicano/*mexicano.* She, like my race, is a synthesis of the old world and the new, of the religion and culture of the two races in our psyche, the conquerors and the conquered. She is the symbol of the *mestizo* true to his or her Indian values. *La cultura chicana* identifies with the mother (Indian) rather than with the father (Spanish). Our faith is rooted in indigenous attributes, images, symbols, magic and myth. Because *Guadalupe* took upon herself the psychological and physical devastation of the conquered and oppressed *indio*, she is our spiritual, political and psychological symbol. As a symbol of hope and faith, she sustains and insures our survival. The Indian, despite extreme despair, suffering and near genocide, has survived. To Mexicans on both sides of the border, *Guadalupe* is the symbol of our rebellion against the rich, upper and middle class; against their subjugation of the poor and the *indio.*

Guadalupe unites people of different races, religions, languages: Chicano protestants, American Indians and whites. "*Nuestra abogada siempre serás*/Our *mediatrix* you will always be." She mediates between the Spanish and the Indian cultures (or three cultures as in the case of *mexicanos* of African or other ancestry) and between Chicanos and the white world. She mediates between humans and the divine, between this reality and the reality of spirit entities. *La Virgen de Guadalupe* is the symbol of ethnic identity and of the tolerance for ambiguity that Chicanos/*mexicanos*, people of mixed race, people who have Indian blood, people who cross cultures, by necessity possess.

La gente chicana tiene tres madres. All three are mediators: *Guadalupe*, the virgin mother who has not abandoned us; *la Chingada (Malinche)*, the raped mother whom we have abandoned; and *la Llorona*, the mother who seeks her lost children and is a combination of the other two.

Ambiguity surrounds the symbols of these three "Our Mothers." *Guadalupe* has been used by the Church to mete out institutionalized oppression: to placate the Indians and *mexicanos* and Chicanos. In part, the true identity of all three has been subverted—*Guadalupe* to make us docile and enduring, *la Chingada* to make us ashamed of our Indian side, and *la Llorona* to make us long-suffering people. This obscuring has encouraged the *virgen/puta* (whore) dichotomy.

Yet we have not all embraced this dichotomy. In the U.S. Southwest, Mexico, Central and South America the *indio* and the *mestizo* continue to worship the old spirit entities (including *Guadalupe*) and their supernatural power, under the guise of Christian saints.

Maximón–San Simón

FRANCISCO
GOLDMAN

*M*exico, you gave Guatemala la Virgen de Guadalupe,
Reina de los indios. Now Guatemala returns the
favor, they give you, the Americas, all the world—Maximón–San
Simón! Whom the times do seem to have been calling out for. A
most morally ambiguous spirit for the *fin de siècle* of the nastiest century, his powers, his *being*, rooted in the ancient Maya lords who
carry the Sun across the sky, and name the days. This cigar-puffing,
aguardiente-swilling, libidinous campesino-dandy in black suit and
red tie, curled mustache, broad-brimmed black Stetson!

So it seems anyway: Maximón–San Simón, Guatemala's most
prominent export since La Rigoberta Menchú went back to live
there. Mexicans tend not to be very enamored of things
Guatemalan (just ask the thousands of Guatemalan refugees still in
camps across the border from their country how welcome *they've*
been made to feel). But I saw San Simón represented by all manner of artifacts, displayed all over the stalls in the so-called "witches'
market," tucked into labyrinthine Mercado Sonora in Mexico, D.F.,
where I'd been living for the last year and a half. You'll find him in
New York City *botánicas* now too. Just the other night I went into
a Mexican restaurant on Fourteenth Street in Manhattan—situated
nearly across the street from the church La Guadalupe—and the
first thing I saw was a large San Simón sitting in a wooden chair,
and on the wall his framed portrait: black Stetson, mustache, and
a baton in his hand, a faintly sinister yet authoritative and patrón-
ish expression. This image, infinitely photocopied, is based, al-
legedly, on the only existing photograph of Francisco Sohuel, a
nineteenth-century wizard in the Guatemalan Maya highlands,

where he was believed to have been the flesh-and-blood incarnation of Mam–Maximón–San Simón.

Maximón and his role at the center of the Holy Week celebrations in Santiago Atitlán, a Tzuhutil Maya town in Guatemala's central highlands, are probably the best-known and most written about of all the modern Maya Christo-pagan ceremonies. Here the venerated idol has an austerely carved wooden face; he is elaborately dressed in traje (as traditional Maya clothing is called), suit coat, several Stetsons worn at once, a collar of knotted silk scarves, with another scarf—the finest of all—worn wedged between hat brims, draped down his back. Last year this scarf was a Hermès, with a pattern of stylized samurai faces, a gift from fans in Japan.

Maximón is his Tzuhutil Maya name, a hybridization of Mam and Simón. But he has many names, many identities. He's the ancient Maya Lord of the Middle. He's Don Pedro Alvarado, the ruthless Spanish conqueror of Guatemala's Maya tribes. I le's Judas Iscariot. He's Old Grandfather. He's "the Filth Eater," devourer of disease. As Dolores Ratzán Putzey, a Tzuhutil friend, put it to me during Holy Week in Santiago last year, "He's crazy, he's a wild man. He's the Any Old Time God. He's the Lord of Everything. He likes to do *many* things." His symbolic journey through the year, from youth to old age, culminates every Good Friday, when Maximón rides out of the little chapel on the plaza fronting Santiago's old (1520) Spanish Mission church on the shoulders of his telenél (that year's ceremonial shaman) to intercept the procession of the Holy Sepulchre from the church for a ritual encounter with the unrisen Jesucristo (which anthropologists describe as a symbolic act of "sodomy"). The telenél tags behind the sepulchre-bier, dancing the idol around while Maximón-Judas "fertilizes" Jesucristo, ending the dry season, inaugurating fecund rains along with the annual resurrection.

Maximón and the San Simón "idols" in their various shrines across Guatemala are banned from entering any church. (Though the church in Santiago is lenient toward Maximón's role in the Holy Week rites; many of Good Friday's Catholic Action bier-bearers come to visit Maximón later to pay their respects.)

Supposedly Maximón has a wife, who also has a number of

names, including Mary Magdalene. According to the poet-anthropologist Nathaniel Tarn and his sometime American collaborator Martin Prechtel (a trained Tzuhutil shaman himself), in his youth Maximón is "He Who Loves Love," the deity of unfettered sexuality, desire, and disorder. Originally "instituted by the ancestors" to be the protector of women whose husbands were away buying and selling in other villages, Maximón "is the violator of all the sexual norms he was instituted to protect; he is "he who defeats the *bad* person only to take on his characteristics and dangers." He's like a cross-dressing, all-powerful local political boss, loved and feared. He may be after your wife and daughter, or your husband and son—but he's the Lord of Everything. He comes to people who need him in their dreams. Part of the year he lives in a tree, and people sleeping under it can smell his cigar smoke.

All of this, I think, helps to explain Maximón–San Simón's trendy international stature, his modern resonance: his play of identities, his sexual ambiguity and subversiveness, his treachery and power, fit nicely with all sorts of "postmodern" notions that have found a place even in an intellectually unself-conscious part of our culture. The Maya way of recognizing evil's intrinsic place in the cosmos goes well with our own times' endlessly finessed moral ambiguities as well, a sense of evil as something that has to be managed and contained, even placated, and thus kept under control, rather than purged or outrightly defeated. That would certainly help to explain why he seems to be striking such a chord in Mexico now—a country so tormented by an economic crisis caused in part by massive corruption and a sense that violence and lawlessness seem an ineradicable part of society. Certainly times in which to summon San Simón, most cabrón of cabrones, to your side.

But the qualities I've just named are only those that might strike a foreigner as the most easily apprehensible and compelling. Most Guatemalan highland communities adhere to a fervent, complex syncretism of Maya and Catholic beliefs. I admit that Maximón cannot be so patly summed up.

Russian Jewish, mestizo Catholic, half American, half Guatemalan: my relationship to religion has always been a confused one. The arrangements I make between myself and that part of me that needs a sense of God are constantly evolving, and conducted in deepest privacy.

My mother has always been more religious, more overtly spiritual, than my father, though she is no longer a practicing Catholic in the formal sense. As a child I found both church and temple tedious. But I was baptized. In my *abuela's* house in Guatemala City, where I spent long stretches of early childhood, there was an altar to the Virgin with a votive candle always burning. On día de la Guadalupe in Guatemala City, December 8, it is the tradition among the city's *ladino*—that is, non-Maya—population to dress their children up as *"inditos"* to celebrate la Reina de los indios. They are dressed in *traje*, and the boys get little charcoal mustaches drawn over their lips, though *indios* tend not to have mustaches. My kitschiest souvenir of all that is a photograph of my sister, cousin, and me, all three of us dressed up in the ceremonial *traje* of Quiché Maya Chichicastenango, posing against a photographer's backdrop of a rural hut. We were living away from my father at the time, so Abuelita sent him this picture, and wrote on the back, in English, "Here are your little Indians."

Years later I had an equally authentic bar mitzvah, mainly to placate my father's relatives, since neither my father nor I were synagogue-goers: the Hebrew words spelled out in phonetic English on index cards which I discreetly held against the open Torah. The other five kids I shared the podium with actually read Hebrew, but when it was over several rosily beaming someone-else's-aunties told me I'd done the best. (A lesson, no? As Frank Bascombe says in Richard Ford's *Independence Day*, "Locution, locution . . ." Y arte.)

So much for my formal religious education.

I spent most of the 1980s living in Guatemala and elsewhere in Central America, working as a magazine journalist, trying to write fiction. Those were the years when I began to learn what religious faith really is; when that part of me that is responsive to the need or desire for such faith occasionally found a way of describing itself, through something closer to fleeting understanding than any actual deeply held faith of my own. I'd have moments of understanding which took me outside my own ironic distancing and into something else, a glimpse into something that other people had, which seemed pure, mysterious, and true. Which might seem a strange thing to say, considering how often I saw religion cynically manipulated by politics and sometimes the other way around, religion even used to justify murder. In the early eighties Guatemala's evangelical Protestant dictator, General Ríos Montt, who claimed God's mandate for all his actions, waged a campaign of ethnocide in the highlands which eliminated nearly five hundred villages and left tens of thousands dead—a more ruthlessly overt cranking up of the "campaign" that has been going on against the Maya in Guatemala since the Conquest. Scores of priests, nuns, and Catholic lay workers were murdered in Guatemala, and the Church pulled all its priests out of the highland province of Quiché, though a handful defiantly stayed behind. Not that there weren't bishops and priests who didn't support the army and their "anticommunist" backers (the oligarchs, big landowners, Generalísimo Reagan, et cetera); or who didn't dare to speak out. The Army and the death squads always picked Holy Week in Guatemala to carry out some of their most heinous crimes, because they knew the newspapers would be closed, and "everybody" away at their vacation chalets on the lake, the beach, the river; everybody except those without enough money to do anything but stay where they already were and witness to the inevitable wave of terror—nearly everyone. Holy Week 1985 was perhaps the most horrifying, when of the six founding members of Guatemala's first families-of-the-disappeared group, three were murdered—Rosario Godoy de Cuevas, the young wife of a disappeared union leader, murdered along with her twenty-one-year-old brother and baby son—two fled the country, and one scaled the Belgian embassy's walls just ahead of a death squad.

Nicaragua is a country whose devotion to the Virgin is so fervent that there are worshipers who venerate the Virgin's Holy Mother, too, her immaculate conception of the Virgin Mary herself. In Nicaragua, during those years, the Virgin suddenly began appearing to people with unprecedented frequency to warn—as the Pope did on his riotous visit—against the new "danger" in their country, i.e., the godless Sandinista revolution. In churches at Sunday morning Mass, statues of the Virgin wept miraculous tears of sorrow. Weeping Virgins, the Virgin appearing to humble campesinos to deliver antirevolutionary messages—these were trumpeted in the anti-Sandinista press and on radio, at least until they were shut down. The Sandinista press denounced reactionary priests for freezing their Virgin statues overnight so that they'd sweat tears in the morning heat. Eventually the Sandinista Interior Ministry passed a law prohibiting mention of miracles in the press unless they had already been confirmed by the Vatican. Archbishop Obando y Bravo, the Sandinistas' most formidable foe, bravely denounced Sandinista human rights abuses at every opportunity, while turning a blind eye on even the most savage atrocities of *la contra*. And the pro-Sandinista Popular Church only denounced *contra* abuses. Padre Descoto, the priest who'd been Sandinista Foreign Minister, went trudging through the countryside with a ten-foot cross, mounted on small wheels, over his shoulder to rally and thereby prove the doubtful existence of the Popular Church's mass base. But one day when the priest was still Foreign Minister, we'd received a knock at our door in Managua: Descoto's motorcade was parked out front, and Padre Descoto himself stood on the stoop holding a newborn puppy dog. He'd seen it out in the street and had ordered his driver to stop. He was worried the puppy might be run over. Was it ours? No; but we took it in. By that night it was obvious the puppy was very ill. It happened to be the weekend of the July 19 Sandinista Triumph anniversary celebrations, and we couldn't find a veterinarian anywhere. The tiny dog howled and yelped in relentless agony. A good friend, who'd been a company commander in a Sandinista volunteer battalion, found an open pharmacy, where he bought some medicinal powders. He held the puppy on his lap for hours, rubbing the medicine into its mangy wounds. But the dog writhed in hideous pain all through the night and into the early-morning hours of July 19, until the woman who rented the house mercifully drowned it in a pail of water. An anecdote—and I don't say this all that glibly— we withheld from the opposition press: it's not hard to imagine the prophetic-religious-political hay they might have made from the Foreign Minister's not-so-miraculous touch.

So many young Sandinista soldiers, both volunteers and

draftees, went to war and sometimes to their deaths with Catholic religious scapulars and other holy artifacts worn around their necks, carried in their backpacks. Often these had been given to them by their mothers.

In El Salvador, in the war and massacre zones, you could go to village markets around Christmas and buy, among the usual adornments for your Nativity crèche, little hand-carved *zopilotes,* or vultures—to stand vigil over the infant Jesus, the Holy Virgin and Father.

I remember the nuns in the occupied town of Nebaj, in the Ixil triangle, way up in Guatemala's Cuchumatán Mountains. It was one of the many towns that didn't have a priest anymore. There was a machine gun nest in the belfry now, and the Army had built its base right around the nun's convent, Medalla Milagrosa. The nuns had to speak carefully inside their own convent, for they didn't know who among the Ixil towngirls who came to do chores might be an informer. Yet late at night one of the sisters closed the door and took out a cassette recorder and placed it on the heavy, darkly polished wood table, and turned it on. The tiny screams we heard coming from it, she said, were from the torture sessions they could hear taking place on the other side of the dense, whitewashed stucco walls. She wanted Jean Marie to hear them. Jean Marie Simon, the brilliant photographer and human rights reporter-activist who, for a few years, was the only source of reliable information Americas Watch and Amnesty International had inside the country. We went up to the Ixil and elsewhere many times together, and it was from her I learned that it was always the nuns, and often only the nuns, who had any real idea of what was going on in a conflicted area, and would talk about it.

Stillness, silence, fear, death and more death, hunger and endless hard work, disappearances and more disappearances and more fear and more silence and deep faith; faith you usually couldn't talk about but could feel all around you—strong brave faith, hysterical screaming faith, the magic faith of centuries, the faith of terror and abjection, and the faith of persistence and truth. And I began to understand what was meant when it was said that in suffering you were never alone, because it joined you to the transcendent suffering of Christ. It was that simple idea that helped me to understand how so many people endured with such quiet dignity and strength. The people who would no longer step inside the church rectory the Army had used as a torture center in Chichicastenango but furtively left lit candles in front of its door for the souls of those who'd died there. The awesome bravery and faith of the Maya women who came from villages miles away for that first Widow's Mass in Chichi . . . (But also the hysterically screaming pastors, electric guitars and organs, the tranced singing pouring from the mushrooming Protestant churches.)

The veiled Tzuhutil women chanting and singing in Tzuhutil Maya, on their knees in front of the altar to the Virgin in Army-occupied Santiago Atitlán, in the church where Father Stan Rother had been murdered by soldiers in 1979. Father Rother's family took him back to Oklahoma to be buried, but his heart was put inside an unsealed peanut butter jar; and when they took it out on the tenth anniversary of his death—it was going to be reburied in a new shrine in the church, in the altar—the heart was still wet with blood.

Over a thousand Atitecos (as residents of Santiago Atitlán are called), out of a population of twenty thousand, were murdered or disappeared between 1978 and 1990. During most of those years the town was caught between ORPA guerrillas dug into nearby volcanoes, and the military. And though the Guatemalan Army wasn't the cause of absolutely all the disappearances and murders, they certainly were to blame for nearly all of them. Often, at night, the town was under curfew, the streets lined with rustic stone huts dark and deserted but for the occasional Army patrol, which often stopped at houses and took people away.

What does Maximón have to do with that kind of faith? He who in his statuette San Simón version sits arrayed along shelves in a Mexico City witches' market just like the Virgin of Guadalupe statuettes sold to pilgrims and religious tourists outside her basilica there. The Lord of Everything. The most ancient and powerful, with all his disguises. Married to Mary Magdalene. He whom la Guadalupe was meant to banish, displace. For, of course, the Virgin of Guadalupe, "Queen of the Indians," had come to Mexico, certainly according to the teachings of Spanish priests, to establish the primacy of the Catholic religion over the pagan. In highland Guatemala, this so-called Spiritual Conquest was never completed. Instead Catholic and Maya were blended, and Catholic icons were often invested with the properties of the very Maya gods the priests futilely tried to banish. In Santiago Atitlán and elsewhere, the saints are worshiped for themselves in the Catholic way, but they are also the Lord of the Wind, of Corn, of various animals, and so on. The cross is the symbol of Christ's martyrdom, but also the Maya World Tree. The Virgin—la Guadalupe, la Virgen de Rosario, la Virgen de Dolores—is the Mother of God, but she is also the Great Mother, and those Tzuhutil women singing so beautifully in Santiago's church were likely to have been praying to both at once.

The Holy Week rituals that revolve around Maximón in Santiago are too rich and complicated for me to attempt to explain with any depth here. Just this then:

For most of the year Maximón "lives" in the Santa Cruz cofradía's house. Cofradías are religious fraternities that oversee traditional observances, costumbre, in towns with Maya populations that still, to varying degrees, live by them. In Santiago Atitlán there are ten cofradías, despite the growing presence of Evangelical sects which have claimed at least half the population in the last decade or so. The Protestants try to gain a moral high ground criticizing not only the cofrades' Maya-Catholic paganism but their habitual drunkenness as well.

Maximón supposedly "sleeps," in an undressed bundle, in the Santa Cruz cofradía's rafters, only to be brought down and put together on special occasions. (But "special occasions" seem to occur all year long, now that the cofrades have realized what a draw a well-turned-out Maximón is to tribute- and liquor-bearing tourists.) I was in the house two Holy Tuesdays ago, on the night that Gaspar, that year's telenél, was about to reassemble and dress Maximón in the dark, as the ceremony demands. There had been a struggle to shut the door against the crowd in the dirt yard outside. But the shamans and elders of the Santa Cruz cofradía could hardly have kept me out—to win their friendship, or at least a certain practical acceptance, I'd been paying for a large portion of the aguardiente and beer they'd been drinking nonstop for days. Maximón's starkly arrogant head—cigar stuffed into the hard slot of his mouth, opaquely staring eyes starred with gashed lashes—rested on a chair, wearing a Stetson. Offerings—fruits, liquor, snacks, candles—lay on the petate mat at the foot of the chair. Shamans and elders swung fuming copal censers. Musical Christmas lights, strung over a glass-encased, flower-draped recumbent Jesucristo, twinkled and beeped "Santa Claus Is Coming to Town." The rafters were strung with vegetables and fruits, fertility symbols; the knobby little squash that Dolores Ratzán told me are called chichas because they represent the breasts of adolescent girls.

Suddenly all the lights in the packed room went off and we were in the most complete darkness. I couldn't even see my own hand waving a bottle of warm beer over my face. The air was thick and stifling with smells: incense, candle wax, overripe fruit, pungent body odors, stale liquor breaths; and the aerosol spray from the cans of scented room freshener with which Maximón is regularly doused, as if it were the distilled essence of the divine. An hour later I was still standing in the clamp of warm bodies while down there in the dark Gaspar was still dressing the idol. Maximón, Dolores had told me, was supposed to have come to the telenél in a dream to tell him how he wanted it done: "This is how I want my scarves . . . my jacket . . . my shirt." About half an hour later I felt warm breath against my ear and then heard a voice speaking into my ear, long emphatic sentences, moving and disturbing-sounding words, words which sounded as if they might have explained everything, though of course I hadn't understood any of it because they were spoken in Tzuhutil . . .

The lights came on, and there he was, Maximón, a four-foot armless mannequin, his radiant collar of scarves curtaining all but the bird-embroidered hems of his pants and his big rubber-soled shoes. The telenél lit Maximón's cigar, an elder held an ashtray to catch ashes. They pour aguardiente through the wooden lips, down the mysterious throat (where's it all go, all that booze poured into Maximón?). So many people brought gifts, asking for favors, health, prosperity. As if pleading for their lives before the Lord of Everything, the gift-bearers approached on their knees, gesturing, so many extraordinary-sounding speeches; so much unhappiness and frightened flattery; now and then extravagant tearful speeches of gratitude for favors granted in the last year; so much conviction and love.

Since the end of 1990, Santiago has been the only town in Guatemala which the Guatemalan Army is not allowed to enter. On December 2 of that year thirteen Atitecos were massacred outside the military garrison during a spontaneous protest against the wounding of a man in town. In the ensuing international outcry, the soldiers were withdrawn, the garrison dismantled; the town refuses, despite all entreaties and threats, to let the military back. (Captured army plainclothes provocateurs have been nearly lynched by mobs; the town is now seen as having something of a Masada complex when it comes to the Army, and the Army, burdened by its image as the Americas' greatest human rights violators, doesn't want to risk another massacre.) Santiago Atitlán polices itself now: groups of unarmed men go out on patrol every night. Santiago has become a peaceful town.

Eleven of the thirteen who died outside the military garrison that day in 1990 were "Catholic." When the Army left, huge mosaic crosses made of bits of colored paper went up on the church walls: on each piece of paper was written the name of someone who'd been murdered or disappeared in the preceding years.

When Atitecos talk now about what gave them the courage and fury to surround the garrison that day, many invoke Maximón. They say things like, "When the people realized the Army didn't even respect Maximón . . ." They tell about what happened a short while before, when military plainclothes agents drove up to the Santa Cruz cofradía in a jeep. Inside, the telenél, Martin Kik, was serenading Maximón with his guitar. The soldiers murdered Kik, and though they shot up Maximón, too, Maximón stood upright until one of the men kicked him over.

In a corner of her house in Santiago, on a steep hillside overlooking the lake, my friend Dolores Ratzán Putzey has a Maximón altar, and near it, a small shrine to the Virgin. Dolores has always wanted to be a telenél, a shaman, herself, but of course women aren't allowed to in Maya culture. So she's a midwife, conducting elaborate birthing ceremonies in sweat baths, contending with the thirteen jealous goddesses who hover about, and make dangerous, the first week of an infant's life. She told me, with a tone of still-awed wonder in her voice, that Martin Kik's widow had come closer to being a telenél than any Tzuhutil woman ever had. For all the rest of that decisive year after the soldiers killed her husband, she took over his duties as telenél: she'd tended to Maximón, dancing him around the cofradía house in her arms, singing to him. And that experience, said Dolores, laughing, left Maximón a little nicer, a little sweeter than he'd been before.

A subjective leap of my own, but such leaps are hardly contrary to the practice of faith in Catholic-Maya Santiago Atitlán: Martin Kik's grieving widow unprecedentedly tending unruly Maximón, isn't this in the spirit of la Guadalupe's tender embrace of the ancient Americas, the Americas the Spaniards had come to subjugate in an opposite way?

At home I keep my own small collection of religious objects on a shelf—I wouldn't call it an altar, since I practice nothing there but an occasional pensiveness. Four objects that mean something to me, that represent a certain balancing of influences and memory. A simple wooden crucifix, slightly smoke-smudged but unharmed and smooth, which I found while kicking around in the smoldering rubble of a farming collective in northern Nicaragua which la contra had attacked and burned to the ground the day before. A framed color snapshot I took in the Jewish cemetery's little museum in Fez, Morocco: a portrait of a nineteenth-century beauty named Solika La Sainte—long flowing hair, gown worn off the shoulder, an actual coil of her hair hung over the portrait on the museum's wall (I don't know who she was, but I love the picture). An antique Virgin of Guadalupe statue of painted wood, with blue-yellow robes and slightly crossed glass eyes which somehow make her expression even sweeter—bought in Guatemala, the only "art object" I've ever shelled out significant money for. And a Maximón—San Simón devotional plaque, that famous image reputed to be of the wizard Francisco Sohuel under a cover of transparent red cellophane, blackened now with smoke from a past stormy love when I did find myself following the rituals outlined in the prayer sheet pasted to the plaque's back, keeping his glass filled with tequila, a cigar nearby, and always, always keeping a red candle lit—red for "Love, Faith, and Will."

El mito azteca[1]

CHERRÍE MORAGA

*S*egún la leyenda, Coatlicue, "Madre de los Dioses," is sweeping on
top of the mountain, Coatepec, when she discovers two beautiful
feathers. Thinking that later she will place them on her altar, she stuffs them into
her apron and continues sweeping. But without her noticing, the feathers begin to
gestate there next to her womb and Coatlicue, already advanced in age, soon discovers that she is pregnant.

When her daughter, Coyolxauhqui, learns that her mother is about to give
birth to Huitzilopochtli, God of War, she is incensed. And, along with her siblings, the Four Hundred Stars, she conspires to kill Coatlicue rather than submit
to a world where War would become God.

Huitzilopochtli is warned of this by a hummingbird and vows to defend his
mother. At the moment of birth, he murders Coyolxauhqui, cutting off her head
and completely dismembering her body.

Breast splits from chest splits from hip splits from thigh from knee from arm
and foot. Coyolxauhqui is banished to the darkness and becomes the moon, la diosa
de la luna.

In my own art, I am writing that wound. That moment when
brother is born and sister mutilated by his envy. He possesses the
mother, holds her captive, because she cannot refuse any of her
children, even her enemy son. Here, mother and daughter are pit-
ted against each other and daughter must kill male-defined motherhood in order to save the culture from misogyny, war, and
greed. But el hijo comes to the defense of patriarchal motherhood,

[1]Thanks to Mexican performance artist Guadalupe García, who first introduced
this myth to me.

kills la mujer rebelde, and female power is eclipsed by the rising light of the Sun/Son. This machista myth is enacted every day of our lives, every day that the sun (Huitzilopochtli) rises up from the horizon and the moon (Coyolxauhqui) is obliterated by his light. Huitzilopochtli is not my god. And although I revere his mother, Coatlicue, Diosa de La Muerte y La Vida, I do not pray to her. I pray to the daughter, La Hija Rebelde. She who has been banished, the mutilated sister who transforms herself into the moon. She is la fuerza femenina, our attempt to pick up the fragments of our dismembered womanhood and reconstitute ourselves. She is the Chicana writer's words, the Chicana painter's canvas, the Chicana dancer's step. She is motherhood reclaimed and sisterhood honored. She is the female god we seek in our work, la Mechicana before the "fall."

And Huitzilopochtli raises his sword from the mouth of his mother's womb and cuts off his sister's head, her bleeding down the belly of the serpent-mountain. Coyolxauhqui, moon-faced goddess, enters the darkness, y la Raza, la época de guerra.

Pero de vez en cuando la luna gets her revenge.

Just a week ago, I returned from a two-month stay in Mexico, the last day of which found me on top of a pyramid in Tepotzlán, an hour outside of Mexico City. At 1:26 pm the sky fell to complete darkness as the moon eclipsed the sun. "Tonatiuh cualo," el sol fue comido por la fuerza femenina. And el Conchero[2] who led the ceremonia in full Aztec regalia de pluma y piel believed it an ominous sign, this momentary and sudden loss of light, this deep silent feminine darkness. The quieting of the pájaros, the retreat of the ground animals into their caves of night. And he prayed to the gods to return the light. And I prayed with him, brother that he is, brother who never recognizes his sister in prayer, brother who

---

[2]A "conchero" is a ceremonial leader who sounds the conch shell and leads the people in their prayers and offerings.

fears her power, as mother and daughter and wife and lover, as he fears the darkening of the light.

But we women were not afraid, accustomed as we are to the darkness. In public, we mouthed the shapes of his words that mourned the loss of light, and in secret we sang praise to She Who Went Unacknowledged, She Who Remains in Shadow, She Who Has the Power to Put Out the Sun's Light. Coyolxauhqui, the moon, reduced in newspapers to the image of a seductress, flirtatious coquette, merging in coitus with the sun. Later, we women, lesbianas from all parts of América Latina, would offer sacrifice, burn copal, call out her name. We, her sisters, would pay tribute to la luna, keep the flame burning, keep destruction at bay.

In those six minutes of darkness, something was born. In the darkness of that womb of silence, that female quietude, a life stirred. I understood for the first time the depth and wonder of the feminine, although I confess I have been awed by it before, as my own female face gazes upon its glory and I press my lips to that apex in the women I love.

Like the others, I welcomed the light upon its return. El Canto de Gallo. Probably that was the most amazing of all, el segundo amanecer. The female passed on y dió luz a un sol nuevo. As the light took the shape of the sky again, el Conchero stood on top of the pyramid mountain and announced the end of El Quinto Sol, the end of a 500-year historia sangrienta that saw to the near destruction of the Indigenous peoples of Las Américas. And from the ashes of destruction, a new era is born: El Sexto Sol: La Epoca de La Conciencia Humana.

The day after the eclipse, I called my mother from San Francisco to tell her I had arrived home safely. And without planning to, when describing the eclipse I told her, "Ahora conozco a Dios, Mamá." And I knew she understood my reverence in the face of a power utterly beyond my control. She is a deeply religious woman, who calls her faith "catholic." I use another name or no name, but she understood that humility, that surrender, before a sudden glimpsed god. Little did she know god was a woman.

I am not the church-goer that my mother is, but the same faithfulness drives me to write: the search for Coyolxauhqui amid all the disfigured female characters and the broken men that surround them in my plays and poems. I search for a whole woman I can shape with my own Chicana tongue and hand. A free citizen of Aztlán and the world.

Extraordinarily Woman

ANA CASTILLO

I was six. Or maybe I was five, or seven. I don't remember and no one talks about it anymore. But six is the age my older siblings agreed upon years ago, when we were growing up. They haven't mentioned it for years now either.

I was thin as a straw, undernourished, my first set of teeth like little brown erasers, decalcified. Later, they were all pulled out at the Cook County Dental School. I was being raised primarily on beans, flour tortillas, and sweetened coffee with canned milk. Juice was an unheard-of delicacy. Real milk never saw its way to our home. Fruit and fresh produce were an extravagance and nonexistent also. Roaches brazenly paraded across our kitchen table and tomcat-size rats made their way about openly too, scaring our cat kept for the purpose of discouraging them. We were not living in migrant shanties or in the slums of Tijuana but in the urban heart of the northern city of Chicago, where I was born.

No one talks anymore about the time I was dying, every day giving out a less audible peep, like a bird that has dropped out of its nest. Death—like the mother bird that threatens anyone who comes near the baby—kept watch over me. In the annals of my family, my near death is a time now too painful to acknowledge.

When we were growing up, my older half brother teased me about it and thereby kept the memory alive. He'd laugh devilishly in the bullying manner of some big brothers. But afterwards, I'd see it in his eyes, *el susto*. He'd had a mean brush with María Guadaña. To the Mexican mind, death is a woman; she is christened with that name. She'd invaded our flat, come and sat on the narrow bed I shared with my older half sister, and held my hand. My brother had looked into Death's eyes and resented me for having invited her.

A nurse came from the social services department to make her rounds in our run-down and soon-to-be-plowed-under neighborhood and gave me a shot, said I should be interned, and then went away. My grandmother, who was my caretaker, didn't learn anything about my illness, which, for all we knew, was simply poverty made manifest in the body of a small child. Abuelita didn't speak any English and white people frightened her. She was afraid that if they took me away, I'd never come back. Like Peloncito, the great-grandchild she had taken in when his mother abandoned him. Apparently he was born completely incapacitated. My grandmother spoonfed him in her bed, changed his diapers, kept him alive with love. When he was twelve or fourteen years old a person from social services came to see my grandmother. When she discovered the sick boy she reported him to the authorities and Peloncito was soon taken away somewhere. My family was simply told that our home was unsuitable for the boy, who needed to be institutionalized; shortly after, my grandmother was told he'd died.

Such dark days in America, long past those of the Great Depression that white America recalls so vividly, still exist. Illness, infant mortality, and all manner of travesty that visit the impoverished are a rolling force today throughout our countryside and cities. The Aztecs named their version of this terrible force Cihuacoatl. Cihuacoatl or Snake-Woman was one of the Mother Goddess's manifestations, thought to take infants at night and in their place leave an obsidian knife as a symbol of their sacrifice to the gods. So the babies and children of the poor today are taken away before dawn with scarcely a whimper.

My grandmother could not read or write in any language. She signed her relief checks with an X. But she was a curandera—loosely translated, a medicine woman—and proceeded to negotiate with María Guadaña, with whom, I seem to recall, she was on first-name basis. I was the youngest of all her many grandchildren and great-grandchildren and, as she also told me later, when I recovered, I was the very nectar of sugar cane in her heart, her consentida, and she was not about to let me go.

Abuelita was the oldest person on earth then and in poor health herself. She was the most wrinkly, soft being I have ever touched. I can still remember curling up on her pillowy lap like a kitten, nestling my head against her sagging breasts, and feeling the eternal, abounding assurance of Our Mother from her warm breath on my brow. Her legs weren't strong enough to get her down the stairs from the second-floor flat where we lived, so it was left to my older siblings to run errands for her.

Abuelita sent my big sister, who would have been about twelve at the time, to the Mexican market around the corner with a list of supplies. My grandmother, illiterate, wise healing woman, was going to cure me, not with miracle-cure injections or nutritious food but with magic. Some people call it faith. Others think of it as procuring the wisdom of ancestors. But here, without going into complicated speculations, we'll call it magic.

My sister brought back two seven-day candles, a small hand broom made of corn husks, and a dozen fresh eggs. On Sunday when she went to Mass at our parish, my sister was instructed to "borrow" a little holy water from the church. San Francisco, the iglesia of the Mexicans migrants in Chicago, was where I made my holy sacraments. Dead center in front of the altar stood a huge image of Our Mother. Quite naturally, I believed then that this pious place was Her home; that this beautiful Indian woman with the enigmatic gaze was Mother God. God the Father was absent, though like the men in my family, who were often shadowy and silent, He nevertheless was the ultimate authority. He watched us with a close and critical omnipotent eye and mostly wielded His power by instilling fear. Our Mother, on the other hand, watched over her children without condemning our acts. Our Mother simply loved us.

Of the two candles my grandmother ordered, Saint Jude is the patron saint of the desperate, the terminally ill, a no-nonsense heavenly emissary when all other hope is lost. His devotional candle is green and dispels the malevolence that has overtaken us as it burns.

The other candle was devoted to none other than Our Lady of Guadalupe, our Mexican Mother who is unfailing when our mortal mothers, all too human and burdened by life's demands, aren't there. Our beloved Mother who takes us back into the folds of Her robe at the hour of our death.

Abuelita lit Saint Jude on the self-styled altar she kept on the bureau in her room, but Our Mother was placed in the room where I slept with my siblings, to watch over me.

The little hand broom is San Martín's wand. It is used for performing the limpieza or spiritual cleansing when a "sweeping" of the patient's spirit is done to remove any spiteful influences causing the illness.

The egg, which in and of itself is a phenomenon, the perfect symbol of life, is also a healing instrument used by the curandera. A single egg in its shell, held in the hand, can be used like San Martín's broom-wand. Later, the curandera breaks it in a clear glass of water to divine who has cast the spell on the patient. I often saw my grandmother "sweep" away evil spirits and use eggs to draw out curses and illnesses from those in our community who came to see her. She accepted no fee and rarely took a gift since her clients were as needy as we were and often, in her opinion, more so.

I don't remember homemade soups like the ones grandmothers are credited with prescribing during fevers and colds. I was never taken to a hospital. No doctor was called in. But with her magic and with Our Mother's assistance, Abuelita rescued me from María Guadaña's grip.

And that is how my own apprenticeship as a healer began. I did not ask for it. I do not believe I ever wanted it. But just as I learned firsthand as a child that death is a woman, I learned that life, too, is a woman and that an intimate relationship with both death and life was my inevitable legacy as a female, as the granddaughter of a curandera, and as a child of Guadalupe.

The Virgin of Guadalupe for Mexicans is as much a symbol of life as María Guadaña is a symbol of death. But perhaps they are two faces of the same coin, a two-headed goddess like Coatlicue, the fierce fertility diety of the Aztecs with a double serpent head. The serpent, too, has universally symbolized rejuvenation, death as a precursor to new life, the endless natural cycle of all living things.

Abuelita—ancient crone *curandera*, disciple of Our Mother, Mexican matriarch—took her smallest, frailest offspring into her apprenticeship and taught me what she could until she died when I was nearly ten years old. When I was twenty, various individuals began to enter my life who would insist I had my work cut out for me regardless of what other plans I had for myself, and so my lessons resumed.

When I was still a child, however, when my grandmother's legs finally gave way and she had to be confined to a wheelchair, she was taken to her oldest son's flat where there was always someone home to keep an eye on her. I missed her profoundly. I have never stopped missing her. But back then, shortly after her departure, an adolescent cousin was brought up from Laredo, Texas, to stay with us, and although she mostly ignored me, the presence of a new family member kept me intrigued. It was because of Berta, the "bad girl" big cousin, that I came to realize the duality of Our Mother's infinite wisdom and unconditional love.

Berta, like my sister, was a teenager, a mystical age for a pubescent girl who marveled at the older girls' underarm hair and the great shared secret of their menstrual cycle, which they referred to as their "friend." (Come to think of it, my sister still refers to it that way.)

The reason for my cousin Berta's temporary stay was also a mystery to me. It was odd that a child in my mother's extended family should be allowed to travel anywhere alone, much less be sent such distances to relatives she hardly knew. It was clear to me, however, that the reason that was given—that Berta was in Chicago to finish high school so that afterwards she could get a good office job here—could not be the cause for so much whispering in the kitchen among the women.

Eventually I gathered, from lingering behind curtains that divided rooms, pretending to be asleep or distracted with a book or a drawing, that Berta was in my mother's care because she had gotten herself into "trouble." According to her mother, she was a young fertile female out of control; beside herself, she sent her oldest daughter to my mother. Chicago was about as far away from Laredo as Berta's mother could imagine. There was much behind-closed-doors discussion before the day I was the one sent to the market for a seven-day candle devoted to the Virgin of Guadalupe. My sister, this time, was part of the closed circle of women and allowed to stay in the apartment, while I was sent on the errand and afterwards told to stay out on the porch.

A distant relative by marriage was brought in, who I later figured out had experience with the kind of procedure Berta was going to have performed on her. Back then among the women, the procedure was referred to in Spanish, as "the cure."

About a week after Berta underwent the cure, we went to visit my grandmother. I was sitting beside Abuelita as I always did—I liked touching her, being close to her—when Berta and she had their little chat. First my grandmother asked Berta a few questions about how she had been "duped" by her boyfriend back home. My grandmother was trying to establish whether Berta was duped because her boyfriend had been that clever or because she had been that naive. But that she was duped, my grandmother had no doubt. In her day, my grandmother said, fifteen was not too old for marriage. But now, a girl could get an education, have other choices than to be tied to a man all her life bearing children from such a young age.

Berta was drinking a cup of bitter rue-and-yerba-buena tea my grandmother had prescribed. Rue would help ease her flow and yerba buena is good for everything. My cousin, who had gone from being a vain and silly teen to an almost woman overnight, looked sad or ashamed. "Don't ever allow yourself to think about what just happened with remorse." Abuelita spoke quietly. Her words were meant for Berta but I caught them and made them mine, too. And I have carried them with me since. My abuelita also said this: "You see that cup filled with that good herb? Think of your womb as that cup." She did not say womb—but pointed to her own. "Hija—everywhere around us spirits are with us. Sometimes they want to come back, to be in this life. They have eyes but see very dimly. They look for a place to transform themselves to flesh. Sometimes one finds its way to a cup that although it is full, is not ready to nourish anything. Don't worry. It will find another cup; it'll have another chance if it is determined to come back, if it has business here. The important thing is that you knew you could not provide what it needed and so you made the best decision . . ."

These are not my grandmother's words verbatim. Her actual words were simple and in Spanish and a long, long time ago. But this is what I remember. I remember Berta crying softly, sipping her bitter rue-and-good-herb tea. I remember my grandmother praying her rosary of white plastic beads. I remember Mami's voice in the other room, abruptly calling out: "Ready, muchachas?" And I remember the long way home on public transportation. My mother seemed not to want to stir up my father's curiosity about our impromptu visit and she wanted us back before she expected him home.

Berta returned to Laredo before the school session was over. She turned out fine; recently became a grandmother, in fact.

When Our Mother is seen only as the one-dimensional Mary of modern times, instead of the great dual force of life and death, She is relegated to the same second-class status of most women in the world. She is without desires of Her own, selfless and sexless except for Her womb. She is the cook, the mistress, bearer and caretaker of children and men. Men call upon Her and carry Her banner to lead them out to war. They show Her off, take Her love and magic to form a formidable fortress, a team of cannons to protect them against their enemies. But for a long, long time the wars that women have been left to wage on behalf of men, on behalf of the human race, have started much sooner, in the home, in front of the hearth, in the womb. We do what we must to protect and provide for our young, our families, our tribes. Because of our humility, we call upon Her privately, quietly in prayer, from our kitchens and bedrooms, as if She had more important matters to tend to besides those of a mother, of all mothers, besides those of any ordinary woman—when no woman born who knows herself could ever be ordinary.

The Battle of the Virgins

ROSARIO FERRÉ

*I*n Puerto Rico the Virgin appears to people often. She has been seen hovering over a mango tree, on top of a water tank, at the brink of a well, even on the pink skin of a sweet potato. People are used to these occurrences and so when the rumor started to go around Ponce that *la Virgen de Guadalupe* was filling the cathedral with a perfume of roses, no one was surprised. Gilda Ventura, my nursemaid, mentioned it to me while she was giving me a bath. "I don't believe it," I answered, eyes shut tight, as Gilda poured water over my shampoo-covered head with a *dita* gourd. I was eight years old.

"We'll go next Saturday to the cathedral and you'll smell them!" Gilda answered.

Ponce's churches were full of Virgins. There was *la Virgen de las Mercedes*, at La Merced Church on Calle Aurora, where all the brides of well-to-do families wanted to get married because of its magnificent baroque *retablo*, with carved golden meringue clouds billowing around them. There was *la Virgen de la Milagrosa*, who stood on a pillar at a Gothic chapel near the middle-class barrio of Río Portugués, glowing next to the stained-glass windows decorated with flowers and golden chalices; *la Inmaculada Concepción* at the bishop's chapel in La Alhambra—the elegant, Spanish-style suburb where my family lived—gazing ecstatically toward heaven as she rose on a supersonic white cloud and left planet Earth—a blue basketball—way below. And *la Virgen de Guadalupe* in the cathedral in the middle of Plaza Degetau, Ponce's main plaza. *La Guadalupe's* image stood high up near the ceiling, on top of a Romanesque altar. The rays that surrounded her were bent and glimmered in the dark like a halo of curved Oriental swords.

All the Virgins in Ponce except for *la Guadalupe* looked like elegantly dressed society ladies; they could have walked into any of the town's drawing rooms and sat beside my mother and her friends, gossiping and drinking coffee all afternoon. *La Guadalupe* was different. She was dressed in an exotic blue mantle covered with stars and stood barefoot on a pair of silver horns, held aloft by a bull. But what really set her apart from the other Virgins was that she was black. She wouldn't have been allowed into a drawing room in Ponce.

La Guadalupe was Ponce's patron Virgin, and she had the largest following amongst the townspeople; every year the *fiestas patronales* were dedicated to her. Perhaps this was so because Ponce had a large black population. The town was in the middle of a sugar cane valley, and sugar cane was cut mainly by blacks, descendants of slaves. They had been brought to the island precisely for that type of work because they were stronger and had more stamina than whites; they could survive the scorching sun better. Black people flocked to *la Guadalupe* every Sunday to pray. They walked all the way to the center of town from the slums, many of them barefoot and dressed in rags, and stood begging in front of the cathedral's door after Sunday's ten o'clock Mass, which was also well attended by the rich.

Although my family went to Sunday Mass at the bishop's chapel in La Alhambra and prayed to *la Inmaculada Concepción*, I got to know *la Virgen de Guadalupe* well, thanks to Gilda. Every Saturday, after the current episode of El Zorro at the Broadway Theater, we ran the three blocks to the cathedral, and Gilda made me kneel next to her while she whispered a hurried prayer to *la Guadalupe,* her hands tightly laced in a little chapel of fingers in front of her forehead. Then we would race back to the cinema's door, just in time to be picked up by Carmelo, our family's chauffeur, who drove us back home to La Alhambra in the gray family Cadillac.

That Saturday after the movies, the minute we walked into the cathedral, Gilda smelled roses. I looked up at the carved wooden image standing high up in her dark niche. "I don't smell anything," I said. "Just dust and candle wax!"

"You must have a cold, your nose is all stuffed up. Juan Diego's apron is full of roses. I can smell them all the way over here."

As everyone knows, Juan Diego was the young Indian man who

knelt at the foot of *la Guadalupe* when the Virgin appeared to him in Tepeyac in 1531. He didn't speak Spanish and the Virgin spoke to him in Nahuatl, because she was a very smart Virgin. I didn't want to contradict Gilda, but even when we knelt to pray in the first bench, right in front of the altar, I still didn't smell anything. I thought maybe she was getting Juan Diego confused with Eusebio Martínez, her favorite boyfriend, who was always secretly bringing her roses to the house. Gilda was very romantic—she had several boyfriends and on Saturday nights she would always sneak out to go dancing at El Tibidabo. I shook my head silently and knelt next to her on the wooden bench.

No sooner had she begun to pray when I asked, "Why is *la Guadalupe* black? All the other Virgins I know are white and blond, and they have blue eyes."

"She's not black, she's brown. She was buried in the ground for eight hundred years. The dirt stuck to her, and now she's the same color as the earth."

"Why was she buried in the ground for eight hundred years?" I whispered.

"Because some bad men wanted to harm her. I saw the story in *Tizoc,* a Mexican movie I went to. Pedro Infante tells how *la Guadalupe* was hidden away in a cave in the mountains because they wanted to destroy her image. It was such a beautiful movie! Every time María Felix appeared on the screen, Pedro Infante and his mariachis played the guitar for her, just like Eusebio does for me in El Tibidabo once in a while."

I knew that what Gilda was saying was fairly close to the truth. In the Sacred Heart where I went to school, they taught us that when the Moors invaded Spain *la Guadalupe* had been buried high up in the Sierra de Guadalupe for eight hundred years, so that the Moors wouldn't find her.

"They weren't *bad* men. They were Arabs, and the Arabs don't believe in the Virgin because they believe in Mahoma," I went on pestering.

"*Shhhhh!* Let me pray, Niña. I need *la Virgencita's* help. Eusebio's going to travel far away soon. Next week he's going to California to pick grapes and peaches, so he can save money and we can get married." I had heard the story before. Eusebio went back and forth from the States to the island so often, he reminded me of a Ping-Pong ball. He not only picked fruit, he was also a composer, and often visited the recording companies in New York trying to sell his songs there, but without any luck. He composed songs for Gilda on his guitar all the time.

Eusebio was very good-looking. He had straight black hair, high cheekbones, and slanted eyes which glimmered in the dark, just like Juan Diego's. I saw him one night when Gilda sneaked out of the room and I followed her into the garden. Eusebio had jumped the fence, and they were kissing under the lemon tree. But whenever I knelt at the Cathedral, I prayed that one day Eusebio would never come back. I didn't want Gilda to leave, and I begged *la Virgencita* not to listen to her prayers.

I kept quiet, out of respect for the sadness in Gilda's voice. I knew she was worried about her boyfriend. She was afraid that one day he'd stay in the States and not come back, that he would never marry her. But I was determined to make her stop praying, so a little later I asked, "Why does *la Guadalupe* have those funny swords around her? All the other Virgins have clouds, cherubs, and flowers. *La Virgen de Guadalupe* is weird."

Gilda turned around and looked at me in horror. "Don't ever say that, Niña!" She shook me by the shoulder. "*La Guadalupe* is a very powerful Virgin. You don't want her as your enemy! Those swords are her thunderbolts. She's not a namby-pamby Virgin, like the ones in those other churches. She gets things done, and she protects people who fight for what they want."

"Well, I don't like her, and I hope she doesn't listen to you!" I said, tears beginning to well up in my eyes. I ran out of the church.

La Guadalupe must have heard me, because Eusebio stopped coming to the house. He had found a steady job in New York and decided to stay there. Gilda still got letters from him every so often, but she didn't want to fill her heart with false hopes, so she turned her attention to the other young men she was dating.

Gilda couldn't have been more than eighteen years old and she was beautiful—tall and willowy like an *almácigo* tree, with nut-brown skin and finely chiseled features. She always wore brightly colored clothes, and her enameled nails looked like cherry-red daggers. Her mouth was a perfect bow which shot little teasing arrows at you every time she laughed.

Mother, on the contrary, was always sad. She dressed only in black, because she was in mourning. First her father had died and she mourned him for three years; then her favorite brother died in an airplane accident, and she mourned for another three years. She never went to parties, or allowed music to be played at our house. She was always traveling to Mayagüez to visit her parents, and to get together with her brothers and sisters.

When I wasn't in school I spent most of my time with Gilda. I was forbidden to step outside the six-foot wall which surrounded our house without her, much less go for a walk by myself out of La Alhambra. Downtown Ponce, with its cathedral, movie houses, plazas, and streets full of shops, was as distant as the planet Mars, even though it was only a five-minute drive from our house. Gilda slept in my room on a small cot under the window. When there were thunderstorms and lightning bolts fell, we stood together under the arched doorway holding hands; and at night, when everybody was sound asleep, we would turn on the radio and listen to Bobby Capó, Rafael Muñoz, and Daniel Santos croon beautiful songs about love until the early hours of the morning, oh, so softly! And only for us.

"Now that Eusebio and I have broken up, I'm going to save every penny, and one day I'm going to attend nursing school. You'll see! I'll pray to *la Virgencita de Guadalupe* and she'll help me become a nurse." I felt sorry for her every time she said that, because I knew Mother gave most of Gilda's salary to her parents. Her father worked at my father's foundry as a smelter, and they had fourteen children. He needed every penny Gilda made as a nursemaid to feed them; his salary alone wasn't enough.

Thanks to Gilda I developed a passion for books. She was a voracious reader, and dreamed of going one day to the university. We began to read *El Tesoro de la Juventud* together, and it awakened our curiosity about a lot of things. Reading about the Greeks, the French Revolution, or the constellations in the sky was like traveling on a flying carpet. It took us out of the twilight zone of boredom and made us feel alive.

In *El Tesoro de la Juventud* we also learned a thing or two about *la Virgen de Guadalupe*. She was known as a warrior Virgin, because she was originally from Extremadura, the province in Spain where the conquistadors came from. In fact, our statue of the Virgin in the cathedral had been brought to Ponce in the eighteenth century by the Spanish soldiers stationed in our town, the encyclopedia said. Ponce had the largest garrison on the island—at least three thousand soldiers were stationed there at the time, and many had previously served in Mexico, where they had heard about *la Guadalupe*. When they came to Puerto Rico, they brought the image with them.

I went on visiting the cathedral on Saturdays with Gilda, and gradually took a liking to *la Guadalupe*. On Sundays, however, I continued to pray to *la Inmaculada Concepción*, Mother's favorite Virgin. Bishop James MacManus always gave the sermon, dressed in eggplant silk and sweating profusely under his cassock. He was Irish and had very white skin; he always drove from La Alhambra to the Cathedral in his car because he didn't like to get sunburned. The townspeople nicknamed him *Marshmellow*. At his chapel he always spoke in English because the people of La Alhambra spoke English perfectly, but when he gave his homilies at the cathedral he tried to reach out to the townspeople—who didn't understand English—and used pidgin Spanish. But no one understood his sermons!

When the bishop talked about *la Inmaculada Concepción* at La Alhambra's chapel he would become inspired. The mystery of how the Virgin had conceived the Christ Child while remaining the "Immaculate Virgin" was a wonderful event, he said. Granted, it was impossible for a woman to remain a virgin once she got married, but she could still remain "immaculate." To be immaculate meant to be without sin, pure like the lilies that grew at *la Inmaculada's* feet. And that could be achieved only if the wife managed to keep herself detached from earthly passion. Even during the holy act of procreation, when her husband was making love to her, she should remain pure. Then, when she died her body and soul would rise up together on a cloud and attain heaven, like the Virgin. Her flesh would never decompose; she would live forever in the bosom of

Christ. The idea immediately appealed to me, and I became a devotee of *la Inmaculada Concepción*.

At night, when we were lying on our beds in the dark, Gilda whispered, "What did *Marshmellow* talk about today at Mass?"

"He said young women must pray, so that when we get married our husbands will respect us during the act of procreation. He said decent men only marry young virgins."

Gilda made a funny noise and screwed up her face. "Does he mean they don't marry old ones? Poppycock! What did he say about women going to the university?"

"Nothing. He said we had to be like *la Inmaculada*. Even when we get married, we must remain pure. Our duty will be to stay home and take care of our children. After we graduate from high school we don't need to study anymore."

Gilda gave a low whistle. "I hope you didn't fall for that! What about the Greeks, the French Revolution, Orion, and all the wonderful things we've read about together in *El Tesoro de la Juventud*? I may never get to the university, but I'll never forgive you if *you* don't!"

Gilda looked at me and I saw her eyes glisten in the dark. I didn't answer. I knew Mother agreed with the bishop and believed that once I finished high school at the Sacred Heart, I should stay in Ponce until I found a husband. Father had promised to send me to a good boarding school in the States if I wanted, but just the thought of going away terrified me. I didn't speak English well and I had never been away from home. And if I didn't go to college on the mainland, I wouldn't go to the university at all. There was no university in Ponce then, and to attend the University of Puerto Rico in Río Piedras was out of the question. It didn't have decent boarding accommodations where young women from good families could stay for long periods and be chaperoned. On the mainland it was different. Girls of good family could go everywhere unchaperoned and study at any college they chose. It was far enough away that no one would know about it, so the people of Ponce wouldn't gossip.

The matter went undecided until 1952. I was thirteen and just about to graduate from eighth grade when something terrible happened. Mother discovered Gilda was pregnant and told her she had to leave. I found out about it when I came home from school; I never even had the chance to say good-bye. She went back to Cuatro Calles, the slum neighborhood she had come from.

My whole world fell apart. I didn't know what street Gilda lived on, and it was dangerous to try to find her. Carmelo would never take me in the Cadillac without Mother's permission. I'd have to wander around Cuatro Calles on foot, asking if anyone knew where Gilda Ventura lived.

I found out what had happened from Aurelia, our cook, who was a friend of Gilda's. Mother had called Gilda all kinds of names to her face when she found out about her condition. She was a *puta*, a *malagradecida* who didn't give a damn about her reputation. She would probably end up with seven children, each by a different man, and have to bring them up by herself because Puerto Rican men were all scoundrels. They made women pregnant and then went gallivanting on to New York. Gilda was a sinner and she would burn in hell. She must stop working at the house immediately, of course, but she could repent and mend her ways. Maybe after she had the baby she could come back and work for us.

But Mother's insults bounced off Gilda. She laughed and answered her. She said she had *hecho el amor*—done love—with her boyfriend who had returned from the States for a while and she wasn't sorry at all, because it made her feel wonderful. She wouldn't come back to work at our house, because in a few months she was going to the States to live with Eusebio, as soon as he sent her the plane ticket.

I didn't think Gilda was a sinner, and I remember being furious at Mother. I grabbed a pair of scissors and sheared off my long mane of hair—both my torture and my mother's pride. She made Gilda brush and untangle it every day, after rubbing my scalp with Tricófero de Barry, a red liquid that smelled like quinine and was supposed to make my hair grow shiny and strong so that one day I would look like Rita Hayworth.

That night I cried myself to sleep, and the next day I took my bike out of the garage and did something I had never done before— I rode out of la Alhambra and went into town all by myself. I dropped the bike in front of the cathedral, ran up to the altar, and knelt in front of *la Guadalupe*. "You're more powerful than *la Inmaculada Concepción!*" I cried, tears streaming down my cheeks. "You protect people who fight for what they want. If you can speak Nahuatl, you can help me learn how to speak English well enough so I may go study in the States. Maybe I'll meet Gilda over there."

That night I told Father of my decision. He kept his promise and sent me to a boarding school in Massachusetts that fall. Later I went to Manhattanville College in New York. I graduated in 1960, and sixteen years went by before I saw Gilda again. I lived in San Juan and wrote articles for *El Mundo*, one of the local newspapers. My first book of short stories was about to be published, when Gilda came to see me at my house. I don't know how she found out my address, but I recognized her the moment I opened the door. She had gone to live in New York and was back for a visit. Eusebio had gotten a very good job as a guitarist in Rubén Blades's orchestra, and had managed to save enough money to send her a ticket. She looked the same as always: tall and dark and willowy like an *almácigo* tree, and she was standing next to a beautiful sixteen-year-old girl that looked just like her. "You must have gone to the university in the States, because I've seen your articles in *El Mundo*, Niña," she said with her little teasing laugh, as I embraced them ecstatically, pulling them both into the house.

Gilda's life had been heroic; she was a fit example of a devotee of the Virgin of the conquistadors. When she got to New York she had worked as a volunteer for a while at Lincoln Hospital in the Bronx, until her little girl was born. Then she had stayed home to take care of her baby for a number of years. As soon as Gildita was old enough, however, she had gone back to Lincoln Hospital and had entered nursing school. Eusebio had paid for her education; he was now a famous salsa composer for Rubén Blades's orchestra, and was making a lot of money. "Congratulations!" I told her, when I heard the good news. "*La Virgencita de Guadalupe* helped both of us win the battle, after all!"

Coatlicue's Rules: Advice from an Aztec Goddess

PAT MORA

Rule 1: Beware of offers to make you famous.
I, a pious Aztec mother doing my own housework,
am now on a pedestal, "She of the Serpent Skirt,"
hands and hearts dangling from my necklace, a faceless
statue, two snake heads eye-to-eye on my shoulders,
goddess of earth, also, death which leads to

Rule 2: Retain control of your own publicity.
The past is the present. Women are women; balls, balls.

I'm not competitive and motherhood isn't
about numbers, but four hundred sons and a daughter
may be a record even without the baby.
There's something wrong in this world
if a woman isn't safe even when she sweeps
her own house, when any speck can enter even through
the eye, I'll bet, and become a stubborn tenant.

Rule 3: Protect your uterus. Conceptions, immaculate
and otherwise, happen. Women swallow sacred
stones that fill their bellies with elbows and knees.
In Guatemala, a skull dangling from a tree whispers,
"Touch me," to a young girl, and a clear drop
drips on her palm and disappears. The dew
drops in, if you know what I mean. The saliva moved

in her, the girl says. Moved in, I say,
settled into that empty space, and grew. Men know.
They stay full of themselves, keeps occupancy down.

Rule 4: Avoid housework. Remember, I was sweeping,
humming, actually, high on Coatepec, our Serpent
Mountain, humming loud so I wouldn't hear
all those sighs inside. I was sweeping slivers,
gold and jade, picking up after four hundred sons
who think they're gods, and their spoiled sister.

I was sweep-sweeping when feathers fell on me, brushed
my face, the first light touch in years, like in a dream.
At first, I just blew them away, but then I saw it,
the prettiest ball of tiny plumes, glowing green and gold.
Gently, I gathered it. Oh, it was soft as baby hair
and brought back mother shivers when I pressed it
to my skin. I nestled it like I used to nestle them,
here, when they finished nursing. Maybe I even stroked
the roundness. I have since heard that feathers
aren't that unusual at annunciations, but I was innocent.

After I finished sweeping, I looked in vain inside
my clothes, but the soft ball had vanished, well,
descended. I think I showed within the hour,
or so it seemed. They noticed first, of course.

Rule 5: Avoid housework. It bears repeating.
I was too busy washing, cooking corn, beans, squash,
sweeping again, worrying about my daughter,
Painted with Bells, when I began to bump into their frowns
and mutterings. They kept glancing at my stomach,
started pointing. I got so hurt and mad, I started crying.
Why is it they always get to us?

One wrong word or look from any one of them doubles me over,
and I've had four hundred and one without anesthetic.
Near them I'm like a snail with no shell on a sizzling day.
They started yelling, "Wicked, wicked," and my daughter,
right there with them, my wanna-be warrior boy.
And then I heard the whispers.

The yelling was easier than, "Kill. Kill. Kill. Kill."
Kill me? Their mother? One against four hundred and one?
All I'd done was press that softness into me.

Rule 6: Listen to inside voices. You mothers know
about the baby in a family, right? Even if he hadn't talked
to me from deep inside, he would have been special.
Maybe the best. But as my name is Coatlicue, he did.
That unborn child, that started as a ball of feathers all soft
green and gold, heard my woes, and spoke to me.
A thoughtful boy. And formal too. He said, "Do not be afraid,
I know what I must do." So I stopped shaking.

Rule 7: Verify that the inside voice is yours.
I'll spare you the part about the body hacking
and head rolling. But he was provoked, remember.
All this talk of gods and goddesses distorts.

Though this planet wasn't big enough for all of us,
the whole family has done well for itself I think.
I'm the mother of stars. My daughter's white head rolls
the heavens each night, and my sons wink down at me.
What can I say—a family of high visibility.
The baby? Up there also, the sun, the real thing.
Such a god he is, of war unfortunately, and the boy
never stops, always racing across the sky,
every day of the year, a ball of fire since birth.

But I think he has forgotten me. You sense my ambivalence.
I'm blinded by his light.

Rule 8: Insist on personal interviews.
The past is the present, remember. Men carved me,
wrote my story, and Eve's, Malinche's, Guadalupe's,
Llorona's, snakes everywhere, even in our mouths.

Rule 9: Be selective about what you swallow.

Coatlicue: in Aztec mythology mother of Huitzilopochtli, the sun god, who is
born fully armed and slays his sister Coyolxauqui, Painted with Bells, who becomes
the moon, and his four hundred brothers, Centzon Huitznahua, who become the
stars.

Virgencita, *Give Us a Chance*

LILIANA
VALENZUELA

*C*amila leans over the bridge's railing, contemplating the water. Lets her mind fly, free as a fish, fragile as the warm air enveloping her. She contemplates the water and sees some bubbles; at first round and soft, barely showing, then larger, popping and forming circles of restless water. A mane of black hair appears, silky, wet, full of green and rose tiny fish. Seems like a woman, emerging to the surface bit by bit and Camila can't believe her eyes. A gorgeous woman, enveloped in steam, enveloped in a rose robe, soaking wet, showing her voluptuous body, her round and firm breasts. Her mouth a seashell. But who is this mysterious woman? an amazed Camila asks herself, yet cannot bring herself to speak or alert Antonia, who is taking pictures of the Basilica di San Marco; Camila watches her in astonishment. The sea smell is so intense it would seem this creature was the sea herself, her hair coral and her body a mermaid.

—Camila, I've been following you. The divine being emits human words.

　　—What? Me? But who are you?

　　—I'm the Virgin, Mother of God.

　　—What are you saying? The Madonna? *¿La mera mera?*

　　—That's right, Camila. I've been wanting to talk to you but you refuse, my words find no resonance in you, says no less than the Virgin.

　　—But, how can that be? The Virgin? Then you existed once?

　　—Camila, Camila, always so unbelieving, always doubting, of course I exist, my daughter.

—Don't call me daughter, and I still don't know why you wanted to see me; we may get to be friends but don't get too familiar.

—Camila, what a temper, girl! Why this aggression toward me?

—Mhhh, I don't know; if you want, climb on the bridge and let's go to a coffee shop, so we can talk a bit. There are so many things on my mind, I don't even know where to start.

The majestic woman emerges completely from the water and rests on the bridge. Her feet are almost normal, except for a pair of small wings on her heels that take her lightly wherever she wants to go. Camila is still dazed by her beauty and the warmth emanating from her, a warmth of sea, of eternal spring. They sit at a table and *la Virgencita* orders cappuccinos.

The prayer Camila learned as a child comes to mind, the words resonating in her mind: "*Ave Maria purísima, sin pecado concebida . . . sin pecado concebida . . .*"

—What are you thinking, Camila? asks the Madonna.

—Mhmmhm . . . tell me, were you really a virgin when you had baby Jesus? I never really believed it.

—Ay Camila, you focus too much on details, why don't you . . . ?

—But tell me, how was it with José, did you desire him, were you really a virgin?

—Camila, I was a woman just like you, with desires, likes, with what they now call a natural desire quite in blossom. I met José in our village, he was much older than me and I liked him so much, you can't imagine what I went through. José was so sweet and soft with me and one afternoon, on the edge of town, it happened. We loved under the olive trees hours before dawn. It took root like fire. It may seem strange to you to hear about the passions of the gods . . .

—And did you like it? asked Camila, now hooked on the conversation.

—Mmmmhmm, José was the best-looking man in the whole region, and the hottest, too. I'll confess to you that I loved it. I became more experienced and each time I enjoyed it more. His soft and burning skin next to mine, I couldn't hold myself back. Until one day I became pregnant.

—How exciting! And what did your mom say?

—In those days mothers knew that if one got pregnant she'd follow the man, and my mother, although sad to see me go, gave me advice, gave me a small pouch with gold coins, and gave me the burro for the journey. Since José was older . . . but wait, why am I telling you all this? What am I saying?

—María, forgive me for calling you by your name, what happened is that you gave me your trust and now we're friends, and I like you. María smiles and her eyes shine with a glint of water.

—Camila, you're impossible! says María, sighing and laughing at once. Incorrigible! Camila smiles too and looks into her eyes, serene, soft, full of wisdom.

—*Virgencita*, give us a chance, the heck with virginity, no? We're up to here with the same old song about honor, let's call it quits.

> Listen, Camila
> in your time there will be transformation
> paradise doesn't exist
> but a life of reason does
> of greater conquests
> of greater powers
> You are like Lilith, mother of all
> curious
> an adventurer, eyes
> shining.
> She was the first to know
> the first to know about
> the first to choose
> the first to feel passion
> Listen, Camila
> in your time there will be transformation
> Like Lilith
> you are free
> free

from now on your guilt has been washed with water
erased from your heart
Follow Lilith
you hothead
it's your time of transformation.

Having said this, the Virgin leans over and kisses Camila's cheek. A soft smile draws itself on her cinnamon face and her coral robe disappears in the air. Camila sees the Virgin's young body, her fresh skin, her wet vagina, everything you don't see in the holy cards. She sees herself nude as well, sees her pubic hair, her tits. Sees *la Virgencita*. Sees herself.

Camila wakes up. The sun filters softly through the window that opens onto the balcony, that opens onto the canal, that opens onto life. She sees sweet Antonia by her side and smiles a tad. After all these weeks of travel sleeping in bunk-bed youth hostels and on friends' couches, they decided to splurge on a decent room with a view in a pensione, a room they share with two other travelers. The real luxury is their own bathroom—an old-fashioned commode and a toilet, the shower costs extra. Camila and Antonia share a lumpy old bed. So different from the water bed Camila and her boyfriend have back home. Roaming through streets nearly empty of tourists in Venice, in the spring, is another unexpected luxury. The whole city seems to pulsate in sensuous images that invade every window and arch, every church and art collection. Fresh images of Botticelli, Bellini, Tiziano, and Giorgione dance in their heads, overloading their senses. Camila looks at her best pal again and is amazed at how her breasts are drawn against the thin sleeping T-shirt. She has seen them a thousand times, since they were girls and had nothing but two painted circles on their chests, past the time when Camila couldn't stop looking at Antonia's breasts that grew excessively, she was almost ashamed for her but fascinated at the same time to see those abundant and soft breasts that grew on their own, morning glory after the rain.

Camila remembers the time she spent the night at Antonia's and while Antonia and her sister slept, Camila got up and tried on Antonia's bra that her smaller breasts could not fill. Using it for the first time gave her a strange feeling. To feel the lace, the tight snap on the back compressing her whole chest, to see herself reflected on the mirror under a blue light, as of night birds, she felt different, aroused. Her curiosity took a step further and wanted to know whether Antonia slept with her bra on and maybe Camila also wanted to feel Antonia's large breasts, fearfully beautiful. But Antonia awoke and Camila, caught in her attempt, said she was trying to climb to the other side of the bed, because she had just come from the bathroom. After this incident Camila didn't worry anymore about Antonia's breasts and started to accept her own with a little more ease, no longer trying to hide them under those two braids she wove for that purpose, to ignore their presence.

But this morning Camila is surprised again, like when she was a young girl, to see Antonia's firm breasts, her hard nipples against the thin T-shirt. She feels shaken by her beauty, her fine and slender body, her lace-and-silk underwear. Camila touches Antonia's breasts over the thin T-shirt. The two virgins embrace over a turquoise green, they float over the blue-green waters of Bellini, they reach for the fruit below. Their breasts are duplicated, quantified, multiplied, a twin image, a mirror image, a repetition, an unfolding, and a rupture. Venus plays with a golden lock of hair over their vulvas. A delicate foot squashes the juice of a red poppy. Raspberries drip from their breasts. The smell of apricot behind their ears. And the smell of the canals, of their own canals, their own rivers and seas.

La Madonna de Latte nurses Camila and Antonia at her breast, envelops them with petals, gives them divine manna while they lie on her bosom of understanding. All of Venice is witness to this miracle. La Virgencita crosses the canal, swimming with her light transparent robes. The priests on the sides of the canal, in their crimson-and-black robes, kneel. Their bald heads shine. They are silent. The maidens watch attentively. A black man steps out of a door facing the canal, still holding a maiden's hand, and is about to jump in the water. The gondolas stop, their passengers look in astonishment, some standing, some sitting, the gondoliers cease their song. La Virgencita swims, Venus in the water, her light robes appear and disappear. Her indomitable long mane of curls floats and tangles, floats and sinks. The monks in their white habits pray, raise banners, the miracle of the vulva is back. Silence reigns.

The sacred places, the corners where centuries melt and doves copulate. Camila kisses Antonia's mouth, juicy as persimmon. All of Venice is witness to the miracle. *La Virgencita* swims across the canal with her light transparent robes. Priests are silent. Maidens look attentively. Monks cross themselves. The black man swims to his white lover's arms. The church bells ring their millenary beat. A newborn nurses from her mother's breasts over a soft and fresh grass. A white silk cloth shelters and provides a seat for them. Spring begins.

The Undocumented Virgin

RUBÉN MARTÍNEZ

I'm Catholic. Not just a *cultural* Catholic, mind you, but a flesh-eating, blood-drinking practitioner of the faith. I beat my chest during the recitation of the confession at Mass. I cross myself whenever I pass by a church, on the plane before takeoff and landing, and always before a performance. I've got as many rosaries, bottles of holy water, crucifixes, and saints (depicted on plastic statuettes, refrigerator magnets, three-dimensional postcards) as a Mexican *abuelita* or a Dominican baseball player. Christian symbolism permeates my writing: my characters are always undergoing Christlike crucifixions and resurrections.

My friends—the poets and performance artists, the godless neo-bohemians—they're the cultural Catholics. They laugh at my Old World ways. The Church! they scoff, the light glinting off gold crucifixes dangling just above the neckline of their shirts or from one or both ears. A genocidal institution! Priests! they say, lighting a stick of incense at their apartment altars and showing off their *Virgen de Guadalupe* T-shirts. A bunch of altar boy–molesting hypocrites!

I admit that the Catholic Church is guilty of many crimes against humanity. But, I tell my friends, there is a vast gulf between the *institution* and what I consider to be the true Rock of the Church: not the priests or the bishops or cardinals or the Pope, but the faithful in the pews. In El Salvador, it was radical Catholic laity that laid the groundwork for the revolutionary movement of the 1970s and 1980s—and, in the process, convinced key church authorities (such as martyred Archbishop Oscar Arnulfo Romero) that acquiescence to the military dictatorship was a mortal sin. Despite the wane of Marxist-influenced liberation theology in this postsocialist era,

Catholic activists continue to be in the vanguard on issues of social justice, whether in the poverty-stricken favelas of São Paulo or on the gang-infested streets of East Los Angeles.

But it is something even bigger than politics, or what is at the heart of any meaningful politics, that is the basis for my spirituality. I am a practicing Catholic because I believe in the strength of communities of faith and, especially, in the role of ritual as a unifying force that allows people to transcend narrow individualism and reach out to the strangers who mirror our own visage: that moment of the Holy Mass when we turn to our neighbors and offer, "Peace be with you."

My Catholicism has its roots in Mexico, where my father's parents were born and lived until they came to Los Angeles as young adults. Mexico is a culturally and spiritually Catholic land: it survives its political and economic turmoil and its *mestizo* identity crisis to a great extent because the solidarity and ritual of Catholicism reunite the disparate pieces of its fragmented self. To the horror of the nativists in the United States, so is most of the Southwest now again a Catholic land—because it was once so and because recent waves of immigration have replenished its Mexican-Catholic self, especially in California.

The most visible symbol of this spiritual transfusion across the U.S.-Mexico frontier is the ubiquitousness of *la Virgen de Guadalupe*, Mexico's patron saint, on the northern side of the border. She is painted on neighborhood walls and on storefronts, emblazoned on sweatshirts and baseball caps; Her portrait hangs in living rooms and in every barrio church from East L.A. to El Paso. There's no quantifiable data on people's prayer habits, of course, but I'm certain that many more prayers are offered up to *la Virgen* by Mexican and Chicano faithful than to the Son of God. For us, *la Virgen* is at least as important a religious icon as Jesus Himself. *La Virgen* is at the center of the Mexican soul.

For Latin Americans, as for people in any colonized quarter of the globe, the legacy of the Church is bittersweet. It was the Church that arrived with the *conquistadores* and burned the last of the Náhuatl codices, erasing thereby the record of one of the world's great cultures. But a third culture arose from the blood and ash of the Conquest, as did what is arguably a third religion—New World Catholicism. In Mexico, *la Virgen* was at the center of this spiritual death/birth.

In the end, there could have been worse matches than that of Indian America with the Catholic Crown of Spain: their religious lives before their encounter had much in common. Catholicism is both viciously hierarchical and collectivist—it is the religion's elemental contradiction. Social and political passivity is inculcated into the faithful as a form of theocratic control, but the sense of community among Catholics is also extremely powerful. The Catholic family, both the nuclear unit and the larger congregation, has survived the centuries and flourished in an incredible array of cultural settings because its public life, in its best moments, mirrors the private: there is familial warmth inside church and at home, a selfless generosity as much between strangers as between parent and child.

Pre-Columbian Indian theocracies shared in this very contradiction. Political control was achieved through the machinations of an elite priestly class that jealously guarded its power, but the Indians also developed harmonious modes of communal living: the public space was an intimate one. Catholicism's cluttered iconography of the Holy Trinity and the endless procession of the saints also resembled the Aztec spiritual world's polytheistic pantheon of deities. It was this similarity, I believe, that offered the possibility of spiritual synthesis rather than outright conquest.

The clash between the European *conquistadores* and the indigenous world of the Americas is as much a story of survival as of death. Just a few years ago, Indian communities across the continent sounded a note of discord during the quincentennial "celebration" of the "discovery" of the New World. That their voices were heard at all is tribute to the survival of Indian America. Increasingly, we come to recognize that the Conquest did not result in the complete destruction of the Indian—and that redress of the historical wrong of the Conquest doesn't require a purging of the European. The Catholic Church in Latin America is not the Church of the Vatican, nor is it entirely indigenous. It is the mestizo Church, wherein commingle all of the Americas' cultural contradictions in an uneasy and constantly evolving tension.

The melding of Spanish Catholicism to indigenous spirituality began with the Conquest itself, in which pre-Columbian deities survived by a process that my colleague transvestite–performance artist–AIDS activist Marcus Kuiland-Nazario describes as "wearing Catholic drag." The spiritual continuum was unbroken: Guadalupe *is* Tonantzin, the Aztec goddess the Indians venerated on the Cerro del Tepeyac before the arrival of the Spanish. "Mother of Mexico," She is called: identifying with the Indian, not the European. Of course, Mexicans venerate Jesus and the constellation of Catholic saints as well (and there are many other cases of spiritual "transvestism" like Guadalupe's in the Americas, especially in the Afro-Caribbean Santería religion). But Guadalupe-Tonantzin was particularly powerful for Mexicans: it gave them a subversive path away from the patriarchal, Jesus-centered European Church toward an Indian, matriarchal spirituality. Would that this spiritual matriarchy were Mexico's political and economic reality as well, but alas, Guadalupe has yet to storm the halls of macho power.

Guadalupe followed Mexicans north as they settled in what was to become the southwestern United States, and she remained at their side after the Mexican-American War. A century and a half later, She continues to accompany Mexicans as they cross the border at the Rio Grande, and remains the most powerful of Chicana icons for Mexicans who've been trapped on the "other side" for generations. Guadalupe, in the end, proclaims a vast spiritual region that ignores the political demarcations that divide California and Mexico. Through Her intercession, a Mexican remains Mexican in California, an Indian remains Indian in Mexico.

Once again, there is no quantifiable data that I can point to, but my personal research shows that there has been a dramatic increase in miraculous apparitions of *la Virgen de Guadalupe* in recent years— on both sides of the border. There was the sighting a few years back of Her blurry image on the side of a modest stucco home in Watts, one of the many barrio destinations of the new immigrants in California. The TV news cameras didn't show much more than a curious play of shadow and light from a tree and the glow of a streetlamp, but thousands of faithful made the pilgrimage anyway. In a small central California town, home to thousands of migrant workers, a statue of *la Virgen* inexplicably shed tears. There is talk of *la Virgencita* luring border patrol guards down dead-end paths while the illegals cruise toward the American Dream on the other side of the arroyo. I even heard a rumor that *la Virgen's* serene countenance appeared before a crowd of hungover homeboys in Montebello, quivering in a big bowl of menudo.

It's no coincidence that She's been appearing more often lately. In times of crisis, She's always there. Today, the crisis is on both sides of the border.

The economic and political turmoil in Mexico began with the Zapatista insurrection of January 1994. Until then, the country had seemed stable enough. Six years of neo-liberalism under the regime of Carlos Salinas de Gortari had functioned in typical trickle-down fashion: the millionaires had become multimillionaires, an optimistic middle class was buying everything it could on credit, and the poor—well, the poor grew poorer (in Mexico, that's roughly half the population). NAFTA, the neo-liberals promised, would result in even greater prosperity for all.

Then, at midnight on December 31, 1993, at the very hour NAFTA went into effect, a ragtag army of mostly Mayan peasants burst onto the world stage, piercing the neo-liberal armor with a simple message: Mexico's relative prosperity was coming at the expense of the poor. In Mexico, the poorest of the poor are the Indians. The Zapatistas described NAFTA as a death sentence on the Indian countryside, where subsidized farming cooperatives lay directly in the path of international competition. Ross Perot talked of that big sucking sound of jobs lost to Mexico because of NAFTA; the Zapatistas saw it the other way around.

What's more, the Zapatistas pointed to the country's biggest existential contradiction. Postrevolutionary Mexico had fashioned for itself an identity predicated on the idea of the Aztec Nation: the governmental project of *la cultura nacional* proclaimed the Indian the cultural heart of Mexico. But the Indians, Mexico's minority culture (thirty percent of the population), didn't prosper from their newfound status as cultural revolutionaries. The Indians were appropriated as poster children, much as environmental activists used Native Americans in the 1970s in the U.S. The Mexican Indians were depicted in Diego Rivera's grand murals, celebrated by poets and composers, and fervently studied by the anthropologists. But the Revolution of 1910 never reached the Indian countryside. In Chiapas, social conditions remained as they had for centuries: death from curable disease and malnutrition, no education to speak of, and an economic status no better than the peonage created by the Conquest.

Because of all this, the Zapatista movement, which had little military might, claimed a tremendous moral authority. The rest of Mexico—mestizo Mexico, the mixed-race sons and daughters of the Conquest—could not help but face its historical hypocrisy. The Zapatistas both confirmed the Revolution's cultural truths and challenged the corrupted (mestizo) structures that sold out the lofty ideals of social and economic equity.

After the January insurrection, a series of events pitched Mexico dangerously close to chaos, easily the most critical moment in the country since the Revolution of 1910. Presidential candidate Luis Donaldo Colosio was assassinated at a Tijuana rally. Another top ruling party official was gunned down on the streets of Mexico City a few months later. Narco-lords fought turf wars openly on the streets of several cities in the north, which in recent years has come to resemble the lawless Old West.

California, meanwhile, was undergoing its own identity crisis. The central political conflict in the Golden State was ostensibly over illegal immigration. In November of 1994, Proposition 187 was approved by California's voters, who are so overwhelmingly white (an apartheid-like situation due to the fact that Latinos are severely underrepresented in the voting rolls).

Prop 187, if it ever beats the many lawsuits brought against it on constitutional grounds, would deny basic public benefits like education and most health services to illegal residents. There was plenty of political déjà-vu in the pro-187 rhetoric: too many immigrants! The same was said in the 1930s during the Great Depression, and later during the postwar recession of the 1950s; on both occasions, hundreds of thousands of Mexican workers were deported back to Mexico. Proposition 187 was yet another chapter in California's long love/hate relationship with its Latino immigrants: loving the cheap labor, hating the natural consequence of Anglos having to share space—and a slice of the economic pie—with big Spanish-speaking, mostly Catholic families.

In the same election, voters also approved Proposition 184, the "three strikes and you're out" initiative, which mandated life prison sentences for a third felony—be it a violent crime or a check-kiting scheme. Propositions 187 and 184 are related: both target California's "people of color"—Latinos and African-Americans. Both target the working poor. Both were passed by a white middle class led by scapegoating politicians to believe that the poor and the nonwhite were responsible for California's economic downturn.

But 187 and 184 were about much more than immigration and crime. The real debate was over what kind of place California is to be in the twenty-first century. Anglo residents in Los Angeles regularly complain that their fair City of the Angels has been "Tijuana-ized," no matter that their middle-class existence depends largely on cheap immigrant labor in agriculture, light industry, and the service sector. Anglo Californians begged the federal government to make a stand at the southern border: Keep the barbarians from breaching the Gates of Rome!

What many Californians fail to see is that the crisis in Mexico *is* the crisis in California, and vice versa. Mexicans are at the center of this whirlwind of history: agents of change. They are scorned on either side of the border. Chicanos and immigrants are treated like Indians in California, while in Mexico the Indians are seen as stumbling blocks to the latest neo-liberal schemes: the Indians of Mexico are treated like the Chicanos or immigrants of California.

The economic crisis in Mexico sends the Indians north; Proposition 187 seeks to send them back down south. And yet, speak to the immigrants, to the Indians, to the Chicanos, and you hear not the siege mentality of the Anglo Californian but the optimism that once characterized the Golden State. There is hope on the "other side" as the immigrant bolts past the border patrol to the dream of a better life in the North; there is hope in the sad eyes of Emiliano Zapata, standard-bearer of the revolt in Chiapas; there is hope on college campuses where a new generation of Chicano students stage hunger strikes and marches in support of their immigrant brothers and sisters or in behalf of their own culture and causes. On both sides of the border, she is there.

Faint murmurs: "*María . . . bendita . . . mujeres . . . fruto . . . vientre . . .*"
 I am snuggled under a thick Mexican wool blanket, warm as in the womb, at my grandparents' house late at night. The whispers are my own and my grandmother's. She stands over me in her long nightgown, her black braids trailing down her back. The prayer finished, she leans down and under her breath rapidly recites another prayer, all the while blessing me with her hand. She places the cross of her thumb and index finger before my lips. I kiss it. "Amen," we say, almost in unison.

 The only light in the house emanates from my grandparents' bedroom, where shadows from a wavering candle flame dance on the wall—and from the towering *Virgen de Guadalupe* that hangs above the fireplace in the living room. From beneath the cherub and sliver of dark moon that bears her aloft comes a red glow that burns night and day. I never, ever saw my grandmother replace the bulb hidden behind the green ceramic corona under the Virgin. In my childhood, it was the eternal flame, protecting me from the darkness . . . from the bitter pain in my grandparents' bedroom—the ghosts of my family's Passion—and from the chaos of the world outside.

 My grandmother did everything she could to turn her house in Los Angeles into one grand Mexican-Catholic altar. There was the Last Supper in the dining room, of course, and little saintly medallions of the mail-order variety strategically placed in every room. A candle always burned before a gold-framed San Martín de Porres. But it was *la Virgen* in the living room—by sheer size, the most important icon in the house—that fascinated me. Terrified me. Could save me. Was my mother. Was His mother. And was a virgin, but that didn't mean much to me; what mattered was that from her all things came: She was the Mother of God, the Goddess, the Witch, whatever you want to call her. And best of all, she was *morena*: her olive skin, tinged with the glow of the omnipresent red light, was as dark as my own.

At Franklin Elementary School, I was the only Latino in an overwhelmingly white student body (I recall one black girl, and a smattering of Asian kids). I became a good student, despite the fact that my English was less than proficient when I entered kindergarten. But there was always the feeling that I didn't quite fit in, no matter how well I ended up speaking and writing English. It was at home that I had a more secure sense of self. At my parents' house, there was a fluid negotiation between Spanish and English, between American ambition and Latino family values, between Vicki Carr and Motown. But the space that I found the most comforting in my early childhood was my grandparents' home. *La Virgen* was the source of a precious thing in my life: the sense that no matter how many costumes I had to wear (socially, linguistically) out in the world, there was a home I could always return to, as warm as school was cold, as secure as the world was scary.

A month after the passage of Proposition 187 in California and just a few days before Christmas 1994, the new government of President Ernesto Zedillo suddenly and drastically devalued the Mexican peso, plunging the middle and working classes into a deep holiday depression. But Mexicans weathered the storm. Because of Her.

I arrived in Mexico City just a few days before the devaluation, as the famous Popocatépetl volcano was belching mammoth gray clouds of ash in a tailor-made metaphor for the country's instability. *¡Feliz Navidad!*

The pilgrims come from all over the republic to celebrate her feast day on December 12, but the party begins the night before. They come as they've come for a thousand years to the Cerro del Tepeyac. The pilgrims come by bus, car, or bicycle. Yet others come jogging or walking from distances greater than the Greek marathon, carrying banners and picture frames and heavy ornate wooden altars, all bearing her image.

A mostly brown nation of Indian and mixed-race heritage assembles on the lava stone before the basilica. Their hair is neo-hippie long or punk short—mestizo kids from the city, *indígenas* from the provinces. I came expecting to see a lot of grandmothers with crinkled faces and long white braids, but mostly the pilgrims are young: teenage rocker types in leather jackets carrying ghetto blasters with stickers of Metallica and Nirvana right next to *la Virgen's.*

It's a Catholic Woodstock attended, according to official crowd estimates, by some four million faithful every year. The biking pilgrims park tens of thousands of machines on top of one another, ceremonial piles of aluminum and rubber. The pilgrims drink, a little rum or brandy to ward off the chill of the night and—why not?—to toast *la Virgencita.* The pilgrims smoke, too. A crew of *rockero* youth at the top of Tepeyac pass the pipe around and listen to Pink Floyd on a battered box. *La Virgen* doesn't suffer from any generation gap.

It's the biggest party I've ever been to. My street paranoia fades as I realize that this is probably the safest place on the planet to be: who would dare diss Lupe by committing the sin of robbery? (Police reported that there was a grand total of seven arrests during the entire festival.) There is virtually no security, except for a few Red Cross crews with stretchers and ambulances at the ready for those who pass out in the crush of the crowd. The few cops are in an uncharacteristically jovial mood (cops are hated in Mexico City as much as they are in the barrios of Rodney King's L.A.). They while away the hours by taking pictures of themselves at Technicolor-bright Polaroid altars depicting *la Virgen's* apparition and munching on traditional egg-and-nut breads along with everyone else.

After two in the morning, the chill grows bitter and the party energy flags. The thousands of faithful turn in for the night: the marathon runners from Hidalgo, the Marian devotees from Morelos, the Indian dancers from Oaxaca, the young former drug addicts-turned-missionaries from Tijuana. They lay out their blankets and huddle together against the cold. It's as if the entire country is in one huge embrace; Mexico hugs itself through the night to keep warm.

This is the greatness of mestizo culture, I think to myself. Everyone's welcome; we can all get along. Because of *her.* Because She is both Indian and Spanish. A rocker and an Aztec dancer. She's olive-skinned, a blend of indigenous copper brown and Iberian white. She's the woman that puts the Mexican macho in his place—

no matter how much he beats his chest, she's the origin of All Things, the serpent-woman Tonantzin.

She is the protector of Family, and lashes out at anyone who would endanger a child's well-being. She is, after all, the Savior's Mother and sees her Son's visage in the face of every Mexican son or daughter. Perhaps that's why most of the pilgrims are so young. It is young Mexico that stares into a bleak future, a violent world, that is looking for itself today in the jungles of Chiapas, along the endless asphalt of Mexico City and in the cold cities of the United States. Young Mexico desperately needs to believe.

Skyrockets burst in the predawn sky as I climb the Cerro del Tepeyac. A tearful nostalgia overwhelms me: I am returning to my grandmother's home country, where she bought that big, beautiful portrait of Her. I'm the prodigal son born in the North returning to wrap myself in the gentle folds of Tepeyac. It's okay that my Spanish isn't perfect, that I eat hamburgers and love rock 'n' roll. All *la Virgen* asks of me is faith.

And I do believe: more in her than in the politics of the country whose passport I bear, the good ol' U.S.A. This is my first December 12 in Mexico City, and it is both a political and an existential pilgrimage. I'm a mestizo twice over: Indian and European blood runs through my veins, plus I was born on the "other side," where my cultural icons, in addition to *la Virgen*, included *Soul Train, The Brady Bunch,* and later, the Beat poets, rock 'n' roll, and rap. So I've "returned" to Mexico not so much to "remember" who I am as to acknowledge my present and seek a future. In *la Virgen*, I see myself. Call Her the first mestiza, the original Chicana. And because she crosses so many borders—walls erected and kept in place by American nativists and Mexican nationalists who refuse to see we already live in a borderless time—call Her the Undocumented Virgin.

Beginning at dawn on the twelfth, thousands of Indian dancers pound the lava stone of the plaza with their bare feet amid clouds of incense. The fierce beat of the drums melds with the church hymns emanating from the cathedral. Pilgrims painfully approach the entryway on their knees, rosaries swinging from their hands, sweat streaming from their brows. I watch one man inch his way toward *la Virgen's* birthplace carrying his sick child in his arms. Mexico comes to Her to heal itself.

We come to pay Her tribute, and to petition her as well, the tradition of the *mandas*. I speak to a family that's come all the way from East Los Angeles to honor Her. "I want to ask Her for better luck with work in the North," the teenage son, a longhaired rocker, tells me. "And for Her to accompany all Latinos in California now that they've passed 187," adds the father.

I have faith that Mexico will survive this turbulent time with its essence intact. That essence is the festival of *la Virgen*, where all of Mexico's children come together to admit that the very pain of our history—the racism against the Indian, the diaspora and conflict of immigration—is what offers us the path toward redemption. It is a hope that brings with it a tremendous responsibility: to live up to *la Virgen's* own faith in *us*.

The Mexican-ness of *la Virgen's* festival would probably be misunderstood in the United States. More than ever, Americans cling to their individual "space"; their generosity grows fickle. A feast like *la Virgen's* would appear claustrophobic, dirty, anarchic. And yet, what Americans misunderstand about Mexicans is precisely what they need the most. Americans need to embrace themselves. I've found in Mexico, through Guadalupe-Tonantzin, what I'd lost in Prop 187, three-strikes-you're-out California.

As the sun sinks into the coppery hues of the smoggy horizon of the most populous city on earth, the festivities of Mexico's most important holiday draw to a close. The Indian elders leave the cathedral, chanting in the Spanish of *la Virgen* and in the dialects of Tonantzin: *"Adiós, Madre de Cielo."* Good-bye, Mother of Heaven. They walk backwards, their eyes never leaving the doorway to the cathedral, as if to say that Mexico will never turn her back on Her faith.

December 1995. I wanted to be in Mexico again this year for her day, but I got stuck in L.A. After joining the faithful at Our Lady Queen of the Angels Church downtown, however, I hardly missed Mexico at all.

I get to the church at about four-thirty in the morning, one of the late arrivals for the traditional *mañanitas*, *la Virgen's* birthday celebration which begins a little after midnight and lasts till sunrise. Everything I'd seen in Mexico last year is duplicated here. The mariachis sing with their dramatic vibratos and hand gestures. People kneel and pray or simply stare in reverential silence before Her image, which is everywhere. There's a portrait hanging in the church, one on a makeshift stage in the courtyard, another at an old altar said to be the site of holy apparitions. The glow from the flames of hundreds of votive candles wavers over the faces of the faithful.

And there She is again, on the necklaces, 1996 calendars, T-shirts, hawked by dozens of vendors. Here She stands at one of those kitschy makeshift photo studios. A few take the picture standing alone, but mostly it's families that gather for the memento: the grandmother with long braids and shawl, the red-eyed parents who'll have to go off to work in an hour or so, the hyper kids scampering around in a world of both magical colors and religious solemnity.

We're immersed in sight, sound, smell: tacos, tamales, hot dogs, sweet *pan dulce* bread, hot *champurrado* and *ponche* drinks. Nothing costs more than a dollar. *La Virgen*, above all, is Mother to the Working Poor. As the pastor's voice booms over the loudspeakers recounting the tale of Juan Diego's encounter with *la Virgen*, the perfume of hundreds of red roses wafts over us in the courtyard, reminding us of the miracle centuries ago: the skeptical bishop had asked Juan Diego for proof that he had indeed witnessed a miraculous apparition, and she obliged by presenting him with dozens of the beautiful flowers in the dead of winter that no rose could survive. Who could doubt the miracle? The roses live on in the middle of December, nearly five hundred years later.

It was another tough year in Mexico, and Latinos would be hard-pressed to say things were much better in the anti-immigrant North. The faithful here are almost all recently arrived; many of them are undocumented. Here in L.A., the *mandas* tell of the hardships and hopes of the immigrants.

Antonio Huanetlcóatl, the father of an Indian family from the high sierra of Puebla, asks *la Virgen* to bless this City of the Angels, for her to "bring food to the hungry, health to the sick, and peace to lands torn by war." His twenty-two-year-old son, Luis, meanwhile begs her to accompany his young wife in her pregnancy, that a healthy son or daughter might join their family. "I hope that by February she'll give birth, and I've come to ask *la Virgen* for everything to turn out all right."

Griselda Facio of Jalisco prays for a change in the government back home in Mexico, an end to the crisis and chaos in her homeland. "Things are difficult everywhere you go," she says. "I'm praying for myself and for everyone else."

Meanwhile Doris Sánchez, a Honduran immigrant in her early twenties, prays for peace right here in L.A., for an end to the urban warfare between rival gangs in her neighborhood. "I pray that people get organized" says Sánchez, "so that there isn't any more killing of innocent people."

And so *la Virgen* is called upon to cure ills north and south, for loved ones or for anyone anywhere who suffers. This gathering in L.A. might not be as monumental as the festival in Mexico City. But there is an intensity here that matches or maybe even surpasses the devotion back home. Perhaps it's the yearning to remain rooted in a rootless time where one's address can be changed by twists of fate like the economy or the border patrol.

Leonor Cervantes, a native of Guanajuato who gathered up her three sons, two daughters, mother, and a sister to be here this morning, says she feels the holiday for *la Virgen* might be more important to Mexicans here than back home. "The farther you are from home, the more She pulls at you," says Cervantes. "It's a great thing—She keeps us united, whether we're in our home country or over here."

And then I meet Rafael Torres, who looks the typical American teenager in his backwards baseball cap and baggy jeans, except that his face is just like Juan Diego's, Indian features unchanged five hundred years after the Conquest. He's made it safely to Los Angeles from his hometown of Puebla, due in no small part to *la Virgen*'s guidance. "Before the immigrants come north," he says, "they go to the church right there in Mexico, to get *la Virgen*'s blessing. Everybody does it. They ask Her to let them come to this country, to cross the border without any problems."

The Undocumented Virgin.

The Mother of Mexico stands at the center of the Mexican family. She may have prodigal sons and wayward daughters, Her children might not have enough to eat sometimes, economic and political storms rage at home and abroad, but she is there, unmovable. She reminds Mexicans who they are, wherever they are. She is their very history, telling them that they have not only a millenary past, but a millenary future as well.

The Undocumented Virgin has accompanied me on my journey through life, from early innocence to my alienated teens to my dark twenties and on into the strange pilgrimage of my thirties. Today, I live across the street from my grandparents' old home. Grandfather died long ago; my *abuelita*, she who introduced me to *la Virgencita*, left us six years ago. My parents live in the house now. In a few months, they'll move away and I'll move in. The towering portrait of *la Virgen* is still there in the living room. She is there to stay, as much a part of the house as the foundation itself.

Guadalupe, Subversive Virgin

MARGARET RANDALL

*I*t was the unpredictable sixties, and the Pope was coming to Mexico. Serafina, who cleaned my house and lived with her extended family in the little room on its roof, harrumphed for days. She told me the priest where she sometimes confessed and took communion wanted his parishioners to contribute to the solid-gold rose the country's faithful would give this Patriarch of the Church, a gift of devotion from Catholics whose history was not as fervent as those from Colombia, not as processional as those from Peru. No one forgot the Cristero Rebellion, that searing separation of Church and State.[1]

Serafina laughed. *"Imagínate,"* she said, "a gold rose! As if he didn't have enough gold in that Vatican of his!"

But the Virgin of Guadalupe. Ah, she was something else. "Our own. A sister in suffering." Or better yet, a benevolent Mother, of the sort few had. Serafina's own mother had kicked her out when she was fourteen—"may the Lord forgive her"—because she gave birth one day, no husband, no warning, her emaciated belly barely thickened beneath the homemade apron. "What did I know, *pues*. My mother never told me anything. That was Concha, my oldest . . . And Our Lady, she's never turned her back on me."

Me, not us. The relationship is deeply personal even when it reflects a veritable movement of collective voice. Subversion is about putting something over on a person or system that abuses

---

[1]Cristero Rebellion, 1927 to 1929. Almost two decades after the Revolution of 1910, the Mexican masses rose up in arms against the power of the Catholic Church, provoking a powerful separation of Church and State which has influenced some but not all of the other Latin American countries.

power in order to keep you down. It may be about rerouting an image back upon itself, creating an unexpected boomerang. Or fighting against an oppressor with weapons or tools taken from that oppressor. Historically, it has often meant turning symbols of inequality against structures of control, thereby facilitating a victim's journey to survival. Within Christianity, the iconography and discourse of the Virgin Mary have traditionally urged women to submit, obey, accept. But with experience come questions, and not all Virgins have been willing to play the oppressor's game.

Take this, one of many examples, rising strong through the mist of ancient Marist culture: "Mary, when they always pictured you with child, did your spirit ever call for something free and wild? . . . Mary, when they cast your body into stone, to stand in churches apart and all alone, tell me, Mary, did you think of fighting? . . . Mary, when they taught you how to kneel and pray, did you want to stand and look straight into your day? . . . Mary, when they took your womanself away, and made you the keeper of our virtue to this day: tell me, Mary, did you dream of being?"

These questions are put forth in "Song to Mary,"[2] product of these years of feminist revisioning. It is one that I, a non-Christian and a woman without official religion of any kind, repeatedly used to help me make it through the most difficult war years in Nicaragua. Listening to those questions became a way of evoking a longed-for mother's solace to fortify my own woman's strength.

Over and over, I have heard this me that contains an us. This was the way Serafina spoke. And it was true of the women whose babies I coaxed to life in Mexico City's misery belt then, in those overpopulated shacks of tin and wood, cardboard and stubborn resignation. *Paracaidistas* their inhabitants were called, parachutists; the idea being that they had somehow fallen upon that pitiful land, taken possession of its meager space. I would have said the running poor, shoved by conquest to the inhospitable edges of a sprawling city, then repeatedly shoved again by colonialism, avarice, greed.

"Don't push yet," I would warn the eyes lowered beneath the upper border of the *rebozo* she held against her mouth. "And take

---

[2]"Song of Mary" is by Carolyn McDade, recorded on her album *Rain Upon Dry Land: Songs of Carolyn McDade with Friends.*

that away from your face. You have to be able to breathe." The single room always held other children. Sometimes sheets of newspaper had been carefully spread beneath the mother's hips and thighs, preparation for a clean birth. At some point—I could be sure of it—Guadalupe would be evoked. Perhaps by name: Our Lady. *Virgencita. La Morenita.* She who stays with us, who understands our pain . . . even when the Church does not. Perhaps an image, cut from a magazine or, occasionally, three-dimensional. The radiant points of sun seemed to leap and shimmer as the newborn fought its way to a life that was destined to be worse than hard.

Students of the only black Virgin on our continent insist that Mexicans, on both sides of the Rio Grande, consider Our Lady of Guadalupe their own, the most familiar and compelling. Experts have come up with statistics; like a 1969 poll showing almost half the working-class populations of Zamora and Saltillo reporting the Virgin Mary as their most important deity. (Only twenty-three percent named God!) It is significant that she embodies two characteristics: femaleness and color. That is, she is a woman within the long history of male deification. And, dark-skinned, she appeared to an Indian in the context and continuing presence of European invasion.

It has been a long hard time of transformation, in which power shifts slowly, sometimes falteringly but always doggedly, from the cruelty of androcentrism to the more egalitarian fairness of a female-centered spirituality. If we revisit the history, we find that as long ago as two thousand years, the prophecies attributed to the apostle John posited the Marian cult of Tepeyac as heralding "the last times." Students of New World Christianity have interpreted this as the end of the Church of Christ, to be replaced by a Church of Mary.

Feminists and others have long argued about women's power and social agency: Was there really a time when goddesses were all-powerful and women controlled society? If so, how and why did things change so completely? Is the retrieval of female power even possible within the growing desecration of our ecology, our social systems, the human relationships we find acceptable? It is not my intention here to reopen these discussions. Enough to note that in every time and place, those in control of social organization have mythologized personae, both male and female, whose job it is to keep the underclasses down. Real subversion happens when these figures are revived, reconstructed, reclaimed by those who need them most.

And so, in Christian iconography, the figure of Mary is no longer simply the woman who joyously accepted her role as the sacrificial mother of a male savior. Mary is no longer essentially virginal (disconnected from her body and its erotic powers),[3] passive (a mere vessel, allowing the story of the passion to be told through her), submissive (acquiescing to a higher, male power), and modest (not the doer of deeds, but rather a compassionate onlooker and servant).

And the brown Virgin: surely she speaks, in this incarnation, of the dual oppressions of race and class. Our Lady appeared to an Indian convert, a poor man, a person of color. In the hierarchy of Mexican religious symbology of the times, the whiter, more European Virgin of Los Remedios was worshiped by *los peninsulares*, the descendants of the conquering Spaniards who were taking possession of a "new" world. Guadalupe was beloved by Indians, creoles, mestizos, blacks, and mulattoes, all those who identified with the color of her skin and also needed her compassion. Not only did she choose a poor Indian as her link with the faithful; she instructed him to speak to the Spanish bishop on her behalf. And she provided him with the proof he would need in order to convince the European Church of her appearance. This is a story that begins with humiliation and disregard, and ends with the Spaniard having to accept and honor the Indian's account.

In the mid-sixties, living in Mexico City, I took to visiting the shrine. Impelled by the imploring voices of those women I midwived, and by frequent stories from other quarters, I drove out one December 9 and parked just short of the broad stone esplanade leading up to the doors of the church. Hundreds, mostly women, advanced slowly, many of them wearing the coarse fabric of dark brown sackcloth looped at the waist with a cord of yellow gold. A

---

[3]Audre Lorde's "Uses of the Erotic: The Erotic as Power" remains a classic among the feminist literature exploring this long-misunderstood source. (Freedom, California: Crossing Press, 1984.)

thick paste of blood stained the approach, imprint of knees torn in slow sacrifice. I couldn't help but think of the blood of the Aztec sacrifices centuries before. I knew I didn't understand either. The reference, though, became a road of inquiry. Blood. Life. But more than blood—that life force—a pulsing *mestizaje* of cultures: the Nahuatl and the Spanish. The conquest which, for women, most often translates into rape. Tonantzin: Goddess Mother who creates and destroys. Coatlicue: the pre-Columbian goddess who ate her children so they would not have to live under the Spanish conquerors, thereby bringing dignity to a life of slavery. And Mary: Mother of the Christian Lord. The conqueror's sixteenth-century seizure of women by force or gift exchange was but one face of the conquest of an entire people. But it was, as always, the greatest victimization that gave mythological substance to the most persistent blame.

Subversion at its most complex.

Doña Marina, *la Malinche*, the fifteen-year-old Indian girl whose parents sold her into slavery and who eventually ended up as an offering to Cortés himself, became the symbol of treason: she who slept with the enemy, who mothered the mixed race. Centuries of patriarchal imaging continued to blame the victim. And so, *malinchismo* became betrayal in Mexican popular speech. Just as the Virgin, this brown Virgin, has been put forth as an image of piety and submission. But change has been pushed into the foreground, is evident in many of the mythological personae, and is here to stay.

Quetzalcoatl, for example, took an understanding of rebirth to qualitatively new levels of anticipation and knowledge. *La Malinche* is being redeemed by contemporary Latin American feminists, not as a treasonous whore but as the victimized mother of us all. For who among us cannot proudly claim something of the racial mixture from which all come? And Guadalupe represents the spiritual shift, within the most patriarchal of structures, from centuries of male control to a feminist vision of power, what the more secular like to call democracy.

Long before Latin American feminists began to retrieve and revise the stories that have been twisted in order to keep us captive, generations of ordinary long-suffering women responded intuitively to Our Lady of Guadalupe's powerful signs. She whose skin is the color of their skin. She who stands upon the moon but is surrounded by sun. She whose star-studded mantle is a deep turquoise, not the pale blue of European Marianist tradition. She who poses, head slightly bowed, her hands in prayerful gesture and with an angel at her feet. This image that appears to be just another incarnation of the Virgin contains symbols that are much more complex.

Our Lady of Guadalupe's story precedes those written accounts that hold the European religious sightings in such precarious precision. It was 1531, at a hill called Tepeyac on the outskirts of present-day Mexico City. The Virgin appeared to Juan Diego on December 9. She told him that he, a poor Indian, must convince the local bishop, Zumárraga, that he build a church at this place. Of course he had trouble getting the Spanish patriarch to believe his story, and was unsuccessful on his first attempt. So he returned to the spot where the Virgin had appeared and placed his dilemma before her.

But the Virgin was ready with a strategy that would work. She told Juan Diego to climb the hill and pick beautiful flowers, that he would find them despite the fact that they were utterly out of season. With these flowers he was to go back to the bishop for a second try. Some accounts have him returning on four separate occasions. But he finally did gain access. And when the patriarch asked for proof, he produced the flowers which, the story goes, fell from his cloak, revealing the painted image of Our Lady, the legendary *tilma*.

It is this image, resisting four and a half centuries and examination by experts from many different fields, that bears initial witness to Our Lady of Guadalupe's power. The *tilma* or *ayate*, fabric of the cloak, is of a crude weave, generally considered too coarse to have been the canvas of a portrait painted by human hands, especially with such time-defying definition. The lines are fine, the facial expression subtle, the colors brilliant. A miracle? Students of Guadalupe, students from the secular disciplines as well as of the faith, have tried to prove or disprove successive theories. I have never been concerned with any of them. My connection is to a story whose time has come, one that is needed still.

Our Lady of Guadalupe is a warrior. From the beginning, since the sixteenth century when the indigenous peoples of Mexico needed the sensibility and generosity of a deity who understood their horrendous suffering, she has never abandoned that role. And she is not the stagnant warrior of regular armies, but is capable of changing with terrain and times. The guerrilla fighter. As is true of all authentic subversives—the underground rebel, the elusive foot soldier—she always comes when needed, appearing in appropriate circumstances and dressed in such a way as to assure recognition, renew faith.

In post-Conquest Mexico this was first in the eyes and then upon the cloak of a humble Indian man. The cloak's weave is coarse, but this is no obstacle to divine imagery. Our Lady's facial expression, her stance, the gesture of her hands, are as subtle as they are unmistakably popular, reflecting the characteristics of the native faithful, who see their own pain in hers. The turquoise of Our Lady's mantle is vibrant and unique, a color of strength. Its stars join the fiery rays of sun, symbols of light and hope through generations of continued oppression, exploitation, physical and emotional battering. Guadalupe has become a highly visible icon for women whose own lives are too often invisible or shamed.

When the cult of the Virgin was born, the vast majority of Mexican and Latin American women, like those in other parts of the world, were expected to repress their own growth needs as they attended to the needs of men. The housewife, the educated woman who perhaps might become a teacher or a nurse, the caregiver, the woman exploited in her home and in the larger community: these were and still are the women to whom Our Lady speaks most clearly. They identify with her gesture of eternal care. They easily enter the circle of her open arms. And it is here that subversion works its strongest magic.

In this image, Our Lady has been the standard-bearer for numerous liberation struggles, in the grandiose as well as more personal spheres. There is the conversation, ongoing and intimate, that Mexican women have with her. She is their personal mother. In her they confide their relegation and loss, entrust their fears and dreams. And this is not a one-way conversation. The Virgin responds, with comfort, advice, or simply a dependable ear.

In the more public arenas, Guadalupe has graced the flags of liberation armies: from a doomed resistance against colonialism's voracious tentacles to Villa's and Zapata's insurgent troops during the Mexican Revolution. "Long live Guadalupe / Yelled the insurgents / She is the Sovereign Queen / of the American Indians" is but one of dozens of *corridos* evoking her power and alluding to her care.[4]

More recently, Our Lady shows up wherever she is needed. In the 1960s she could be found in the vineyards of California, when César Chávez used her image to organize descendants of those earlier Mexicans to unionize against the same exploitation in more modern disguise. She appears in the art of Chicanos, particularly in that by some of the great Chicana muralists, who are reclaiming their race, their gender—in some cases even a difference of sexual identity. And she is central to the new theology, especially being formulated by religious women who describe with clarity and brilliance what their ancestors certainly intuited.

Each historic period brings with it the imaging and naming necessary to a retrieval of collective memory. Thus the stories of the ancestors or elders, the mentors and teachers, empower those whose oppression they place in social focus. First the rebel leaders take up an image, exalt a name, and these then become the standards for an expanding community. This ability to name makes it possible for a generation to specify its discoveries and pass them on.

Secrets fade. Silences and lies are less relevant to the sequestering of our lives. Our voices become more and more our own. This linguistic progression is evident around the Virgin of Guadalupe. Her initial appearance was greeted with reverence but also with concern; Juan Diego honored the Lady but complained he would never be believed—a poor Indian trying to gain access to, let alone convince, the representatives of Spanish power. Once she was established as an accepted icon within the Church, the Virgin's subversive qualities continued to endear her to ordinary women and men. They talk with her and she talks back. The naming becomes direct, conversational, harbinger of successful struggle.

---

[4]*The Mexican Corrido, A Feminist Analysis* by María Herrera-Sobek (Bloomington and Indianapolis: Indiana University Press, 1993), p. 42.

In Nicaragua, during the decade of the Sandinista government, the Virgin also took on trappings of struggle and working-class identification. She became a warrior like no other. Nicaragua, just like Mexico and most of the Latin American nations, has a rich Marianist culture. Doña Violeta de Chamorro[5] took full and deliberate advantage of this during her 1990 electoral campaign. She frequently dressed in light blue and white, the traditional colors of the Virgin. In a society seeped in Marianist devotion, her stance, body language, gestures, and discourse were all calculated to simulate that of the Holy Mother of a suffering people.

The feast of the *Purísima* is in early December. In Nicaragua, altars are constructed in living rooms or outside people's homes, in public buildings and parks. Churches, from the great cathedrals to the humblest chapels, show themselves resplendent. In the popular neighborhoods, especially, people make their nightly rounds: singing the seasonal songs and receiving handfuls of special sweets and favors. My initial *Purísima*, in 1979, was just after the Sandinistas had defeated Somoza, tyrant of almost half a century. All expressions of popular fervor were grateful, exuberant, and charged with revolutionary innovation.

It was in this context that I saw my first "proletarian Virgin." Beneath the crossed palm fronds that sheltered an altar in one of Managua's most combative neighborhoods, María wore the red and black neckerchief of those young men and women who had so recently won a people's war. Of course she also bore the more familiar raiments of Marianist iconography: the crown, the mantle, the jewels. Large paper flowers circled her domain, and a single light bulb illuminated the scene. But around her neck the tiny bicolored swatch of combatant cloth was unmistakable. And a simple sign pinned below her proclaimed: *"María . . . ¡Madre proletaria!"* I asked the friend I was with if this was common. "Yes," she said,

---

[5]Violeta Barrios is the widow of Joaquín Chamorro, progressive newspaperman martyred by Somoza's forces in January 1978. Although she herself lacked experience or even an interest in politics, her husband made her the Right's ideal choice as a straw figure who might be able to unite the disparate opposition forces against the Sandinistas. They ran her as presidential candidate, the U.S. poured money into her campaign, and she won the 1990 elections. Real power was consolidated in the person of her son-in-law, Antonio Lacayo.

"you'll see a lot of reclaimed Virgins here. The young woman who lives in this house, her uncle demanded that she remove the neckerchief. But she insisted on leaving it in place."

Each era's dominant culture creates figures that function as immobilizing examples to the various social groups that must be kept in place. Just as, in this age of technology, TV images target specific populations, historically an iconography of saints and martyrs, statesmen and entertainers, personae both religious and secular, has helped nurture those human characteristics that maintained the servant classes in line: characteristics such as blind reverence, a lack of self-esteem, fear of authority, piety, obedience, inhibitance, and subservience, among others. Sometimes a real man or woman appears on the scene, becoming mentor to a particular group. In these cases, those with the power to do so handle the presentation of these historic figures in such a way as to produce the desired allegiance.

What is most interesting is when the targeted group relates to a particular figure and turns that figure around, pointing it toward its own desperate need. Then people look it in the eye, converse with it one on one. A saint or secular being may be spawned by the orthodoxy, but claimed, or reclaimed, by people in need. More impressive still is when groups of people gain self-knowledge and power enough to produce warriors of their own. Control of our history, of our stories, has traditionally been in the hands of those who hold power over our lives. Social change is largely about people retrieving their stories (Joan of Arc as a great peasant leader instead of the simple country girl too obsessed by hierarchical power to be able to save her own life; la Malinche as victim rather than betrayer of the race).

From a faith-centered position, Our Lady of Guadalupe appeared to Juan Diego, through him convinced the Spanish power of the times to honor her appearance with the construction of a church, and remains through almost five centuries the Virgin most beloved among Latin American Catholics. A secular feminist, I am not as concerned with her religious authenticity as I am with her meaning, especially for Mexican women. In the sixteenth century, women's identification with the Virgin had to be rooted in ideas of purity, sacrifice, closeness to God. As the centuries unfold, it is clear that women, in Mexico and elsewhere, have searched for an escape from bondage, sufficient compassion to empathize with their pain, support and solidarity. And so it is in her layered symbology, in her multiplicity of meanings, that Our Lady's true power of subversion lies.

Our Lady of the Cannery Workers

CHERRÍE MORAGA
for Celia Rodríguez

*I*n June 1992 in Watsonville, California, a U.S.-Mexican town of cannery and agricultural workers, a woman reported that la Virgen María
had appeared to her near the county park lake where her son had drowned a few
years earlier. Nearby, a tree took on the Virgin's form in its bark.

> Returning from Watsonville
> the road, a forest of apparitions
> the Mother Creator
> in every Standing
> Sequoia
> every Virgin Forest.
>
>
> Ehécatl
> follows me
> reminds me to listen
> to the stillness
> observe
> her subtle and violent
> appearance
> in pine-scented breezes
> copal dancing smoke
> in icy san francisco winds
> whipping through open bedroom
> windows, sudden slamming
> doors: *did she enter just then?*
> *was she taking leave*
> *of her senses?*

she, the pinwheel descent
of an aging
oak
leaf

Is this the same tree
sheltered beneath the giant
umbrella of sequoia
that bears the shape of Guadalupe
in its breast? A tattoo
emblazoned into the scaling bark flesh
that same slight inclination
of shrouded head, the same
copper rose shade
imprinted on the tela
of Juan Diego's prayer?

Tonantzín
te traigo flores.

Pilgrims hold up mirrors to the sun.
Beams of light ricochet in all directions.
Earthmother colors
illuminate
coastal gloom,
factory shut-downs
migra raids.

Ahora, ¿la ves?
Sí.
Dios te salve
María.

Juanita vestida de blanco
advises the faithful,
"Let go de su coraje."
I thread
my angry fingers
through the chain link
a sagging fortress
of protection.
My swollen knuckles
woven into the rusting wire
like rosary beads
of pink, turquoise-colored glass
carved pine wood
draped from curling polaroids.
Family prayers hang
by a thread
of christmas ribbon.

There is one who refuses
to pray the catholic words
buries small ties
of tobacco at the four corners
she is Diego's living relative
her anger, righteous
and unforgiving.

If la virgen appeared to me,
what would she look like?
Not cannery worker
but pintora?

Sequoia Virgen
I see you in every crevice
of your burnt red flesh
vagina openings split

into two thick thighs
of female eruption.

you grow old and tall
you fall

you turn to seed.

"Forgive Me, Mother, for My Crazy Life"

LUIS J. RODRÍGUEZ

*A*mong some of the Latino barrio youth of the U.S. Southwest, bodies are tattooed testaments to the wounds, pains, trauma, and beauty of *La Vida Loca*. Invariably, many have tattooed *La Virgen de Guadalupe,* in all her glory, across their arms, backs, or chests (in prison, *pintos* often tattoo her image on their backs to protect them from "backstabbers"). Her image has been held high during major Chicano battles for our rights and dignity. She is carried by the oppressed, the dispossessed, the outlawed, and the repressed.

Even as the rich and privileged across this continent exalt and exploit her image, they rarely consider her sacred, despite her "Patrona" status in the Americas.

"She is the unifying religious factor between households, between towns, between countries among the poor," writes Stephen C. Holler in his recent dissertation, "Mary and the Poor in Latin America since Vatican II: Responses of the Church to Marian Popular Religion."

Holler points out that in Brazil, for example, "many titles and pictures [of the Virgin] deal with issues of great interest to the poor and their lives of utter simplicity and insecurity. Over half the titles directly given to the Virgin Mary refer to the great physical and emotional needs of the poor, and to their appreciation for the small things of life."

It is no surprise that among the *cholo* gangs in Los Angeles, the use of crosses, roses, serpents, eagles, and images of Jesus and the Virgin abounds. Many churches have excluded these youth, as have schools and public places. L.A. *cholos*—Mexican and Central American—often find themselves cut off from their own communities, making them easy prey for the drugs, guns, and law enforcement operatives of the city.

Marginalized and excluded, these young men and women see themselves as bound to the *locura,* compelled to be crazy (signified by the tattoo of a spider in the web—a spider weaving its own prison). Some *vatos* tattoo the following words in Spanish: "Forgive me, Mother, for my crazy life." These *vatos* grieve in this life, but feel they can do nothing to change it. Their *locura* is their best defense against the insanity of a racist, exclusionary, and spiritually fractured world.

One young man in Chicago, who had the Guadalupe's image emblazoned on his shoulder blade, says he felt "protected, watched over," by her presence. He is in the street, often in the path of bullets.

"Violence is everywhere around me," explains Chikis (not his real name) from the Two-Six Nation. "I feel she makes sure the bullets won't claim me."

As strange as this may sound, it is indicative of people who feel their fates are not in their hands, who have relinquished their destinies to powers beyond this world. Yet what comfort—and personal power—there is in this! Although people with such faith can often restrain their social energies, they have also been some of the most single-minded and accomplished individuals in the world (one example that comes to mind is Martin Luther, who, responding to why he was so adamant in challenging the Catholic Church, and helping set in motion one of the most sweeping social movements of our time, stated, "Here I stand; I can do no other").

My experience with even the most hard-core of gang youth is that they *are* on a spiritual quest. What some of them give to the gang is more than a name. It is love, their heart, and thus their life. Chicago Latino gang youth often greet and say good-bye with "*¡Amor!*" Of course, without the proper spiritual guidance from community, they often become lost in their quest. But the searching is still quite evident.

Recently, through a voluntary network in Chicago called Increase the Peace, seventy young people, including rival gang members, and ten adults participated in a Native American sweat lodge, facilitated by a Guatemalan Mayan who was also a Sundancer, schooled in the Lakota ways. The sweat lodge is a sacred ritual in which participants may express feelings, thoughts, prayers, chants, or silence within an enclosed structure heavily steamed with water over heated rocks.

At first, there was tension. But as soon as we began to work together, building the lodges from the ground up and firing up the rocks in the traditional manner, the young people set aside their differences. The newness of the experience—even though most of them were of indigenous Mexican descent—and the sacredness helped change their disposition. Soon they talked to each other, shared experiences, opened up to each other's stories. By the end of the event, no one held grudges or hatred in their hearts; part of their spiritual search was being attended to.

I also understand that since most male gang youth hang out primarily with other men, their connection to Mother has to be reestablished or they sense a vital part of themselves is missing. The spiritual road has to include this aspect. While men can take other men to the edges of their psyche, it is women who can take them to their depths.

Only women can birth new life. This is true even for men entering a new phase of life (for example, maturing from adolescence to adulthood), which is often done through a woman (what the *cholos* call a *jaina*—a "main squeeze," if you will) or a significant representation of the Mother through ritual: violent males honoring *la Virgen* with proper respect and clarity (female gang members also need to connect with the Goddess; however, they are usually entering the male's domain, thus disconnecting from their natures; a Mother ritual is vital for violent females as well).

Known as Tonantzin among the Nahuatls, but also as Saint Moon, Queen of Nature, or Earth Mother in other parts of the Americas, *la Guadalupana* is the poor people's agent, not bound by form, or by a name, or by the limitations of time, space, or race. She returns as vessel of the indigenous spirit, as the shamed land crying back its blood. She returns speaking in the inflections of an ancient tongue, before Christianity, beyond Christianity.

La Diosa's face is resurrected in all the faces of all the mothers, of all the young women and children of our *gente*. She is among the bearers of the myths, the rites, and the ancient quests. She reemerges throughout the hemisphere with many titles—*Nuestra Señora de Zapopan, Nuestra Señora de Soledad, Nuestra Señora de San Juan de Los Lagos, Nuestra Señora de Suyapa, Nuestra Señora de Quiché, Nuestra Señora de Altagracia, Nuestra Señora de Caridad del Cobre, Nuestra Señora de Providencia, Nuestra Señora de Monserrate*—and she often appears dark, like the poor who honor her, who embody her with their resistance, with their collective memory and identity.

I see her and I see them all, tribes of this continent, tribes of other continents, who are daily born of woman, Mother Creator. I see them and I know that Tonantzin has risen again and again.

The Church built a shrine to *la Virgen de Guadalupe* in newly conquered Mexico in an effort to contain her; people still approach it on their knees, bloody and raw, depicting their suffering at the hands of a dominant class and culture. The body is wounded, the body dies, but the challenge to tyranny never ends.

Tonantzin-Guadalupe can never be hemmed in, enshrined and unembraced. She lives in the eyes. On the skin. Alongside the poetry. She is within *la Chicanada*, untainted, siren to all nature, in endless song, on the thread of timelessness. She is the eternal which anyone can possess, proof we are never truly conquered, never truly defeated. Through her we are before time, beyond time. Through us, she is flesh.

Known as Aztecs or people of the "umbilical," the ancient Mexica built their home in a place they considered the center of the center of the center—which connected the four cardinal points of the known universe—called the dwelling place of God, the "place of the Duality." They saw the Duality as one person, one God, but it was male and female. This complement was perfect in itself. They called this God many names, including Lord of the Duality, Lady of the Duality, Mother-Father of the Gods, or Brilliant Star. Other Gods were but manifestations of the same God in differing aspects and attributes.

The Duality appeared broken with modern Christianity. Christianity came to the Americas bearing the sword of conquerors who accumulated wealth from stolen gold; the trade in flesh was the impetus for establishing a world capitalist order. Ruled by a Man-God, intolerant, vengeful, and nonfeminine, this religion justified the destruction of the God-centered cultures and peoples of this land (and of other lands, such as Africa, which had also honored the Duality).

The appearance of this brown-skinned Virgin on the rock of Tepeyac supposedly blocked out the sun, but it did not crush it.

"The God-Sun was the principal God in the pantheon of the people," writes Padre Luis Ignacio Gameros of St. Christopher's Parish in Marana, Arizona, who has studied and defended the Aztec religion and culture. "But she does not extinguish it—she is greater than their most important God, but she does not destroy Him."

The Duality is thus restored.

There is power in this, that Mary would come not in pale skin, but in the skin of the land, of the people, in a multicolored image on a maguey fiber cloth; that she would appear to Juan Diego, the "least of them" (and, therefore, the greatest of them), who tells her in Nahuatl: "For I am pitiably poor, for I am harness, for I am hod, for I am all elbows, all haunches, for I am of the dispossessed, for I am a pack carrier"; and that through Juan Diego, the people's deeds, the people's dreams, the people's stories, would be exalted.

"Let nothing scare you or distract you," Mary responds to Juan Diego. "Do not let your heart ache. Do not be afraid of any anxiety. Am I not your Mother? Are you not under my shadow, my protection?"

My own experiences with the Church were not always good. I was baptized a Catholic, born in a now defunct Catholic hospital in El Paso, Texas, that was known to allow births by undocumented people, such as my mother. I first went to catechism classes as a small child in Watts, South Central L.A., where two parishes, St. Lawrence and San Miguel, served the large Mexican community there.

The predominantly Irish priests and nuns then were plainly racists, uncomprehending and unkind to the Mexican and black children who attended those classes, with ages six to nine crowded into one room.

I have a poem called "String Bean" that addressed some of the injustices that I felt at the hands of many of these nuns and priests. The poem ends with the following lines:

> *Children piled into Sunday school classes.*
> *Nuns in black with wrinkled faces*
> *punished some for speaking out,*
> *For laughing behind their backs or being late.*
> *There are bottle caps where children knelt*
> *for what seemed hours.*
> *One time a nun asked a little girl,*
> *"Who is God?"*
> *The girl got up from her seat,*
> *nervous, fearful.*
> *Finally, after a slow start, she replied:*
> *"God ees a string bean."*
> *The class went into an uproar.*
> *The nun gasped in horror.*
> *She grabbed a ruler from her desk,*
> *rushed up to the trembling girl*
> *and smacked the inside of the girl's hand.*
> *It took a while before she realized*
> *the girl had said,*
> *"God is a supreme being."*

After moving to the San Gabriel area, my mother continued our Bible and church studies at St. Anthony's Church, where I made my first communion. But the rectors and sisters there didn't seem much better to me than the ones in Watts.

A sense of shame was slowly and methodically ingrained. I rebelled against it. To me there was nothing redemptive or spiritual about the meanness, the degradation, the ongoing abuse, and guilt. The elaborately carved icons and endless liturgy began to disgust me. Before long, I never wanted to set foot in a church again.

Yet my spirit was still wanting. Once, in my late teens, I turned to Pentecostal beliefs when my fifteen-year-old niece had gotten involved in drugs and was arrested. She was finally released to one of those barrio evangelical programs that emphasized being "born again" in Christ.

One evening when I went to visit my niece, the pastor invited me to receive the Lord. I went up to the front of the room, wanting nothing more than to be open when the Lord's grace came upon me. The pastor had me raise up my arms to heaven; he closed his eyes, placed his hands around my neck (a laying of hands, as they called it), and began talking in tongues. People prayed. People swayed. But nothing happened. I wasn't "saved."

At first I thought this meant that God didn't want me. But to be honest, I wasn't moved at all. The pastor, quite upset, told me this usually worked on "homeboys" because they have been trained since early childhood to accept a higher power. The next week, when I went to visit my niece, everyone's demeanor had changed. They moved away from me; some even refused to look at me. I was being shunned. My niece later told me that the pastor had told the group I was influenced by the Devil.

Of course, I know many homeys who have been saved through organizations such as Victory Outreach (which started in the barrios of East L.A.). Although my mother remains Catholic, many members of my family turned away from the Catholic Church to become "born again." In some instances, mostly by removing themselves from "things of this world" so as to, in their view, enter into God's grace, family members were freed from quite debilitating addictions.

As for me, I turned away from spiritual concerns, although, with my spirit wanting, I ended up seeking "church" in political meetings, in dance halls, in poetry events, in bars and cafes.

Over time, I hooked up with revolutionary activists, poets, and "priests," in and out of the Church. For a few years now I've been reacquainting myself with the Bible, along with Aztec and other native rites, and with belief systems of people from around the world.

I've recently read thinkers such as Joseph Campbell and Mircea Eliade, who "surfed" the spiritual internet so to speak, drawing from all religious experiences, and clarifying the interconnecting threads that link human myths, rituals, and spirituality. They helped make this subject compelling, alive, and real for me.

I pursued my own path, accepting the fullness of spirit and its mysteries, while deepening my understanding of the nature of religion in society. Because of the limiting pressures of class society on God's bounty and knowledge, I could appreciate how vast, expansive, and often incomprehensible spiritual truth can be. So I let it speak to me, without a great need to "explain" it, and often when I tapped into the most creative and poetic part of my being, I came to see that in creativity, you can touch the transcendent within you.

I now feel I can connect to the Mother Goddess, to Jesus Christ, and to the Great Spirit of our native peoples. I've learned that the Creator has many faces, many languages, and that all religions worship the same transcendent reality, but give it a different name.

As a revolutionary, I believe that human action, human intervention, is as vital as spiritual intervention. People make their own history, but they do so under certain conditions, within certain stages of social development. Until we recognize and appreciate the restrictive ideas and structures of our present economic and social foundations, and in the process work to transform them, I believe it will be virtually impossible to enter into a spiritual realm, uncluttered and undeterred.

Over the years, through my experiences and studies, I have learned much about science, dialectics, and the laws of nature, and I have learned much about spirit and mystery. Like the Mexica, I understand and accept the oneness of the Duality—that there really is no separation between the male and female within us—even as they collide and coalesce, as do all opposites. No person can be truly complete, truly alive unless they draw on the mother/woman in all of us.

I believe we are all God's instruments, Its embodiment, capable of manifesting the light, of reaching wide and beyond, capable of expansiveness and openness, of great imagination. It takes time and effort to develop this understanding of Duality. Factors such as class, race, gender, and family can stand in the way. Over the years, in relations with my companions, children, friends, and lovers, I was often lost, confused by alcohol, rage, impulsive behavior, self-sabotage. For three years now, I've been sober, with the help of a recovery program that emphasized the power within each of us to transform our lives (it wasn't about twelve steps, it was about one: either you drank or you didn't; either you controlled your life or you didn't). The spiritual was an essential part of this change.

"Religion is for those who want to stay out of hell; spirituality is for those who have already been there"—these words, used often in recovery programs, were written on the walls of a prison that Michael Meade, friend, master storyteller, and author of *Men and the Water of Life,* once visited.

La Virgen's resurgence at Tepeyac was proof we have been living in an imbalance. Now is not a time to remove oneself from struggle, from the world, but to enter it again, guided by the spirit of justice that I believe *la Virgen* represents.

I contend that to be reconnected means to accept and honor the Mother, the Goddess, *la Guadalupana* inside us all, in the birthplace we all carry, in our ceaseless capacity for imagination and creativity. I contend this means opening up our hearts and minds, not closing them.

"We stand at the end of prehistory," states American revolutionary Nelson Peery. "From now on . . . our skills, clarity, astuteness, and determination become the decisive factors."

Today, I struggle to live my life truthfully, vibrantly, as a revolutionary, with the Mother within, the poet within, reconnecting to her with a gesture, a smile, a prayer.

The Warrior Queen: Encounters with a Latin Lady

YEYE' WORO

LUISAH TEISH

I encounter Her walking through the Latin quarter. She always waits for me in our special meeting place. Between the refried beans and the epazote, the Virgin of Guadalupe and I harbor secrets. We meet in the supermarket, we pretend to be regular, we appear to behave ourselves. Anyone looking would think that I am simply shopping in the ethnic foods section of the market. I push my cart, pick up corn on the cob, a bottle of spring water, and a fresh bouquet of roses. Perhaps some cans and bottles of ordinary food find their way into my basket. I mutter the names of products that must be bought. Milk and juice, eggs and bread, fish and blood oranges. No one suspects us yet.

I stop casually in the middle of the ethnic foods section and suddenly I am elsewhere doing "that other." Now I am in the deep bush of Africa, dancing around a fire under a moonlit night sky, listening to tales of my ancestors and wondering if the spirits will come out tonight. Now I am running through the swamps of Louisiana or over the mountains of Jamaica, leading myself and others to freedom with little more than a torch and a heart in flames.

I look at the many rows of candles lined neatly on the shelf. They vary in size and colors and cost two dollars less than the exact same ones sold in the candle shops and *botánicas*. Some of these candles come in plain clear glasses. I prefer these and gather as many as I can. But at last it becomes necessary to choose between the many saints whose images are wrapped around the wax-filled glass. Now, in order to choose wisely, I must remember my history.

> I am Your Dark Sister's daughter
> the Ones Who Came over the Waves

Rattling chains, and in bondage
Ripped from Her belly as slaves.

It was not so long ago that the ships arrived on the shores of West Africa. White men who came found a land of immense beauty and abundance. They discovered a seemingly endless source of ivory and gold, of food and music, of animals, and of human slaves. Millions of Black people were taken from their motherland. The transatlantic slave trade extended across the vast expanse of Mother Africa. Her children were gathered from the north as far as Senegal, to the south as far as Angola, and inland to the Congo. Among them were healers and warriors, musicians and priests. We were stacked into the bottom decks of ships and carried across the great ocean.

The Africans were systematically separated in an attempt to prevent organization, revolt, and revolution. Igbos, Yorubas, Congos, Bantus, and many other people were sent to Brazil, the Caribbean Islands, and to North America, where they were forced to participate in the colonization of another people's lands.

The English, French, Dutch, Portuguese, and Spanish slave traders operated under the sanction and with the blessings of the Catholic Church. The Church justified its exploitation of the native people and the Africans with the cry of Christian conversion. So upon arriving on these shores, the Africans were stripped of their names, branded with the mark of their owners, and cracked over the head with a crucifix in baptism. The Black Codes, which governed the conduct of slaves, forbade the practice of African spiritual beliefs under penalty of death.

But the use of force and violence is no match for ancestral memory and natural law. Like most people around the world, the Africans acclimated themselves to the land and the people around them.

The indigenous peoples of the Americas and the islands practiced ancestor reverence and nature worship, as did the imported Africans. In places such as Cuba, Haiti, Brazil, and New Orleans where there was close contact between us, acculturation has produced magnificent spiritual traditions. The Church, which had already usurped the deities and sacred lands of European pagans, handed everything over to the saints and forced their worship upon the people of this newfound land. But the ceremonial practices of the Church were pagan. The Crucifixion and the priests' ability to turn bread and wine into the "body and blood of Christ" were seen as sacrifice and cannibalism. The Africans examined the saints and their miracles and saw the folklore of their deities. In order to continue their own spiritual practices, they drew correspondences between the African ancestral deities and the Catholic saints. And Mary, the Mother of God, lent Herself well to the beliefs of the people. They examined Her many faces, Her miracles, and the fervor of Her devotees. And this Benevolent Mother provided a protective mantle under which the Africans could worship the Earth and the Sky, the Ancestors and the Yet Unborn. It is this tradition of examination and association which has me whispering to the Virgin of Guadalupe in the supermarket.

The canned music which plagues public places acts as a friend to me. Those passing by cannot hear our whispers. They only see a brown-skinned woman hovering a little long over refried beans.

I remind myself that after many generations of living beneath the skirts of the Divine Mother Mary, I am *free!* Free to call my deities by their own names—Orishas; free to pray in my native tongues, to sing my own songs, and to honor my own rituals. But standing here among the sainted candles I survey what's available to me. There are no candles designed for the Orishas. This culture does not honor me or my past. But I can honor the creativity of my ancestors, the genius of their camouflage in war. I choose my candles for the various Orishas, at two dollars less.

For Elegba the Trickster and Lord of the Crossroads, a red Saint Michael slaying the Devil. This choice is of special importance. The West African spiritual system had no all-powerful devil as in the Christian tradition. It did, however, have a very powerful Trickster who was responsible for spinning the wheel of fortune for good or for ill. It was missionaries who associated Elegba with the Devil. Whenever I use this candle I think of Elegba slaying the fear instilled by Western thought and belief. Three of them go into my basket.

Much to my pleasure I find a candle for *la Caridad del Cobre*, the Mary chosen to represent the Goddess Oshun. Her candle is usually yellow or a bright gold. She is the Goddess of Love, Art, and Sensuality, the Queen of the River, and the High-Flying Vulture. I stock up on these, for She is my personal Goddess and I need them all the time. This process continues: A *Virgen de Regla* for Yemaya, the Goddess of the Ocean and women's menstrual cycles. A Santa Barbara to represent Shango, the Lord of Thunder and Justice. Glass jingles in my shopping cart.

Then it begins again and She is there. Ava María Morena, the Virgin of Guadalupe. I talk to the Lady on the candle. Who are you today, Ms. Lupe? Shall I choose a green one for Tonantzin, the sustaining power of the Earth? I pick up the green candle and remember the coronation of *la Morena*. She was declared the "Queen of Mexico and Empress of the Americas." I recognize in Her Ala, the Igbo Earth Goddess; Asase Yaa, the Great Mother of Ghana; and Nana, Mother of All the Gods in the Kingdom of Dahomey. I take a moment to thank Her for welcoming my ancestors to these shores. I thank Her for the knowledge of the herbs of this land which the Native Americans shared with my people. And even now as I stand in the grocery store, I acknowledge that this little girl from Louisiana has found a place in Oakland, California. I am snug and safe in Her belly.

She smiles at me, winks an eye. I move down the row of candles and again She whispers my name, Luisah. There She is again; this time, I am thinking of Her dedication to Her people, the way She intercedes for them through fire, flood, and warfare. "Long live the Virgin of Guadalupe. Long live independence." I remember Her image being paraded through the streets in Mexico and Puerto Rico, in Europe, and in the Philippines. The Lady travels. "Ahh," I say to the Lady, "you must be an Oya, the Wind Mother, the Warrior Queen, a freedom fighter, courageous, dutiful, and bold." She answers, "Yes . . . my daughters are many . . . their struggles continue . . . and how are you today?"

Lowering my head, I whisper to the Virgin. "Remember the men who shot your flags and bombed your churches . . . ?" We are both silent for a second, just long enough to catch our breaths. She sighs, "Yes." I inform Her, "They are at it again: poisoning our children with guns and drugs, destroying the water and the trees . . ." My hand reaches for the white candle, the one I will light for the souls of the dead, the one that will help to clean the blood from the streets. I offer Her an Oriki, a praise-poem in the African tradition:

> She Who Inspires Her people,
> She Who leads them to fight.
> Shine like the Sun in the daytime,
> Soothe like the Moon in the night.

Dark or Black Virgins are favored by people involved in struggles for liberation all over the world. It is interesting to note that theologians are fond of claiming that the black Virgins found in Europe were not originally Black. They love to say that the statues were charred during a fire in the church or that some vandal painted the face as a way of disgracing the Church. This is so much bullshit. It is, I feel, a neurotic attempt on the part of the Vatican to deny Mother Africa and the dark races as the foreparents of humanity. It is a foolish attempt to place the Garden of Eden in England, to say that Egypt was created by the Greeks, and to claim that some Northern European sailor arrived in the Americas before the native people got there. While students of culture can argue over Eurocentric versus Afrocentric viewpoints, or whether myth is history, the Virgin of Guadalupe stands firm in Her own center.

Guadalupe chose to present Herself to the people as *la Morena*, a brown-skinned native woman, dressed in the robes of an Aztec princess. She chose to appear to a humble corn farmer, "He who speaks like an eagle," Juan Diego, on a hillside, amidst a choir of birds, in his native language. There can be no doubt about who She is! She forced the Church, in spite of great resistance, to recognize Her. And most importantly, She persists in the hearts of the people, holding together the very fabric of the culture, uniting them always! I am excited by this warrior woman, this uppity brown babe. She and I have some work to do, today, tomorrow, and always . . .

The radiance of the sun shines behind Her, the moon rests at Her feet. Her image is held in relief by mock stained glass, vulva-shaped and in the colors of the rainbow. She reminds me of other soul-sisters, of Ochumare, the Yoruba Rainbow Goddess, and of Aida-Hwedo, the Serpent in the Sky. I think of Maria Lionza, the wild woman in the woods of Venezuela. These women command the wind, fan the flames, and push the flow of the waters. In my mind, Guadalupe is a queen in this court.

Many times I have walked past this shelf of candles and chosen them by colors and corresponding spirits. My conversations with the Guadalupe always led me to interactions with local people. I'd light a Guadalupe and shortly thereafter I'd receive a telephone call from a Latin kindred or co-worker or storytelling engagement at a multicultural festival or an invitation to take part in a political action in the Mission, in San Francisco.

Once I lit a Lupe which resulted in my participation in a women's spirituality conference in Los Angeles. My own presentation was successful and I enjoyed attending the workshops of others. In this way I keep abreast of the concerns of my sisters.

At the end of the conference I was invited to the home of a pagan practitioner, where I would rest for a few hours, then board a plane to Oakland to resume my busy life. I asked if the woman would take me to the Latin quarter so I could shop for fabric. I have a few serious addictions: book buying, exotic flowers, tropical fruit juices, and the great monster—fabric mania. The women in my extended family believe that she who dyes the most fabric wins! I am their Queen. Wherever I travel in the world, I always try to bring back a book of folklore and a piece of the local fabric. Then I can flash and tease them because I have something special. I extort gifts and favors with the promise of revealing where I got that piece of fabric. This is the behavior of marketwomen in Africa, Jamaica, and Mexico. So I was highly disappointed when my hostess informed me that we could not go shopping. It seems that there was animosity between the Anglo and Latin women in the Goddess movement there. According to my informant a battle raged between devotees of *la Morena* and those who have dedicated themselves to Mary Queen of the Angels.

The ancestral past comes to haunt us now. I remember that native people carried the banner of Guadalupe in the war for their independence from the Spanish. The books tell us: "The royalists countered with their own banner of the Virgin of the Remedies, whose image was supposedly brought to New Spain by one of Cortes's men, and lost on La Noche Triste (30 June 1520) when Cortes had to abandon Tenochtitlan (later Mexico City). When one army captured the banner of the enemy, its troops shot the rival Virgin for a traitor. The powers of the Dark Virgin are still evident."[1] I ask myself: Is this story to be repeated in the streets of Los Angeles? Or can women recover from our past?

In the precolonial spiritual cultures of West and Central Africa there existed a position called "The Women of Peace." These women performed particular menstrual rites, studied the history and the law of their tribes, and embodied the power to balance public affairs. When the men of two tribes at war failed to resolve their differences, the Women of Peace in both groups could bring the fighting to an end, simply by laying down a leaf or branch from a sacred plant or tree. The Council of Clan Mothers served a similar function in the cultures of Native America. It is my opinion that we (all of us) need to become the Women of Peace.

A Ritual for Women of Peace

In the spirit of Peace, I would like to offer a ritual to be performed for the Guadalupe during times of strife in the community. For this ritual you will need:

1. A pink candle for the Virgin of Guadalupe. (Note: The pink candle is scented with rose and usually cost fifty cents more than the white or green one, and it's worth it!)
2. A quarter of a yard of rainbow-colored fabric.
3. Four red roses, one for each of the four directions.

[1] *Folktales of Mexico,* edited and translated by Américo Paredes. Foreword by Richard M. Dorson. University of Chicago Press, 1970, from the foreword, p. xix.

4. A clear glass of spring water.
5. A tree branch, flowers or stalks of fresh herbs (palm, marigolds, epazote).
6. An earthenware plate (a terra-cotta saucer from a nursery will do).
7. Images of other Goddesses and any offering you wish to make.

Ideally this ritual would be performed by a circle of women representing the diversity of the community (Latin, Asian, Native, African-American, and Anglo). If you must perform it alone, invoke kindred sisters to come for future rituals.

A. Begin by clearing your minds of any other obstacles and concerns by deep breathing, by chanting the letter O, by doing simple stretches, or by shaking the body vigorously. If in a group, stand in a circle and hold hands as you do this; if you are alone, mentally connect with the other women in your city by visualizing them moving through the streets coming toward you.

B. Dip your heart finger (the longest finger on the left hand) into the glass of spring water and make the sign of the earth on the clay plate. The sign of the Earth is a circle with an equal-armed cross in the center. Then dip the heart finger again, this time touching the third eye (called Iwaju or Eleda, the Eye of Character, the Little Creator), the heart center, and the navel. Now place the rainbow-colored cloth over the clay dish. Take another deep breath and remember that we are all Daughters of the Earth.

C. Lift the candle of the Virgin of Guadalupe above your head to the heavens, then bring it down, and touch the earth. Acknowledge that She is Tonantzin, the Empress of the Americas, and that you are standing on Her land. Give thanks for the privilege.

D. Now take the four red roses. These represent the four directions and the ancestors of the people who have built the country you live in. Acknowledge some contribution of the ancestors of the East (silk, railroads, tantra), ask for their blessings, and place the rose in the East position around the Virgin. Acknowledge the ancestors of the South (African music and dance, the folklore of the South American rainforest, the artwork of the Maori people) and place the rose in the South. Acknowledge the ancestors of the West (Native American ceremony, California cuisine, Hawaiian folklore) and place that rose in the West. Acknowledge the ancestors of the North (Inuit art, the conservation of the north woods, European technical skill) and place that rose in the North. In each direction acknowledge and give thanks for some contributions that all our ancestors have made.

E. At this point, the group may want to discuss some of the problems faced by the community: unemployment, homelessness, violence, and drugs. It is wise to discuss how to protect oneself from these negative influences, to assess one's skills and interests (individually and collectively), and to determine what contribution each woman can make toward addressing the concerns.

F. Sprinkle the branch, flowers, or herbs with spring water. Each woman will clean by passing the plant through her aura. While doing this she asks that all negativity be removed from her and that she be given the power of peace. The sweeping should be thorough. Emotions should be allowed to rise and fall and the cleansing should not stop until the woman feels confident that she can embody peace in this situation. When this is accomplished each woman will vigorously throw down her branch and pronounce the word for peace in her language.

G. Now light the candle of Guadalupe. Lift the plate and walk around the space, as if in a public procession. The women may take turns carrying Her image. Remember that She has traveled around the world bringing courage, strength, and organizational ability wherever She went. As you parade the Goddess call out the positive energies you wish to see manifested in your community: an end to racism; employment and housing for all; health and peace. When all these things are named, place the Virgin on the earth or on the altar.

H. Put images of other Goddesses and ancestors around Her. See them as visitors and members of Her court. Feed them corn and yams, rice and peas, whatever your ancestors ate. Allow them to stand together for seven days while the candle burns. Allow them to share in the sweet scent of the roses, the scent of domestic tranquillity. Allow them to bask in Her pink light, the color of honor and of universal love. Allow yourself and each other to be at peace for one week. Then expect a clear vision of what She would have you do.

I arrive at the front of the supermarket. Now I have twenty-one candles to stack up on the counter. The people behind me wait impatiently for me to finish lining them up. The people in front of me get out of my way quickly. The black woman behind me asks, "Why you buying all them candles?" I answer, "Because they're cheaper here." The Latin cashier rings up seven Guadalupes—three green, three white, and one bright pink. She looks at me quickly and lowers her eyes. Gold *Caridads*, Red Miguels, Blue *Reglas*, and a host of others, unmarked, unnamed.

I walk out of the store to the music of candles dancing and change jiggling in my pocket. Before I get to the car I hear the woman who was behind me say to her husband, "She ain't fooling nobody, that woman working magic with them candles." She knows. I turn around and look at her. We both try not to smile.

Once Again Sor Juana

ROSARIO CASTELLANOS
Translated by Maureen Ahern

*T*here are three figures in Mexican history that embody the most extreme and diverse possibilities of femininity. Each one of them represents a symbol, exercises a vast and profound influence on very wide sectors of the nation, and arouses passionate reactions. These figures are the Virgin of Guadalupe, Malinche, and Sor Juana.[1]

Only positive elements seem to converge in the Virgin of Guadalupe. In spite of her apparent fragility, she is the sustainer of life, the one who protects us against danger, the one who comforts our sorrows, presides over the most pompous events, legitimizes our joys, in short, the one who saves our body from sickness and our soul from the devil's stealth. How can we help loving her, revering

[1] The Virgin of Guadalupe, Patroness of Mexico and Latin America, who first appeared to the Indian Juan Diego in 1531 at Tepeyac, a hill outside the city of Mexico that had been the shrine of the Aztec goddess Tonantzin. The popular devotion that developed to this virgin spiritually unified the conquered and the conquerors, becoming a national cult that is celebrated each December 12 at the basilica in La Villa dedicated to her. Malinche, born near Veracruz around 1500, was the daughter of the local Indian ruler whose family sold her into slavery to Mayan-speaking peoples to the south. Given as a present to Hernán Cortés in 1519, she became his interpreter, counselor, and mistress. As the voice who spoke for Cortés, she played a key role in the rapid Spanish conquest of Mexico and Central America. Her name has become a symbol of betrayal to foreign interests, a stereotype that ignores her original betrayal by her own mother. Sor Juana Inés de la Cruz (1648–1695), was the most brilliant intellectual of colonial Mexico, author of baroque poetry, plays, and scientific studies of philosophy, astronomy, geometry, and music. Her *Letter in Reply to Sor Philotea* was the first document in the New World to defend women's rights to study, write, and teach. See *A Woman of Genius: Sor Juana Inés de la Cruz*, trans. Margaret Sayers Peden (Salisbury, Conn.: Lime Rock Press, 1982), and Octavio Paz, *Sor Juana Inés de la Cruz: The Pitfalls of Faith*, trans. Margaret Sayers Peden (Cambridge, Mass.: Harvard University Press, 1988).

her, converting her into the dearest, most beloved core of our emotional life? That is precisely what Mexicans do—even to the point of separating their religious beliefs from the personality of the Virgin Guadalupe in order to safeguard her, in the event these beliefs conflict with each other, undergo crisis, or must go into hiding due to circumstantial pressures. A classic example is the case of our atheists, who suffer no pangs of conscience when they make their annual pilgrimage to her shrine at La Villa.

Malinche incarnates sexuality in its most irrational aspect, the one least reducible to moral laws, most indifferent to cultural values. Because sexuality is a dynamic force that is projected outward and is manifested by deeds, Malinche has become one of the key figures of our history. Some call her a traitor, others consider her the foundress of our nationality, according to whatever perspectives they choose to judge her from. Because she is not dead, she still wails in the night, crying for her lost children throughout the most hidden corners of our land, just as she still makes her annual appearance disguised as a giant at Indian festivals and she continues to exercise her fascination as a woman, a female, and a seductress of men. Before Malinche, consciousness remains alert, vigilant, and forced to qualify her and understand her in order not to succumb to her power, which like Antheus' is always renewed whenever she comes into contact with the earth again.

The attitudes toward the Virgin of Guadalupe or Malinche are clear ones because their figures are also very clear-cut: the former, a woman who sublimates her condition in motherhood; the latter, a woman of our roots, uninterested in the process of its development, indifferent to the results. But Sor Juana? The initial enigma she poses for us is not her genius (sufficient to worry many doctors) but her femininity. She speaks of it in different passages of her writing, not in terms of a consummated and assumed fact but rather as a hypothesis that perhaps cannot be proven. She states, for example, in a ballad:

> I don't understand these things,
> I only know that I came here.
> So that if I be woman
> No one can truly say.

Such explicit confession and evident purpose constitute the stumbling block for scandal among Sor Juana's admirers. Either they look through her, or they prefer to ignore evidence that in the long run has the value of being firsthand and prefer to continue to construct her according to their own tastes: frivolous damsel of the viceregal court, a bird that allows herself to be caught in the snare of an impossible love from which her only escape is to beg asylum behind the consecrated walls of a convent. There she finds the solace of solitude and drowns her sorrows in sonnets and other minor matters. Like all the chosen of the gods, Sor Juana dies young and fee fi foe fum our story is done.

There's a paragraph written by Sor Juana in her *Letter in Reply to Sor Philotea* that is a type of autobiography, in which she spoke of the many doubts that assailed her before she took the veil. She knew her own character very well, her preference for solitude, how difficult it would be for her to submit to the discipline of a community life. In the end she chose the convent because the only other alternative was marriage, for which she felt an unconquerable aversion.

That paragraph has not prevented many persons from praising her monastic vocation, finding her obedience to the orders of the several superiors that she endured to be irreproachable, her zeal in the fulfillment of her vows excessive, and her final sacrifice and her charity toward her suffering sisters nothing less than saintly. For all of these reasons there has been no lack of those who, carrying their admiration to the utmost, have begged the pertinent authorities to canonize her. Naturally, the cause has not advanced. The Church straddles the Rock of Ages and resorts to very painstaking procedures before elevating anyone to its altars.

However, the attitudes that we have just described are, in the final instance, naïve and thus inoffensive. There is another attitude that takes on all the trappings of science, placing the curious specimen under the microscope in order to classify it.

Why so curious? Not because she chose the convent, a very commonplace deed in the New Spain of her time. Not because she wrote somewhat charming verse, because it was already a saying that in this newly founded metropolis there were more poets than fertilizer (and fertilizer was very abundant). No, it was because it was a woman who wrote those poems. Because she was a woman who had an intellectual vocation. Because, in spite of all the resistance and barriers of her environment, she exercised that vocation and transformed it into literary work. It was a body of work that provoked the astonishment and admiration of her contemporaries, not for its intrinsic qualities but because it sprang from a hand whose natural employment should have been cooking or sewing. A body of work greeted by silence, beset by the scorn of centuries, now comes to light once again, thanks to the research of scholars, among whom first place goes to Father Alfonso Méndez Plancarte.[2]

Thus, Sor Juana returns to the present, not only as an author but as a person. We see her dissected by the instruments of psychoanalysis, thanks to the Germanic curiosity (and being Germanic it is thorough and solemn) of Ludwig Pfandl.[3]

His diagnosis does not do her any favors. Moreover, it is a catalog of all the complexes, traumas, and frustrations that can victimize a human being. Naturally, in her relationship with her family there are all those ambiguities that are explained, thanks to the dummy card of Oedipus. Naturally, due to her beauty and her talent, she was a narcissist. Did she confess an eagerness to know more? She's a neurotic. Does she use symbols? Was she effusive to someone? Careful! That's either mistaken affection or an unconscious urge to kill.

A book conceived in this fashion is insulting, not for its partiality but because criteria like these have been superseded by other, broader ones. Wouldn't it be fairer to think that Sor Juana, like any other human being, possessed a backbone, that it was her own vocation, and that she chose among all the different kinds available to her the one she was most able to count on achieving?

[2] A reference to Alfonso Méndez Plancarte, editor of the complete works of Sor Juana, *Obras completas de Sor Juana Inés de la Cruz*, 4 vols. (Mexico City: Fondo de Cultura Económica, 1951–1957).

[3] A German Hispanist who wrote *Sor Juana Inés de la Cruz, la décima musa de México: Su vida. Su poesía. Su psique*, ed. Francisco de la Maza, trans. Juan Antonio Ortega y Medina (Mexico City: Instituto de Investigaciones Estéticas, UNAM, 1963).

Retablo

RONNIE BURK

1.
Was it Woman in the shape of a Tree?
pink breasts on the bark wood
the leaves of her hair change color
tiny incisions of light follow Her
to a meadow

streams of Mercury run through
Her body heavy with fleshy,
stubborn, octopus-child

a Star in her belly foretells
the goodness She is
Athanor, Vase, Flower of Milk

2.
She said, "make me a poem of Guadalupe"
I said I cldn't do it not green stars
nor the bliss of Her Presence
would shine from the pages
the folds of clumsy paper

3.
Mother of the Stars, Mother of the Neters
Mater Materia's *Al-Kemi*
weaving the nets of Mother Maya
I stood on the hills of Tepeyac
the city fell behind me

4.
The sky people will drink
my blood. I will pass
through Gate or arbor.
Maguey thorns will pierce
my arms. I will pass before
Her dark forgiving Face
as I fly into
the sun

Novena Narrativas y Ofrendas Nuevomexicanas

DENISE CHÁVEZ

*N*ovena Narrativas was inspired by cultural traditions of *cuentistas* (storytellers), *santeros* and *ofrendas* (constructed and assembled collage mementos), especially popular during All Souls Day in the Southwest and in Latin America. Inspiration came as well from the *altares* and *nichos* one finds in the family homes.

Novena Narrativas are nine narrations to be performed in monologue by one or more actresses. The characters vary in age—from 7 to 78—and are familiar to those of us who love New Mexico, its traditions, cultures and daily life—full as it is with significant detail. Specifically linked as they are to New Mexico, the women are universal in spirit. They appear one by one, and the great delicate flame of their burning hopes, dreams and devotions rises to the maternal figurehead.

The *Ofrendas Nuevomexicanas* consist of a clay Madonna (in the style of Nuestra Señora de Leche y Buen Parto), which is set on a chest, suggesting an altar in the home. Her garments, corona, and *esplendor* (halo or aura) are constructed of fiber, handwoven and embroidered commercial cloth, ornamental tin and brass work. The setting will include other items, token memorabilia representing parts of the women's lives and culture. The narrator(s) portray(s) the women and assembles the *ofrendas* as she performs on stage.

Novena Narrativas y Ofrendas Nuevomexicanas was first performed in Taos, New Mexico, in February 1986 by Kika Vargas. Since that time, the play has toured throughout the Southwest.

This labor of love began as a collaboration between five women artists: Juanita Jaramillo-Lavadie, a weaver; Sandi Roybal Maestas, a potter; Patricia Vargas-Trujillo, a tinsmith; Denise Chávez, a writer; and Kika Vargas, an actress.

List of Characters
(In order of appearance)

María Isabel González, the narrator
Jesusita Rael, a storeowner and spinster
Esperanza González, the wife of a Vietnam veteran
Minda Mirabal, a foster child
Magdalena Telles, the mother of seven children
Tomasa Pacheco, a nursing home resident
Juana Martínez, a factory employee
Pauline Mendoza, a Chicana teenager
Corrine "La Cory" Delgado, a bag lady

The set: A tall chest, covered by a lace mantle. On it stands a statue of La Virgen de Guadalupe. On either side of the Virgen are two tall candles, and fanning out in front are nine small votive candles, unlit. Nearby is a table and a chair. The space is untidy, scattered with paper; the props, a blanket draped over the chair.

At rise: Isabel comes in breathlessly, with a bag of groceries that she sets down on the table. She leaves the food in the bag and organizes the area. The lights come down, and she throws the blanket on the floor, then lies down on it. She is tired and wants to meditate awhile. It has been a busy day and she wants to relax. On the floor near her is a large pile of papers, some collated, some not. After a long silence, in the darkness, she turns the lights up slightly and begins to exercise. She does various yoga positions, stretching slowly, first on the floor, then in a seated position. With her back to the audience she begins talking.

Isabel

Somebody asked me what I do for a living. I am an artist I said. I write. I am a writer . . . (*Stretching, she grabs a foot, then jumps up, yelling*)

Green tennis shoes! That's it, I forgot the shoes! *(Turning up lights, she goes to a pile of papers on the desk and jots down the note)* . . . Jesusita Rael, *green tennies* . . . *(Back to floor, adjusting self, with Jesusita's voice)* Buenos días le dé Dios, hermana . . . *(Practicing, trying to get voice just right, high, with an S lisp)* Buenos días le dé Dios . . . *(In a shoulder stand, struggling, then falling back and lying there, she turns to one side and begins to collate papers. She talks and collates)* Jesusita, Esperanza, Minda, Madgalena, Tomasa, Juana, Pauline and Corrine; Jesusita, Esperanza, Minda, Magdalena, Tomasa, Juana, Pauline and La Cory, one, two, three, four, five, six, seven, eight. . . .

(Isabel does this for a while, then goes to the bag, finds juice, has a sip; she takes out a can of peas and leaves it on the chest, near the altar. On her way back, she picks up a pile of bills, opens them, and then places them face down on the table. She starts to put out the prop pieces; we follow her, as she mumbles and works out the play. She talks as she puts out the props, which include: Jesusita's lace collar, Esperanza's peas, Minda's doll and blanket, Tomasa's wig and cane, Juana's goggles, feathers and cedar, Magdalena's comb, brush, makeup and robe, Pauline's jacket and red headband, and Corrine's bag. She goes into snippets of the characters' speech)

¡Adrede iba a bailar! *(Dancing around the room singing "El Rancho Grande")* . . . I didn't care with who! *(Sitting down and hunching over, she becomes Tomasa)* I'm going to live to a ripe old age! *(Then sitting up straight, as herself)* My name is María Isabel González . . . *(Sighing)* When people tell me it's an easy time to be a woman, me río! As far as I'm concerned, when you're a woman, no time is easy. And when you're an artist, it's worse. Those born rich suffer as much as those born poor. But I'm not complaining. I might worry, but then I either sing or pray or laugh. Ríanse, as my gramita used to say. And love! One of the greatest powers we all possess is the ability to love.

(Getting up and beginning to set the altar) Just last week I was cleaning up in here, you can imagine what it was like, and I ran across a letter from my mom. She's been dead for years. I sat down and read it, and it was as if she was talking to me. Isabel, Isabel, what are your priorities? Mija, you need some lipstick, you're so pale, are you wearing a bra? It was as though she was right here next to me telling me how much she loved me, how proud of me she was, and to keep on working.

(Isabel is moved, she pauses in her work. She goes and lights a candle for her mother's spirit) When I feel alone, I remember behind me stand my grandmother, my mother, all the women who have come before me. Their spirits are always near, watching over me, guiding me, constantly teaching me. Today, when I went out for groceries, I heard one woman telling another, "La vida es una canción." I could have sworn I heard my grama's voice. And then I thought: This woman is a thread that connects me to all women, everywhere. Wherever I go, I *know* the women. I know their deepest joys and pains.

(Setting things on chest) Jesusita, Minda, Esperanza, the others . . . They are familiar to me. On the surface, their lives are really different from mine. And yet, when I look at them, I see a light shining from and through them, and in that light I recognize my gramita, my mom, my sister, my friends and myself as well. I understand the passion of their lives. I see that it has made them strong, patient and faithful. They have come full circle to that place of peace we all move toward when we pray or sit in silence.

(Stretching) Ay . . . Look, I've really been talking, que habladero! I have to get back to work, I have a deadline, excuse me . . .

(Becoming Jesusita, she puts on the collar Jesusita wears. Throughout the play, Isabel will become the characters, donning costume pieces and assuming the posture and voice of characters. All is done on stage, without a curtain, in full view of the audience. Each character should have one or two costume pieces that identify them. A basic black turtleneck with pants and skirt should serve as the primary costume)

Jesusita

(A mouse-like spinster, she speaks in a high reedy voice, with a certain lisp. She runs a store of curiosities, sells thread and needles and little yellow candles that are so old that when you lift them, they break. The store has ceased to really serve the public, but Jesusita would not dare think of closing it. She wears her little hat, green tennies, and dusts as she talks)

Buenos días le dé Dios, Hermana Dioses. Muchísimas gracias por la manzanilla que me trajo la última vez. Siéntese, hermana, a platicar. Not too many customers yet. Todo ha cambiado. ¿Por qué? La gente se levanta tarde, come demasiado, y nobody va a misa anymore, y por qué? El H-B-O. HBO! La television! Pues sí, tengo cable, falta de esa novela desgraciada, *Seducción*. *(Pause)* Oh, I been pretty good. I'm not dead yet, gracias a Dios! *(Sighing)* People don't need different colors of thread anymore, nobody sews. And ahora nadie usa dedales! My mother always used a thimble. She thought anyone who didn't was a fool. One time in this very room, bárbara, she was working on a dress and she yelled to me, "¡Jesusita, ven pronto!" She had stabbed herself with a small needle and it was moving up her arm into the bloodstream. Oh, yes, she finally got it out. And then she sat down and cried. If she'd lost it, it would have gone through her blood, gone to her heart, and killed her! ¡Bárbara! Have you heard of anything? That was mamá.

(Looking around) Rael's Tienda de Abarrotes. Someday it will just disappear. If I'd gotten married . . . Oh, tuve chansa. His name was Prudencio Sifuentes. El Ermitaño, they called him, for his role in *Los Pastores*. Oh, I was too busy with the store. Finally, Prudy moved to Santa Barbara, California. And about a year later, he drowned in the ocean. ¡Bárbaro! No, no, no tuve ganas de casarme con él. Era muy chapito. His ears were small as well. I could never marry anyone with ears smaller than my own. ¡Ni lo permite mi Dios! Oh, I missed having children, but then I started with the Foster Children's Program. They became my kids. Rosella, she lives in Roswell, Rini's in Tucumcari, and Donacio's a dentist in Downey, California. All the kids . . . They call me mamá and everything. And they always send me cards pa' Crismes, you know?

(Confidentially) Pero ya me cansé. I'm ready to devote more time to the church. I take communion to the prisoners and up to the Four Directions Nursing Home. Vi a la hermana Tomasa. ¡Bárbara! She don't look too good, that's what I say. Tenía una peluca güera. She was never a blond! but what can you say? *(With resignation)* I'm too busy with God to be worrying about people.

(Hedging a bit) ¿La muchachita? She's still with me. Pobrecita Minda. Me da lástima con ella. Es que her father wants her back,

ni lo mande Dios. And Magdalena says she'll take her, ni lo mande Dios. And she can't stay here, ni lo mande Dios! *(Crossing herself)* Pobrecita niña, all she really wants is a mother and to be close to God, if God's not a man! *(High, nervous laughter)*.

No, I never married . . .

(Rearranging things on the altar) ¿No necesita unas velas, hermana? Cera de abeja. They don't make them like they used to, you know?

(Sighing) Nobody buys thread anymore. Or buttons. Or needles.

(Swatting at a fly) ¡Malditas moscas! Oh, I understand, hermana, you have to go. Lleve esta velita a la hermana Tomasa, if she ain't dead yet, pobrecita. El cancer. I'll see you next week at the Third Order Meeting of Las Franciscanas! Vaya con Dios, Hermana María. ¡Adiós!

(Going back to altar to light a candle and rearrange a little bit more) ¡Pobrecito Prudy! Como me contaba del amor de California . . . del mar de California. *(She shakes her head as a look of fondness, sadness, almost regret comes to her face)* No era porque era chapito . . . not really . . . eran esas orejitas! Pobrecito Prudy. Que mi madrecita lo tenga descansando en paz . . .

(Isabel sheds Jesusita and becomes Esperanza)

Esperanza

(A plain-looking, tired woman; she goes to the altar and lights a candle immediately)

No tengo mucho tiempo, Madrecita. I have to rush back to work. I just came to check the mail and to eat lunch. *(Making the sign of the cross)* You know my needs better than I do myself. Take care of José, bring him home and help him to stop drinking. Take care of Isabel, ay Isabel, her and her art! She's a wonderful girl, a beautiful woman, Madrecita. Make her strong like all the other women of her family. Take care of everyone else in the family, tía Panchita, Reis and the twins, my ahijado, el Jerry . . .

(*A bit sadder*) Take care of all my hijitos who are already with you in Heaven. El Hector, pobrecito, ni tuvo chansa para vivir. Take care of all the others who were killed in Vietnam, and all the others who suffered from it, like my José, who never got over that terrible war. Take care of todos los alcohólicos y los que sufren de las drogas y mueren de las drogas! Take care of our men and all the women who love them. ¡Cuídalos, Madrecita! Lift them to your loving heart, hold them in the palm of your hand, have mercy on them.

(*Tiredly, to la Virgencita*) Ay, sometimes I'm so tired I can't even pray. All I can do is sit. Sit and be quiet.

(*Getting up and opening a can of peas with a can opener*) I don't have much time, excuse me, Madrecita. Voy a comer mi lonche. Con su permiso, mi Reina.

(*Isabel transforms into the character of Minda, a seven-year-old girl who sits on the floor playing with her doll and blanket*)

Minda

I have a little friend. Her name is uh . . . uh . . . Jennifer . . . Marie . . . something. Something anglo. She's seven years old, like me. No! She's not fat! She's real pretty. It's not me, I told you, it's my friend, Jennifer Marie. Anyway, it can't be me 'cause she has a mom. And a real father. And she doesn't live where there's garbage and broken beer bottles all over the place! She doesn't have to take shortcuts through Mrs. Ruiz' faded towels and stinky baby diapers or Mr. Ruiz' baggedy-raggedy shorts on the line! (*Giggling hysterically*)

(*Whispering confidentially to the doll and pulling the blanket over her and the door to make a tent*) Now, you can't tell anyone, okay? This is a secret for always and forever. You can't even tell God, understand? Jennifer's father hurts little girls. He beats her and does ugly, dirty things to her. What he does is bad! And he told her if she ever told anybody, he would kill her! (*Crying hysterically*)

(*Dramatic change into the present and herself*) I never even told God. I didn't even know God until Miss Rael took me to church.

(Does switch-over to Jesusita Rael, with a high voice) ¡Minda, Minda, Minda, buenos días le dé Dios!

(Back to herself) I can't talk to Miss Rael. Her voice is too high and her bones stick out, real sharp! And she never even had a baby! But I can talk to you, mi'jita. You're my best bestest friend! And I can talk to Magdalena, the neighbor. She tells me, "Don't be afraid of your body, Minda. All women are the same that way. It's beautiful! A gift from God the Mother. The female thing won't kill you, or your mother being dead. All things have to die. It's natural."

(To her doll) Come on, let's you and me and Miss Rael go to church. *(Pretending to be in church)* Shhh. We have to sit back here with the other old ladies and Miss Rael.

(Looking around and daydreaming. She then becomes attentive and begins to imitate the way the old ladies sing) Bendito, bendito, bendito sea Dios. Los ángeles cantan y alaban a Dios. Los ángeles cantan y alaban a Dios . . .

(Daydreaming again and having a conversation with the doll) I want a dog. But Miss Rael says, "No. It will only die." Oh, let it! It's natural! Ay, ouch! Don't pinch me. I wasn't daydreaming! I know I have a lot to be grateful for! I'm not fat and ugly! *(To doll)* Miss Rael always pinches me when I talk in church . . .

(Pointing) See God on the altar? He's got big black strange eyes and silver lightning coming out of his head. Look the other way!

(Pointing the other direction) And that's the God Mother. She's not old and ugly. She's real pretty! I never had a mother, except when I was born and was real sick and almost died. That was when the tubes were in my mouth and nose and the doctors said, "She'll probably die. If she lives, don't expect much."

(Suddenly changing, becoming violent with the doll) You're retarded, retarded! That's what Jennifer's father says to her all the time.

(Back to earlier conversational tone) The funny thing is that I lived and my mother died. *(Pause)* Her name was Carmen.

(Seeing that Rael is after her again, she prays fervently) Dear Mother of God, save me from the fires of Miss Rael's Hell! I don't want to be afraid of the dark or of God the Man, or spiders, or tunnels that never end, or having babies . . . I want to be a mother someday, when I'm not afraid anymore, okay?

(As if saying to herself, "Is this a prayer?") I wish I had a mother . . .

(*An idea just dawned on her, with a sense of wonder*) Mary, if you become my mother, I'll become a nun, and then a saint . . .
(*Getting pinched again*) Ouch! Maybe I won't become a saint . . .
Dear mother God, let me forget everything! Everything! Except love . . . like in a fairy tale . . .

Magdalena

(*A youngish-looking woman in her late forties comes out carrying a makeup case, fixing her face and hair as she speaks to someone behind the screen*)

¡Duérmete, mi amor! It's still early, about four. I'm sorry I woke you up. Yes, I'm going. I told you I was. ¿Por qué no vas conmigo? You promised me before Johnny was born that you would climb with me every year as a thank-you to la Virgencita. That was seven kids and no marriage license ago!

(*Laughing coyly*) Okay so I'm plenty married now! When you left, I climbed to bring you back. And one year I climbed for el Señor Gallegos, el vecino. It just happened, Mikey, like I told you. Una noche se presentó. His wife, Chila, se estaba muriendo de cancer. He was lonely. Me dio lástima con él. No, I didn't tell him about the baby. He was on the school board, pobrecito. Then there was the climb for el Compadre Juanito. When his wife, Dora, left him with the four kids to run off with his cousin, Humberto, he didn't know what to do. So I told them to move in. There's always room for more. Don't worry about it, Mikey. She missed him and they got back together. They're very happy now. I climbed for them that year. And then one year I climbed for el poeta, Maggie's sobrino, from Portales. Se llamaba Toribio. He was a poet looking for construction work. He didn't have no money and I was getting food stamps, so no problem. But you were the only one I loved, Miguel, you know that!

(*Continuing with conviction*) And then I climbed for all my kids. Yes, and for all their fathers too. They were all good men. And now you've come back. So today I'm climbing for you. And for the baby . . . (*Patting her stomach*)

(*Falling over imaginary shoes*) ¡Ay, Mikey, mi amor, cuidado donde pones los zapatos! It's so good to have you home. Put your shoes under the bed, where you used to keep them? ¡Cómo te extrañé! ¿Por qué no me llamaste? Why didn't you at least write? They don't let you write in prison. Duérmete, mi amor . . . Okay, okay, it's all right.

(*Putting on coat and hat*) There's food in the icebox. Me and the kids will be back tonight after the mass. I have to go, mi amor! Es mi manda. Mikey, mi amor, I love you so much. You don't know. I love life so much! I just want to help people. That's the way it is with me. I see the good in all the men. Me dio lástima con el señor Gallegos. Y también con el compadre Juanito. Y especialmente con el poeta, pobrecito, ni tenía barbas, lleno de espinillas. But you're the only one I've ever loved, mi amor! You gonna stay? I'll get my food stamps any day. When the kids get bigger I'll get a job. The rent is low. We'll get back on our feet, mi amor, you'll see. (*With resignation*) We'll stay together, you and me and the kids.

(*Going to the altar*) Sometimes when I think about you, mi amor, and then I look at you, I love you so much I want to cry. Que la Virgencita me perdone. She understands everything. Everything. And she forgives everything. That's why I have to go on this pilgrimage today, mi amor, that's why . . .

Tomasa

(*A 78-year-old woman wearing a tousled blond wig and hospital gown, walking with a cane; she sits*)

¡Ay, Esperanza, qué bueno que viniste a visitarme! Take me home, hermanita, please! (*Starts to cry but quickly snaps out of it*) You never come to see me anymore! Oh, you came last Thursday. We went outside and sat in the sun . . .

(*With terror*) What's going to happen to me? (*Petulantly*) I want to go home!

(*Seriously*) Can I walk? What's today? Saturday? Already? Crismes? That's a long time off. I'll be dead by then.

(*Angrily*) I don't want to go outside! We just came in! ¡Acuéstame, por favor! They never do what I tell them. Where's Ida, she's the one who put me here.

(*Crying again*) Oh, I'm better. Except for my head. I can't think anymore. (*Patting her hair*) Well, at least I still have all my hair. (*Testily*) No, no quiero nada. Today's Monday. That's right. I forgot. What did you say today was? My daughter Ida never comes to see me. She's got her family, I'm in the way. (*Hopelessly*) ¿Qué me va a pasar?

(*Planning*) Llévame al banco. How much money do I have? It should be enough to get me out of here. I'm moving to San Diego. Ahí tengo unas primitas, Gussie and Tenoria.

(*Suddenly deflated, crying*) ¿Por qué no me he muerto? Diosito, Diosito, ten misericordia. I know, I know. It's not my time. I'm going to live to a ripe old age. That's what Elena, la flaquita, tells me. I don't feel old. Seventy-eight? I'm not that old!

(*Angry again, hitting the air*) ¡Acuéstame! I want to go to sleep and never wake up!

(*Suddenly getting a dreamy, faraway look, she softens with wonder*) ¿Mamá? ¿Mamá? ¿Comó está?

(*Quietly, sober*) Oh, that's right. She's dead. It's my head! What time is it? ¿Ya te vas? ¿Tan pronto? You're the only one who comes to see me. You and la monjita ratoncita Rael. She brings me communion. Antes que te vayas, ¡acuéstame!

(*As if grabbing someone's arm*) ¿Qué me va a pasar? I'm going to live to a ripe old age. That's what la gordita, Elena, tells me. Dale gracias a la Hermana Rael por las velitas. Vuelve, Esperanza.

(*Alone now, she sinks into remembering*) Esperanza! Esperanza, I forgot to tell you. ¡Mamá me vino a visitar!

(*Like a little girl, she sits up with her eyes shining beautifully*) Me acuerdo de mi altarcito. Con la Virgencita tan bella. Con su vestido de blanco y su manta de azul. Su carita tan linda, su boca cantando.

(*She gets up, lights a candle and sings*) ¡Oh, María, Madre mía! El consuelo del mortal, ampárame y guíame a la patria celestial.

(*Watching the candle and Virgencita in wonder for a while, she breaks out of her reverie and turns to her mother, who she imagines is next to her*) ¡Mamá! ¡Mire que bonita se ve la Virgen!

Juana

(A 56-year-old factory worker, a nativa. She wears goggles, a scarf, apron, and holds a pair of panty hose in her hands)

En esta fábrica hay mexicanos, anglos, vietnameses, latinos, and everybody else ain't got a job. Si no fuera pantyhose, it would be boots or jeans or moccasins . . . or turquoise jewelry . . . algo pa' los turistas.

(Motioning) The work starts back there. Little by little it moves to me. I do the inside seams. People don't like you to talk about pantyhose. ¡Yo ni las uso!

(Pausing to place a bingo chip on an imaginary card on a nearby table) I used to work in the hospital, in the kitchen throwing away the garbage. ¡Ese era trabajo! I had to wear unas botitas verdes, de plástico, como los niños. ¡Todos creían que yo era doctora! When I told them I worked in the kitchen, their faces got sad . . .

(Suddenly animated as she places a chip on the imaginary bingo card) Bingo! Bingo! B-12. Over here! Bingo! I just won ten bucks! A month ago I won fifty! See, we have this bingo goes on all the time. "Something for you to think about," nos dice el Señor Wiley, el patrón. No es de estas partes. Ever notice they always bring in the boss from other places? Me conoce. Me dice, "Wuanita, how you doing this fine day?" "Oh, pretty good, pretty good," le digo. "Mucho bueno," me dice. Le gusta hablar español. "Wuanita, you're the best inside seamer I've got. Keep up the good work and one of these days, one of these days, I'm gonna raise you . . . to $3.50!!" "Oh, thank you, Mr. Wiley, thank you!" "Okey, dokey, Wuanita, now git along . . ."

(Suddenly a change takes place and she becomes quiet, moving in slow motion as she begins to remove her goggles, apron, etc.) One of these days, the noise gonna stop! It won't be so long. Tengo cincuenta y seis años. Fifty-six years of my hands working. Making tortillas, changing pañales, burning eyes and lyes, boiling water and stabbing needles.

(Pause) Mi abuelita me enseñó a trabajar. She taught me the healing life of the herbs, what to do with cota and osha, como sobar con aceite while praying. Cuando se murió, I took her ashes to the

pueblo and I scattered them in the wind. She was the only person I had in the world. Estas manos son mi herencia.

(She has been redressing herself by taking off the scarf and putting on a medicine wheel necklace. Now she lights cedar and picks up macaw feathers) I remember my abuelita telling me, "Acuérdate que eres india, y que la Virgen María, la mestiza, es tu madre querida. The Mother's Mother is your mother as well. Never forget that. You are a child of many worlds: say your prayers, praise the sun, glorify the moon, and send your spirit in the wind." *(She ends with a chant, singing to the Virgen and the four directions)*

> *Hey oh hey, hey ya no*
> *Hey oh hey, hey ya no*
> *Hey oh hey*
> *Hey oh hey.*

Pauline

(Transformation to a 14-year-old girl who sits facing away from the audience responding to an imaginary teacher's questions and demands)

(Facing the back wall) Pauline Mendoza.

> *(Turns partly towards the audience)* Pauline Mendoza.
> *(Turns full face to the audience)* Pauline Mendoza.
> *(Mad)* Pauline Mendoza!
> *(Sulkily)* Taos.
> *(Told to say everything again loudly, she yells out)* Pauline Mendoza. Taos. Sixth grade. Fourteen years old.
> *(Bitterly)* I'm a freak.
> *(Naming things she likes, staccato-like)* Boys. Cars. Makeup. My leather bracelet. My red headband. Black T-shirts. My jean jacket. My hair cut long in back and short on the sides and front. Tattoos. Can I sit down now?
> *(In response to a question)* I made all the tattoos. Myself.
> *(Withdrawn)* I'm working on one now. No, you can't see. Can I go back to my desk? Okay, okay. So what do you want to know

for anyway? I already told you what I liked! I don't want to be nothin'! My teacher, Mrs. Espinoza, makes me sit behind the screen, in the corner, facing the wall. I'm jittery, she says. Hell, so I work on my tattoos. Nothing better to do. I can't barely read or write. I'm dumb. I'm a freak. Don't yell at me!

(*Yelling*) She always yells at me! It's embarrassing!

(*Trying to get back to her seat*) I've got work to do, okay? (*Sits*) Nine times eight? How the hell should I know? Okay, okay. (*Stands*) Yeah, I like my mom. She's pretty young for a mom. I hate school. I hate homework! Thinking? I hate thinking! Maybe I could like it. You want me to read that book? I can't read the whole thing! Don't you understand? I thought substitutes are supposed to know everything! I'm dumb. I'm a freak. I sit in the corner all the time. Can I sit down now? (*Sits*) I been in sixth grade three years. I'm going to move next year. (*Stands*) Okay, okay.

(*Picking up book, trying to read*) The . . . his—hist—history of a . . . ah . . . a . . . p-e-o-p-l-e.

(*Angrily*) Yeah, I know the word people! Don't you, or what? The history of people . . . This is boring! People are boring. I don't know. I don't know. I can't read, I told you. I just can't. Can I sit down?

(*Exasperated*) You still want me to talk about myself? Mrs. Espinoza never makes me read out loud. She lets me sit in the corner and be quiet. That's all she wants from me. Yeah! I try to read in church . . . I try to read the prayer books. One . . . one . . . one . . . ho—ly . . . that's as far as I get. I'm a freak even there. So I look at the statues and pictures and I feel better. A freak? What's a freak? A freak is someone who wears a you-know-what in the sixth grade. A freak is someone that has already started their you-know-what in the sixth grade. That's a freak!

(*Off guard*) That? Oh, that's my tattoo. No. Oh, okay, since you asked. It's Our Lady of Guadalupe. It don't look like a lady on fire; that's rays of gold, stupid! Don't you know nothing? I just started working on it. Yeah, I told you, I go to church. Why do I like tattoos? I don't talk good. I don't think good. It's something cool. A picture like in church, you know, one . . . holy . . . okay . . . the history of a people, okay? Pictures, pictures!

(*Not so harsh now*) I'm working on my tattoos, back there see, where nobody bothers me. It's my art work. I'm working on my tattoos and my drawings. I'm gonna be an artist.

(More confidentially, but still hard) My girlfriend, Gloria, she says I'm changing. I don't want to go out and get rowdy and drunk all the time now. Ever since this lady came to our school. She made me stand up and talk. She's an artist. Her name is Isabel Martínez. She's Chicana. I never known anybody . . . a lady and a Chicana and an artist . . . It surprised me, you know?

(Stands up straight and takes a deep breath as she moves to light the candle) Pauline. My name is Pauline Mendoza. I do tattoos. And I draw. Next year I'm going to move to a new school. And someday . . . someday . . . I'm gonna be an artist!

Corrine

(An aging, very tough bag lady. She drags around a big and colorful bag which she empties on the floor. Throughout the scene she will put on clothing from the bag)

Antes me importaban las cosas, pero ahora, sss—I take every day as it comes. Some good, some pretty bad! Like the weather. If it looks like rain or snow, I head down to the Holy Bible Rescue Mission para agarrar mi espacio. I stay there or at the Good Faith Shelter, or one of my other spots. Near the Interstate, that overhang with the old colchón . . . that's my bedroom! Or behind Bennie's La Paloma Bar, by the vents. ¡No te apenes! No sweat! Rain or shine, Corrine got it covered, ésa! Ssss.

(Taking a drink from her wine bottle in the bag) I don't want your stupid pity, okay? I got enough problems of my own, you start worrying me about your shag rug and your color t.v. . . . I don't need it, okay? I had a family once . . . kids . . . the whole . . . But don't get me wrong, ésa, it's never as good as it looks. I got into writing bad checks. I needed things, you know? I got sent up. That was when they still had the women in the pinta in Santa. Anyway, I was in my thirties ésa, and they took it all away—the kids, the house— and then el tonturio went to live with his novia in Belén. They all

disappeared. Yeah, I tried to find them, but my family didn't want to have anything to do with me. So, I did my time. Met me my Sophia. Ay, Sophia, ¡Sophia! ¡Que corazonada! We wanted to get married. We did, in our hearts. Later we got separated, she started seeing somebody else, you know? So, I said okay, anyway, I was getting out. The kids in Belén, jefita in 'Burque, you think she's gonna welcome me back a la vecindad? ¡Tattoos hasta el copete! María and Jesús on my knuckles, my hair dyed blond, my eyebrows shaved and then painted black . . . Una pinta jotita, no less. ¡Niel, ésa! Nobody wanted me back the way I was. So I took to the streets. Oh, yeah, I got me a little, here and there, you know, just enough to spend a night, take a shower, get some beer. But didn't last. I was getting old . . . that was over twenty years ago! Pero no te preocupes, ésa, I got it covered!

(Takes another swig) Met this lady wanted me to take care of her jefito. Uh-ummmmm! He got this and that wrong with him. Used to be a big man, now look at him. Pobrecito, medio muerto. Anyway, she tried to give me her mother's old clothes to wear. And I said, I don't want them, dammit! You keep your dead woman's things! You think because you're a Mexican with a little bit of money you can treat me like hell? I'm not your slave! Keep your damn job and house and clothes and car and leave me alone. I oughta report you to the authorities—IRA, INS, NBC, CBS—for cruelty to an old woman! I don't need your pity! They think they can give you the slop once they see you in the streets. ¡Qué va! Lo que necesitamos en este estado es una gobernadora como esa Madre Teresa, ¿no? Anyway, I left her holding the clothes and walked over to the Senior Citizens pa' mis enchiladas. It was Friday and I decided to stick around for the baile. Johnny and the Huipiles were playing. Siempre me ha gustado tirar chancla, ¿sabes? Anyway, I went up to this cute viejita to ask her to dance—that's all it was, I swear—y se puso media weird. So I went up to this dude then, adrede iba a bailar, and I didn't care with who. The dance was over at five-thirty so I walked over to the Holy Bible to see what was happening, you know? It was too late. From there I went over to the Good Faith. ¡Estaba lleno! The mattress was gone and Bennie's was taken. So me fui al bus depot a ver a mi novela, María de Nadie. And from there, I came over here. I thought maybe the padrecito would let me sit in the portal . . . *(The actress may name any place she is performing)* ¿Quién sabe?

(Goes over to the Virgencita to light a candle) Mi Madrecita sabe, ¿no? Me conoce. She know that when Cory got it, she got it! And when she don't got it . . . ssss . . . it don't matter!

(Fondly touches the face of the Virgencita) Te debo, ¿eh Madrecita? Next time.

(Opening umbrella as she turns away) Jesús y María . . . *(Motioning to the tattoos on her knuckles that spell out these names)* I got it covered, ésa!

Isabel

(Isabel takes off Corrine's clothes, putting them in the bag. She rearranges herself a bit; as herself, excited)

All this time I've been thinking about what that lady at the grocery store said, about life being a song. Well, it's true. Life really is a song. ¡La vida es una canción! The song of childhood, the song of love, the song of parting, the song of death . . . Each of our lives is a song, or a prayer, like a novena.

(Picking up some of the papers) When life gets to be too much, I simply lift my hands to the Virgencita and the Heavens and I just pray—or sing! Or I sit quietly at my desk thinking about all the lives that pass before me. Sometimes I have to control myself from reaching out and grabbing someone . . .

(Excited again) And in total love and acceptance and friendship saying to them, "¡Signe adelante, Hermana! Keep going forward! And keep on singing that unending song of love and life—in the fullest, strongest, most beautiful voice you have!"

(Looking around with joy) ¡Ay! ¿Qué familia de mujeres, no? What dreams! What hopes! It makes me want to sing!

(Isabel sings "El Corrido de Las Mujeres." After she finishes singing, she picks a few things and goes out, the pages still on the floor)

End

Framing an Icon: Guadalupe and the Artist's Vision

FELIPE EHRENBERG

*I*n October 1986 I left my home in Mexico for a visit to San Diego. I hadn't been there more than three days when the TV set at La Raza Cultural Center in Balboa Park showed us the first pictures of the devastation: San Salvador had been slammed by an earthquake and the death toll was rising rapidly. So the long-distance call home was justified. After all, we in Tepito, in the heart of Mexico City, knew well about the blind pain and the sense of irremediable loss that such a cataclysm provokes.

"Stop dreaming, José. What good is it to send supplies," I told José Vega on the phone, "if they're bound to be stolen by politicians or the army?"

Vega was the man I'd left in charge of our very own victim's-aid camp in Tepito.

"We could . . . ah, channel it, ah . . . through the Church, couldn't we?" he asked. I could hear the doubt in his voice.

"I think we'd better fly down ourselves," I said. "We're veterans, aren't we? The best we can offer is our expertise."

I took the first plane back to Mexico to join José and the other camp coordinators. Four days later, with the cargo we'd collected all crated, passports in order, donated plane tickets secured, the first fourteen of us were all aboard the two pickups bound for the airport. The other half would follow by land. An expectant crowd of neighbors surrounded us.

"The Virgin! We're forgetting our Guadalupe!" cried Grandma Amelia. "Get a framed one," we all shouted as she hailed a cab and headed for the basilica, to buy a chrome of the brown-skinned Virgin.

The San Salvador airport was in chaos as we disembarked.

French rescue experts and their dogs, German nurses, and a multitude of harried foreigners mingled with well-dressed and bejeweled Salvadorans on their way out, can't-take-it-any more expressions on their faces. Fierce-looking soldiers armed to the teeth patrolled the building. Customs officers chewed gum, scrutinized documents with hawk eyes, and searched luggage, hats, and handbags with exasperating care.

"Jeez, José!" I mumbled worriedly under my breath. "This is gonna be tough. I don't think we'll be out before midnight . . . if they let us into the country at all." El Salvador, after all, was still at war.

Suddenly, tiny and wizened Grandma Amelia showed us what faith is about. She raised the large, framed image of the Virgin of Guadalupe over her head and, waving it like a banner, shoved her way through the harried multitudes and up to the immigration officers. Porters, Mexicans, a few soldiers, crossed themselves. The barriers disappeared and we were whisked through, past the bewildered looks of those who'd arrived before us. The Virgin over our heads shone brightly in her frame in the sweltering heat of the street.

We were nobody, our little group, rather a nuisance compared to the impressive presence of the International Red Cross, the Doctors without Frontiers from France, or the many other task forces that went to San Salvador. But by midnight we'd had a meeting with Archbishop Rivera y Damas, had held conferences with the radio and the press, had survived a confrontation with Salvadoran government representatives at the Mexican embassy (they wanted the supplies we'd brought along!), and had finished setting up the mammoth old tent we'd lugged with us. We raised it on the site where forty-four little girls had been crushed to death when their school collapsed.

Next morning, under the watchful eyes of our Guadalupe, we began working side by side with the quake victims.[1]

This experience was not, of course, the first time I had felt the

[1] During the month-long duration of the operation, named *Barrio a Barrio* (Neighborhood to Neighborhood), five emergency programs were successfully implemented: homeopathic first-aid assistance, community organization counseling, networking with foreign nongovernment organizations, emergency educational services for the young, cultural activities. One year later (1987) the *Barrio a Barrio* operation was awarded the Roque Dalton Medal for our services to the San Salvadorean earthquake victims.

supernatural power of the Virgin of Guadalupe. Friends, neighbors, relatives, all have experienced the miraculous at one time or another, as bestowed by Guadalupe-Tonantzin. Faith in the Virgin helps solve everything from the deepest spiritual unrest to the most minuscule daily problems: a broken back, a broken pocket, a broken heart, the Little Mother of Guadalupe heals all. Neither was it the first time I, a Mexican of Jewish descent and more or less an agnostic, had stopped to think about the power of an icon.

A year before the Salvadoran experience, in the aftermath of our own earthquake in Mexico City, Guadalupe had succored panicked earthquake victims in the face of the otherwise unsolvable problems posed by incompetent urban planners, opportunistic politicians, and corrupt authorities. Like those of the garbage and refuse mountains that mushroomed up around us in the disaster zone, spawning invasions of mice and rats and cockroaches, ravaging our makeshift camps with skin diseases and intestinal infections. When this happened, all we did was proceed to install her well-lit effigy in the trouble spots, and *zap!* they were clean once again.

This is the stuff of faith, of a faith in one of the most powerful images ever designed, the "diptych image of synchretic power"[2] that needs in fact no religion to uphold it, of a faith carefully constructed through the years, through the centuries, and which responds in an immediate manner to the idiosyncratic requirements of downtrodden societies, strongly matriarchal by tradition. Her cult, says the scholar Félix Báez-Jorge, can only be examined *beyond* the limits of religious (or indeed anticlerical) considerations, rather as a "formidable ideological construct which balances the history of Mexico."

Focal point of all the hopes and wishes of Mexican Catholics, the core of almost every Mexican hearth (be it in Mexico, the U.S.A., or elsewhere), Guadalupe-Tonantzin's *effectiveness* is radiated by her very image: an elongated, seedlike, vulva-shaped figure which of-

---

[2]Félix Báez-Jorge: "The Virgin of Guadalupe," *Mitos Mexicanos*, coord. Enrique Florescano et al., Editorial Aguilar, Mexico City, 1995.

fers unending possibilities of transformation, its own *visual* transformation, and as a consequence, its ability to adapt to a people's changing needs.

I am convinced that credit for the *dehispanizing* and *mexicanizing* of the Guadalupan icon must be given to the numerous artists of every caliber who, through the ages, have pictured the Virgin. After observing closely the myriad prints, paintings, murals, wood and stone sculptures, tableaux or retables, ex-votos and folk art produced throughout the years, I noticed that as time passed, the Church texts also varied their explanations of the Virgin's epiphany. This process, that of images provoking texts, perforce legitimated the gradual darkening of Guadalupe's skin, making her, in the process, kin to the vanquished. I've often thought her transformation can well be likened to that of Lenin's effigy reproduced by the millions: as one travels east toward Mongolia, his European phenotype gradually changes to become markedly Asian, high cheekbones, slanted eyes, and all.

Elisa Vargas Lugo, in a substantial text that deals with Guadalupan iconography,[3] traces the development of Guadalupe's image, from a small xylographic print made by an anonymous carver in medieval Europe to the ubiquitous mechanical reproductions of her likeness sold in our day. Vargas Lugo's study extends only so far as portraits of the deity created by Mexican artists—mostly painters who specialized in religious themes—of the early twentieth century. Still, her illustrated work serves well to show how Guadalupe's skin, indeed her complete presence, took a turn toward Mexican darkness as early as the latter part of the sixteenth century.

The early *criollo* artists who portrayed Guadalupe painted her skin not as "Spanish" but with the hues of the Moorish complexion, a marked olive-green tint. A large number of paintings, all made by unknown hands before and after these dates, do show a bronze-skinned woman. As time passed, it is conceivable that, uncultivated as they may have been, the visions of vernacular painters pressed the more educated, *criollo* artists of New Spain to portray

---

[3]Elisa Vargas Lugo; *Iconología Guadalupana*, p. 57; *Imágenes Guadalupanas Cuatro Siglos*, exhibition catalogue, Editorial Centro Cultural Arte Contemporáneo, Mexico City, 1988.

her in a shaded manner, with the acquiescence—seldom if at all enthusiastic—of the princes of the Church, their patrons. After all, the changes for the darker could be—and were—most useful to the proselytizing purposes of a religious institution bent on total expansion, for the glory of Catholicism and, of course, Spain's treasury.

One of the earliest known depictions of Mary of Guadalupe is housed in the Sanctuary of Guadalupe de Cáceres, Extremadura, in southern Spain. A twelfth-century Romanic wood carving, very different from the way she is pictured today, it has been identified as one of the black Virgins then worshiped by the sturdy, sun-baked peasants of the Iberian Peninsula. The shining halo of spiky rays, symbolizing the Sun of Justice, is typical in Marian iconography of her portrayal as an apocalyptic Virgin.

On the American continent, the earliest known image of Guadalupe, considered by the faithful to be the miraculous apron of the Nahuatl Juan Diego, hangs in the basilica in Mexico City. Some scholars maintain it was painted by a Nahuatl artist called Marcos around 1556, the year cited by historian Edmundo O'Gorman as the date of the formal recognition of Guadalupe's cult in New Spain. Beyond this legendary canvas no other depictions of Guadalupe are known to have been made in the sixteenth century.

The next painting still extant was made in 1606 by the skillful hand of Baltasar de Echave Orio, and during the next 150 years a large number of images show the slow mutating process whereby the image gradually became that of a mestiza. Her mantle changes from blue to green, her robe from pink to red, and the little angel's wings beneath her turn red, white, and green. It is worthy of note, however, that the latter three colors were fixed by artists portraying the Virgin long before they were proclaimed the colors of the national flag.

In its gradual transformation through two hundred years, the image suffers only a few conceptual changes—minor ones in the 1920s and 1930s, somewhat more radical ones in the early 1960s. There is, though, one notable exception during that span of time. It is the depiction that hangs hidden on one of the vestry walls of the cathedral of the city of Morelia. Its author, of whom very little is known, was Pur'hepecha, which may partly explain the obscurity to which he was relegated. Master Pitacua painted his innovative work probably in the mid 1700s.

Not only does this Pur'hepecha artist portray the Virgin inclining her head in angles different from those prescribed by tradition, the artist has Guadalupe hovering over the three Magi. Melchior—white-haired, balding, and bearded—is portrayed as a European; he is, predictably, the wisest since he is depicted as the eldest of the three. Balthazar is black, and remains the representation of Africa. But Master Pitacua's allegiance to his own people shines powerfully through in his rendering of Caspar, who is brown-skinned. It is not certain whether Caspar's beard was a concession to the work's commissioners (who may have suggested portraying a mestizo rather than a full-blooded Pur'hepecha), or whether it was added by its renovator, Pérez de la Busta, in 1877. A banner at the bottom of the painting proclaims, "*Only Mexico has this great happiness.*"

What makes this work so significant (and most likely the reason it was banished to a vestry wall) is the fact that the city of Morelia, at the time called Valladolid, was the capital of the Pur'hepecha nation (today the state of Michoacán). At the time Master Pitacua painted his version of Guadalupe, the city was the intellectual capital of the insurrectional movement in Mexico's struggle for independence from Spain.

Whoever decides to study the Virgin's image and its mutations in the latter part of the twentieth century will have to pay very special attention to the Marian visions created *beyond* Mexico's borders, specifically in the United States of America.

In Mexico as well as in the United States, the orthodox image of Guadalupe is most ubiquitous as a printed chrome that reproduces José Amador's 1823 rendering of the Virgin, based in turn either on Luis Cabrera's 1776 painting or on José de Alcíbar's oil of 1783.[4]

But of late, *la Virgencita Morena* has been appearing in guises and

[4]Elisa Vargas Lupo, op. cit.

stances very different from the norm: as a sock-darning grandmother; as a long-distance runner in tennis shoes; holding hands
with Emiliano Zapata; as an almost naked table dancer; even as a
pious skeleton, in direct reference to José Guadalupe Posada's famous Day of the Dead imagery. Her contexts change continu-
ously: she hovers protectively above farmworkers or urban gang
youths. She assumes the form of a tree or is viewed in the company
of Coatlicue and Tlazolteotl. She has even lent her spiky, apoca-
lyctic halo to other iconic figures of the past and the present.

Credit for this renaissance must be given to Chicano artists who
have in the past twenty-five years featured the revered icon in murals, carvings, and multimedia art. Once again, her other, more ancient self, Tonantzin, has come to the fore. Their iconoclastic
depictions, forceful and dynamic, have been transforming the *vision* of Guadalupe-Tonantzin in direct response to issues that concern their communities, whose inhabitants readily identify and
sympathize with her new look. So much so that the Catholic
Church seems to have refrained, at least openly, from expressing
its objections.

In the same manner as Pitacua in the mid-eighteenth century,
Chicano artists like the visionary Yolanda López of California or
the muralist group *Artes Guadalupanas de Aztlán"* of New Mexico
dared defy tradition and orthodoxy and render *their* versions of
Guadalupe.

The Chicano's unabashed use of Guadalupe's image is, in fact,
a new epiphany that deals with self-empowerment. It is about a people, downtrodden, mostly brown-skinned, who seek to *reconstruct*
the deity's presence, and in doing so, manage to define her useful-
ness to their causes.

This in itself marks a hiatus in contemporary art: whereas Mexican art had been a source reference for Chicano artists, the tables
have turned, and the Chicanos have become an important influence
on contemporary Mexican art. More and more artists in the "mother"
country are now offering their own versions of the icon's image.

It is foremost a pragmatic relationship, the one all Mexicans—at
home and abroad—have with *la Virgencita*, the little Virgin. It is what

allows me, a non-Catholic artist of Jewish background, to consider myself a Guadalupan Jew. I am by no means being facetious. My regard for her, both as an artist and as a believer, has nothing whatsoever to do with Catholicism or even religion. I think the trust I have in her is simply a consequence of being Mexican, much like marking the Day of the Dead every year. It is in fact a feeling that allows me, for example, to accept with pleasure any news of the whereabouts of our very own Guadalupe, the one that accompanied us to San Salvador in her frame.

"She now lives in a very nice brick chapel the barrio built for her as an annex to the church. We call it the Mexican Chapel," reported a couple of Salvadoran teenagers, a brother and sister who had worked with the *Barrio a Barrio* project in San Salvador. They stayed a few days in my house a couple of years ago on their way north—illegally—to the United States. They made it—thanks to a Guadalupan organization.

The Two Guadalupes

GUILLERMO
GÓMEZ-PEÑA

When Ana Castillo first asked me to write a text about the Virgin of Guadalupe, I must confess that I was somewhat troubled by the idea. Why? Growing up under the agnostic fog of the seventies counterculture in Mexico City, I learned that religion was often used as a demagogic tool of control; and that the *movimiento guadalupano* was essentially a fundamentalist Catholic movement operating out of fear of modernity and change. The Virgin was certainly not aware of the way her powerful image as the "Mother of all Mexicans" was being used by zealots. She didn't know, and still doesn't know that, in her name, many people in Mexico have been forced into social submission, political passivity, and fear: fear of religious and cultural difference, fear of sex and "sin," fear of eternal punishment, fear of contradicting the majority, fear of being an inadequate Mexican. And ultimately, fear of metaphysical orphanhood, of not belonging to the great and harmonious Mexican family.

Mexico's ruling party, the PRI, has always been keenly aware of the importance of nurturing a mythology capable of unifying an otherwise extremely diverse society. In the official Olympus of *la mexicanidad*, "la Reina" Guadalupe stands proud next to Moctezuma, Cuauhtémoc, Father Hidalgo, Benito Juárez, Emiliano Zapata, and a few other mighty Mexicans. And together, they guard our identity, our national character, and our sovereignty. Again, *la Virgen* doesn't know it.

In the late 1970s, I realized that although I was a strong critic of institutionalized Catholicism, whether I liked it or not I was culturally and ethnically a Catholic, and that my (ex-Catholic) agnosticism was merely the other side of the same coin. In other words, five hundred years of Mexican Catholicism couldn't simply be erased with political awareness. When I began to write poetry and practice performance art, inadvertently Catholic images and ritual ceremonies began to appear in my work, right next to my confrontational politics, my pagan (and eclectic) spirituality, and my wild sexual explorations. Despite a conscious rejection of formalized religion, my sensibility and my symbolic languages were soaked in the pathos, the high drama, and the excessive aesthetics of Mexican Catholicism. And this of course got me into serious trouble.

In late 1983, I was abruptly made aware of the dangers of recontextualizing Catholic imagery, especially that of *"the Chida One."* My performance troupe, Poyesis Genetica, and I were rehearsing a piece titled "Ocnoceni" (Nahuatl for "In some other place") at the Casa de la Cultura in Tijuana. In one scene, a slide of the Virgin of Guadalupe was projected onto the white *hábito* of a gigantic nun (on stilts). In the piece, the nun suddenly broke into a sweaty tropical dance, and began doing a striptease. The night before the opening, during dress rehearsal, a group of conservative-looking women in their fifties sat quietly in the back row of the theater. We didn't pay much attention to them. They stayed for an hour and left. The next morning when my colleagues and I went back to the theater we were told by the security guards what had happened. A group of militant *guadalupanos,* tipped off by the women who witnessed the rehearsal, had broken into the theater at night and trashed the set. They took a gallon of theater blood and painted religious slogans all over the floor and back wall. The message was clear: You simply don't mess around with the Great Mother of Mexico. We cleaned up the mess in silence. Despite the chilling effect this incident had on us, we had to open the show and perform it for four consecutive nights.

In 1987, an artist named De la Rosa had a more frightening experience. He opened a show at the Museo de Arte Moderno in Mexico City with collages in which he superimposed pop cultural images onto Catholic iconography. One of the pieces was a Virgin of Guadalupe with the face of Marilyn Monroe. Another one presented a Christ preceding the Last Supper with the face of legendary Mexican actor and ranchero singer Pedro Infante. Soon after the opening, a crowd of fierce *guadalupanos* stormed into the museum and demanded the removal of the director. It was election time, and in order to appease the conservative opposition, the Mexican government complied and fired the troubled museum director. It was a sad day for Mexican freedom of speech.

Effectively, *la Guadalupe* is an untouchable icon. If we research the myriad *chistes* (irreverent jokes) with Catholic references, we can find Jesus Christ, Mary Magdalena, the apostles, and even the Pope engaging in outrageous behavior, but *la Virgen* is conspicuously absent. There might only be one or two *chistes* about her, and they are pretty tame.

When I came to California in 1978, my relationship with what I saw as official Mexican iconography began to change. Suddenly the political and religious images that I used to question as icons of authority and as artificial generators of *mexicanidad* began to transform themselves into symbols of contestation against the dominant Anglo culture. I also discovered that my Chicano colleagues had a very different connection to Guadalupan imagery. They had expropriated it, reactivated it, recontextualized it, and turned it into a symbol of resistance, something that Mexicans have never been able to fully understand. (Progressive Mexican intellectuals still see Chicanos as naive *guadalupanos*.) In the Chicano movement, *la Virgen* was no longer the contemplative mestiza Mother of all Mexicans, but a warrior goddess who blessed the cultural and political weapons of activists and artists. She was against racism, the border patrol, the cops, and supremacist politicians. And in the Chicano feminist Olympus, *la Guadalupana* stood defiant and compassionate as a symbol of female strength, right next to *la Malinche*, Frida, Sor Juana, and more recently, Selena. (Again, the Mexican intelligentsia cannot quite comprehend the mysterious connection between these icons, which they find extremely corny.) She was no longer just standing motionless with praying hands and an aloof gaze. She actually walked; she showed up in demonstrations and strikes, and lent her image for barrio murals, album covers, T-shirts, and political posters. She could even sit down and take a break, abandon temporarily her holy diorama and jog, or let a working-class woman temporarily take her place, as in the artwork of Lopes. Clearly Chicanos were able to reinvent and activate the icon of *la Guadalupe* in a way that would be unthinkable in Mexico. And this became apparent when the Mexican feminist magazine *Fem* decided to publish on its cover an image of a jogging Guadalupe by Yolanda López. They received several bomb threats and were forced to pull back. It really wasn't until the mid to late 1980s when Mexican artists, mainly the *neomexicanista* painters, began to use images of Guadalupe in their artwork. And even then, she was merely a decorative and somewhat neutral folk icon; a playful yet depoliticized symbol of *mexicanidad.* It wasn't a coincidence that some of these painters were heavily promoted by the Mexican government as part of its diplomatic cultural agenda.

My secondary hesitation to write this text was irrational. For years I felt that the mythology of *la Guadalupe* was an exclusive domain of Chicana artists and writers. Ana spelled out this fear for me: "Precisely because of this, I want you to write about it. There is very little writing on *la Virgen* done by men."

Now that I have accepted the challenge of my literary *comadre,* I am slowly beginning to disentangle my contradictory feelings about Guadalupe. Despite my continuous critique of the way her image has been used by conservative movements, my house in Mexico City is filled with *guadalupanobilia.* Throughout the years, I have collected 3-D portraits, bakery calendars, and electric figurines that light up. I also have key chains, mugs, bolo ties, belts, pillows, and even a towel with her image. And every year, on December 11 at midnight, I "religiously" go to the Basilica de Guadalupe to spend the night and witness the arrival of the largest pilgrimage in the Americas. Like every other Mexican, whether I like it nor not, I may suffer from an acute oedipal complex. Like most agnostic Mexicans, I might in fact be a very religious individual.

With the great spiritual crises of the end of the century, my performance colleagues and I have undertaken a dangerous spiritual challenge: to create ritual contexts capable of containing and expressing our fears and contradictions, our political uncertainties and cultural complexities. In the past two years, we have engaged in what appears to be extremely religious/(anti)religious artistic behavior. *Verbi gratia:* In early 1994, I crucified myself on a twelve-by-sixteen-foot wooden cross dressed as a stereotypical "undocumented *bandido,*" next to my *compadre* Roberto Sifuentes, who crucified himself as a "generic gang member." In this activist performance piece, Roberto and I were not exactly commemorating the death of Jesus Christ. We were commenting on the climate of xenophobia currently afflicting California, and the fact that Mexican immigrants and Latino youths are being blamed for all social ills and publicly "crucified" by nativist politicians and the mainstream media. With a flyer we asked our audience "to free us from our martyrdom and bring us down from the crosses as an act of political commitment." Mesmerized by the melancholy of the image, it took them over three hours to figure out how to get us down without a ladder. In another project titled "The Temple of Confessions," Roberto and I exhibited ourselves for three-day periods inside Plexiglas boxes as "living (border) saints." We asked our audiences to "confess" to us their innermost fears and desires about Mexico, Mexicans, immigrants, and Spanish language. My colleagues and I have also created performance characters who comment on the great cultural wars of the 1990s, and many of them are religious hybrids: *chola*/nuns, holy gang members, crucified Zapatistas, border shamans, and pop cultural madonnas. In our end-of-the-century mythology, Guadalupe has emerged with an entirely new meaning. She is a media star, *"la tele Virgen,"* an anti-NAFTA heroine, and a pro-immigration activist. And her flamboyant colleagues, Virgins of sorts—*del cruce, de la contaminación, de la crisis de identidad*—stand for pertinent political causes.

Understandably, since Proposition 187 passed and California once again became a xenophobic nightmare for Mexican immigrants, there have been several sightings of the Virgin in Mexican barrios. The sense of orphanhood and fragility currently experienced by the Mexican population in the U.S. has increased the faith in her. She simply cannot abandon us. She's got to be on this side of the border; in our own neighborhood and workplace, guarding our vulnerable backs against racist policemen, insensitive employers, and citizen vigilantes.

For the first time in history, the Virgin might have a similar meaning for Mexicans in Mexico. Last December 12, at the basilica, the three million Mexicans who gathered to celebrate *la Guadalupe* were there with a different purpose than other years. They went to ask her to help them outlive the crises; to fight unemployment, urban violence, and corrupt politicians. They were looking for a highly politicized Virgin. Paradoxically, when my friends and I arrived at the altar, we saw President Zedillo in the first row. And the masses behind were hoping to fight everything he stands for *through* her.

Today in 1996, I don't think I am more or less "religious" or "spiritual" than I was twenty years ago. I simply think that as a Mexican immigrant in process of Chicanization, I have learned to understand that symbols, no matter how charged they might be, can be emptied out and refilled; that religion in postmodernity is intertwined with pop and mass culture, and that I, as a border citizen, must constantly reinvent my identity using all the elements that my three cultures have provided me with. For this purpose, *la Guadalupe* has been good to me. She understands my multiple dilemmas and contradictions. She stands next to me on every battlefront. And like my mother, she has the unique capability of making me feel extremely guilty when I fuck up.

The Doll

LUIS ALFARO

We used to have this *Virgen de Guadalupe* night-light. Every time you connected her to an outlet, she would turn and bless all sides of the room.

We bought her on one of my dad's surprise drunken trips to Tijuana. He would come home from the racetrack at about midnight, wake us up, get us dressed, and we would all hop into the station wagon. My mom drove and my dad lowered the seat in the back and he slept with us. My grandmother, *la Abuela*, lived in one of the *colonias*. She hated our three a.m. visits. But you see, *blood is thicker than water, family is greater than friends, and Our Lady watches over all of us.*

When I was ten, I gave the *Virgen* night-light to my *tía* Ofelia. My *tía* Ofelia lived across the street with my *tía* Tita, who lived with my *tío* Tony, who lived next door to my *tía* Romie. Back in those days, everybody was either a *tía* or a *tío*. They lived in a big beautiful two-story house with a balcony overlooking the street below. We were crowded in by downtown skyscrapers, packs of roving *cholos*, the newly built Convention Center on Pico, and portable tamale stands. But our families always managed to live together, because we all knew: *Blood is thicker than water, family is greater than friends, and Our Lady watches over all of us.*

My *tía* lived on the second floor, and on the first lived the Eighteenth Street Gang. There was Smiley, Sleepy, and La Sadgirl, and a bunch of other homeboys who hung out in the front yard playing Bloodstones' "Natural High." They split, like *cucarachas* exposed to light, at the sight of a cop car slowly cruising through our Pico-Union neighborhood, like tourists on Hollywood Boulevard.

My *tía*, she hated *cholos* and she would spit the seeds of grapes she ate out the window, just to annoy them. She was like all of my relatives back then—a grape picker from Delano, California. She claimed to have dated César Chávez, and to know everyone in McFarland, Tulare, and Visalia, the farmworker capitals of *el mundo.* I couldn't call her a liar, because she had *breast cancer.* My mom told us this in a voice reserved for nights when we didn't want to wake up my dad after one of his drunken soccer celebrations. Doctors at County General took away her tits in hopes of driving away *la Bruja Maldita,* who was slowly eating at her insides. When she was feeling okay, my *tía* would tell me stories about the farmworker movement and picking cherries one summer.

The day I brought her the rotating Our Lady doll, I knew she was in pain. I knew I probably should have waited, but I asked her quite innocently if I could see her chest. She slapped me hard on the face, calling me a *malcriado.* While she sobbed, her hand searched for medication. I felt so bad that day. Even I could feel *la Bruja Maldita* eating at my heart. I never got the nerve to go back up there again.

Weeks went by and my *tía* continued to rock in her chair. When the weeks turned to months, she slowly started to forget us. People would walk by and offer up a *"Buenas tardes, Señora,"* but you could tell she was having trouble remembering faces. My grandmother sent a crate of grapes to help her remember, but nothing worked. My mom and my *tía* Romie said that my *tía* Ofelia was becoming a baby, *otra vez. La Bruja Maldita* ate at her bones and slowly she started to melt like the G.I. Joes that my brother and I set fire to with burning tamale leaves. Her cheeks caved in like the plaster *calaveras* that you could buy at the border on *el día de los muertos.* And one day, on my way home from school, I looked up and she was gone.

Phones rang, food poured in, little envelopes with twenty-dollar bills. Hysterical screams from aunts on a Mexico-to-L.A. party line. Dramatic uncles openly wept and the tears of my relatives were covered with huge veils that they wore to our parish, Immaculate Conception. My grandmother, *la Abuela,* got into the drama when, at the burial, she jumped onto the coffin, screaming.

A few weeks later, the Crips drove by and shouted, *"Chump Motherfuckers. Greasy-assed Messicans. Go back to Teehuana!"* And they firebombed the Eighteenth Street Gang on the bottom floor. A great ball of fire and light filled the downtown sky, and for just a moment there, it was better than fireworks at Dodger Stadium. But it lasted for just a moment. Then seriousness took over. Followed by weeks of tears and sorrows and that same story about my *tía's* escape from the second story. Crazy relatives would start crying every time you turned on the burner on the stove.

Smiley, Sleepy, and La Sadgirl died, but we couldn't go to the funeral because my dad said they were *perros desgraciados.* Instead, we rummaged through charred remains looking for usable clothes and my *tía's* collection of Vicki Carr records.

My brother found what was left of the Our Lady doll and he used her head for BB gun practice. My mom cried because the memory of my *tía* Ofelia would now be an empty lot where bums would piss and tires would grow. Every day she watered a little flower she had planted in memory of my *tía* Ofelia, until the Community Redevelopment Agency built the Pico-Union Projects over her memory.

When I was eighteen, I met this guy with a rotating Our Lady doll. He bought it in Mexico, so, of course, I fell in love.

His skin was white, he ate broccoli, and he spoke like actors in a TV series. He was every *Partridge Family/Brady Bunch* episode rolled into one. He taught me many things—how to kiss like the French, lick an earlobe, and dance in the dark. Once, my grandmother, *la Abuela,* sent us lovers a crate of grapes. We took off our clothes, smashed the grapes all over our bodies, and licked them off each other.

When he left, *la Bruja Maldita's* hand replaced his in my heart. And she pounded on it. She laughed like Mexican mothers laugh while hanging *la ropa* at a clothesline. My sorrow was so strong, but I kept it hidden with smiles that were like the veils my aunts wore at Immaculate Conception church. But my sorrow bled through, like stigmata, like rushing waters, and my relatives would say, *Ay mijo,* don't you understand? *Blood is thicker than water, family is greater than friends, and that old Virgin, Our Lady, she just watches over all of us. . . .*

Our Lady of Guadalupe and the Soup

NANCY MAIRS

*T*aking an unfamiliar shortcut through a residential neigh-borhood on Tucson's west side, my husband screeches to a halt and throws the van into reverse, bobbing me around like one of those dashboard puppies in my wheelchair in the back. "Look at that!" George cries, pulling up beside a mural depicting La Virgen de Guadalupe painted on a hole-in-the-wall grocery, La Tiendita, at the corner of two empty streets. "Isn't that wonderful!" Such wall art is common here, especially in the barrios, and it often features La Guadalupana, as do jewelry, scarves, and other articles of clothing, and even the hoods of automobiles. This is a relatively crude production, not signed: the figure faces the wrong direction, and most of the significant details are missing. But she stands upon the head of a truly glorious fanged serpent, painted a violet so in-tense that it shivers in the opalescent light of an overcast winter day in the desert, surrounded by scowling brown pre-Columbian heads. The overall effect is exuberant and, indeed, wonderful, a trea-sure stumbled upon in haste.

Perhaps because we're in a hurry, it doesn't occur to me until hours later, as I settle in to begin this essay, that I am, both aes-thetically and spiritually, not the woman I used to be. I was cer-tainly brought up to know that the colors in that mural clashed. Except the brown, of course—but oh! those hideous lowering pro-files with their huge noses and pendulous lips! And besides, images of saints, even those painted in the most delicate pastels, though marginally tolerable in museums, simply weren't to be put on dis-play in the everyday world. The Mary on the Half Shell decorat-ing a front lawn, the pale plastic statue on a dashboard ("I don't care if it rains or freezes, long as I got my plastic Jesus . . ."), the Saint

Christopher medal around a traveler's neck: revolting! And now here I am admiring a garish Virgin painted on a public wall. I guess that shows what Catholicism—even a relatively late conversion—can do to you.

On the whole, I do not regret my Protestant girlhood. With advancing age and accelerating physical debility, I have gotten out of the habit of regret. The alternative, I am afraid, would drive me mad, and I no longer wish to go mad, a state I endured with horror during my Protestant youth, not ever again. And anyway, the memories of Catholic girlhood I've read and listened to suggest that although I missed a great deal, most of it wasn't the sort of experience to be coveted. I've known woman after woman of my generation who still seethes about some elements of her religious upbringing: obtuse and even abusive nuns and priests who wielded church doctrine along with yardsticks or birch switches to intimidate their young charge, inculcating superstition and self-hatred so poisonous that, even after decades at a safe distance, she still can't speak of those dreary years without a frisson of revulsion. In the long run, Congregationalism left me a little flat, all the mystery scrubbed out of it by a vigorous and slightly vinegary reason, but hardly furious.

All the same, I do wish (and in this I may be more curious than rueful) that it had offered me the Blessed Virgin Mary. Or any feminine figure, for that matter. It may not have been altogether wholesome for a girl to grow up venerating women who leaped out of coffins and soared to the rafters to escape the stench of human flesh, like Saint Christina the Astonishing, or in response to compliments on their beauty rubbed pepper on their faces and lime on their hands, like Saint Rose of Lima. But another kind of soul-sickness, even more enervating in its way, arises in those deprived of any sense of identity with the divine. In Congregationalism I encountered a rather abstract but unequivocally masculine God and, of course, His Son, as well as a Holy Ghost, suitably attenuated and untainted by any association with Sophia. No saints, except the guys who composed the Christian Scriptures. And no holy representatives on earth, except maybe the minister, who was invariably—and without question—a man.

Prayer, within such a structure, was always to an Other, who could be counted on to judge but not always to understand, if you had your period, say, and needed the cramps to stop, or if you were crazy in love with your boyfriend and wanted more than life itself to go all the way and had no idea where you were going to find the strength to say no. This latter situation was especially troublesome, since in Congregationalism the loss of one's virginity was strictly prohibited without any notably spiritual point being put upon the matter. Since the King James Version, like others, reproduced the mistranslation *parthenos*, "virgin," for the Semitic term for a young unmarried woman, we referred to Jesus' mother as the Virgin Mary when we referred to her at all, which wasn't all that often, but no one ever suggested to me that I should preserve my virginity in order to emulate her chastity and obedience to God. No, mine was being "saved" for the husband I would inevitably have (though it wasn't until I discovered feminist theory twenty years later that I figured out why society thought it important enough to save). Not just her virginity, however, but also her motherhood would have provided a valuable model, in my struggles as a daughter and, not many years later, a mother myself.

Because I sensed a mysterious element here for which the utter virility of the Congregationalist godhead failed to account, from early adolescence onward I coveted the saints, what little I could gather about them from books and films, having no Catholic friends, and especially Mary, whose multiplicity—maiden and mother intertwined—authenticated the personal mysteries I was destined to experience yet feared to endure without guidance. Her presence, if I could make it real in my life, could create spiritual space not for the encounter of God and man but for the bond between the holy and me.

Sometimes when alone I'd cross myself and murmur a Hail Mary, which I must have learned young from hearing the Rosary prayed as I twiddled the radio dial, and this habit persisted as I grew older. I did not pray to the Madonnas I studied in art class in college, but I contemplated their images—the severe dark skinny Byzantines, the luminous Italians—until they became a permanent part of my interior furnishings. Although I later named my daughter for my mother, I knew that the name Anne had belonged to Mary's mother, too. At last, I began to walk boldly into Catholic churches, forbidden me in my youth, staring—amused, awed, appalled—at painted statues got up in silk and stiff lace with browning bridal bouquets at their feet. In these ways, I suppose, I was preparing myself for the conversion I would eventually choose, whereby I claimed her for my own.

I don't know whether I'd have become a Roman Catholic had I remained in New England. But if I had, I feel certain that I would never have developed a devotion to Our Lady of Guadalupe. In fact, I'd probably never even have heard of her. In the area around Boston where I grew up, Catholic parishes tended to be identified ethnically. The Irish who went to St. Jude's would never have strayed into the Italian—or Portuguese or Polish or French-Canadian—Sacred Heart across town. Even though Pope Pius XII designated Our Lady of Guadalupe "Empress of the Americas"—from Eagle, Alaska, to Tierra del Fuego, North, Central, and South—in 1945, only a church attended by Mexicans or Mexican Americans would likely be dedicated to her. And certainly none would be in Enon, Massachusetts. (Of the 106 such churches in the United States as of 1980,[1] I doubt that any are in Massachusetts.) To find her, I really did have to move to the Southwest.

Thanks perhaps to a persistent Protestant intractability, I have an uneasy relationship with the miraculous. In fact, the notion of a miracle as an act of God for my benefit, which seems to underlie the use of the word by the devout, embarrasses the hell out of me. When a woman tells me that she has just escaped death because, at the last moment, God deflected an onrushing car off the road and into the desert, I wonder how she accounts for all the collisions that do take place. Does God find those people unworthy of rescue? Or does God blink? Even though my joyous life is made possible by a miracle, George having survived metastatic melanoma for some years now, and even though the wailing infant in me petitions constantly *Dear God please please don't ever let him die and leave me*, I prefer not to look on his good health as a special favor from the Almighty lest I should, at remission's end, be forced to believe myself personally abandoned.

And so my mind scuttles away from flood and pestilence and

[1] Philip E. Lampe, "Our Lady of Guadalupe: Victim of Prejudice or Ignorance?," *Listening: Journal of Religion and Culture* 21 (1): 9.

La Guadalupana's mysterious eyes. With the political features of her manifestation, however, I can engage quite comfortably. In *indigenista* terms, her image and message clearly inform the issues of social justice that first drew me into Catholic practice and, against all odds, sustain me there. The figure, according to this interpretation, encodes the concepts necessary to effect the conversion of eight million Indians in the seven years following the apparition.[2] (The desirability of becoming a Catholic is a moot point, I recognize, today as four centuries ago, but I won't get into it here. What's done is done.) To begin with, "Guadalupe" is probably a mistranslation, influenced by the shrine in Spain, of the name she spoke when she appeared to Juan Diego's uncle; she might more accurately be referred to as Our Lady of Tepeyac. Several Náhuatl alternatives have been suggested, the most widely accepted being "Coatlaxopeuh," that is, "she who crushed the serpent's head,"[3] which suggests the overpowering of the native gods by Christianity.

The icon itself reinforces this idea. It represents a woman with dark skin and hair (La Morenita, she is therefore sometimes called), her eyes downcast, in contrast to the straightforward gaze of Indian gods, and her hands raised before her in an Indian offertory gesture. She wears a rose-colored shift filigreed in gold, and over it a cloak of blue-green, a color reserved for the chief god Omecihuatl, or Ome-Téotl, scattered with gold stars auguring a new age. The black maternity band at her waist signifies someone yet to come, and below it, over her womb, may appear the powerful Mesoamerican cross to suggest just how mighty that Someone will be. The rays surrounding her form show her eclipsing the Sun Lord Tonatiuh; and the blackened crescent beneath her feet may be a phase of Venus, associated with Quetzalcóatl, the sacred Plumed Serpent. Hence the appropriateness of the name Coatlaxopeuh. She is borne by an intermediary "angel," the carrier of time and thus of a new era.[4]

[2]Harold J. Rahm, S.J., "Our Lady of Guadalupe," pamphlet, no publishing information.

[3]Miguel Leatham, "*Indigenista* Hermeneutics and the Historical Meaning of Our Lady of Guadalupe of Mexico," *Folklore Forum* 22 (1/2), 30.

[4]James E. Fiedler, reprint from the *Denver Catholic Register*, December 7, 1977; Leatham.

Some of these signs seem hardly less fanciful than do miraculous remedies and mysterious ocular reflections, but that's not really their point. Their power lies in the suggestion that the Virgin appeared, long before the establishment of political boundaries in the "New World," to indigenous people whose old world had begun to crumble even before the Spanish invasion; she may thus signify both the "liberation and salvation" their prophets had predicted and the new spirit early Christian missionaries hoped to find here.[5] In this sense, she is a thoroughly American[6] saint, and her relegation by U.S. Catholics to Mexico and the Southwest, identifying her dark-skinned image with "an economically and socially unsuccessful and, hence, unacceptable ethnic group,"[7] probably does reflect bias against a minority woefully underrepresented among the clergy.

Ironically, however, this possibility strengthens her appeal for those of us, whether of Mexican heritage or not, who believe, as Virgilio Elizondo puts it, that "the role of the powerless is to evangelize the powerful."[8] A reviewer of one of my books once took me to task for accepting the tenets of feminist and liberation theology merely on faith, as though one could not possibly, after long contemplation and appraisal, continue to affirm them. But God's preferential option for the poor—expressed at least as far back as Isaiah's cry for the protection of widows and fatherless children—rings true to my understanding of the Christian ethos. I must accept it, both on faith and on reflection, and act upon it if I am to carry out God's will. And in the tale of a dark-skinned peasant carrying to the conquistadores for their veneration the image of a dark-skinned Lady who promised her compassion to all humanity (even, I must suppose, the conquistadores) lies a model of the care I am, I believe, required to give.

She entered our urban, white, middle-class lives slowly. George

---

[5]Fiedler.

[6]A term only residents of the United States would arrogate exclusively to themselves.

[7]Lampe, 11, 12.

[8]Quoted by Fiedler.

and I had converted to Catholicism not for its saints but in spite of them; and not knowing quite what to do with them, we politely ignored them, the way you might some atavistic eccentricity in an otherwise sophisticated friend. This is rather hard to do if, every week of your life, you ask Blessed Mary Ever Virgin, all the angels and saints, and your brothers and sisters to pray for you to God. Clearly these holy figures were integral to spiritual health in a way we didn't quite fathom. Still don't, I might add, and probably never will. When I hear my elderly friends talk about Our Blessed Mother, I suspect you may have to be brought up Catholic to fully apprehend the role of an intercessor in devotional life. I still tend to talk to God directly, a habit fixed by the time I was thirteen, and probably nowhere near as courteously as Our Blessed Mother would do for me.

Rather than a repository of prayer, Our Lady of Guadalupe was initially for me an exhorter to social action. In order to avoid being shut down by resentful neighbors, Casa María, the Catholic Worker house of hospitality in Tucson, was consecrated to her. The kitchen there is known as Our Lady of Guadalupe Chapel and Free Kitchen, and any tramp in the city can probably direct you to "Guadalupe's," identifiable by a brilliant painting of her on the wall beside the front door, where a sack lunch with soup is offered every day and Mass on Monday mornings. As George and I became increasingly involved in the community there, we began to think of her as the guardian of the thousand and more *pobrecitos* who lined up each day to be fed. And so it seemed natural, when our daughter left us to live in Africa, to light a candle in the lady chapel of our church after Mass each week and ask her to watch over Anne as her human parents could no longer do.

For my birthday one year George gave me a framed poster of her image. "What on earth will Mother say?" I wondered as we hung this icon on the bedroom wall. "Next thing you know, we'll be getting statues!" Sure enough. Above me as a write, in a niche formed by an old cooler duct, stands a porcelain Virgen (too white, but I was politically ignorant all those years ago when I bought her) surrounded by two garish plastic flowers made at a local senior center and the likenesses of the Dalai Lama, Dorothy Day, and the deep-blue Medicine Buddha. Now she is everywhere in our lives:

on the painted tiles outside the front door; on a plaque enameled by Salvadoran refugees in Guatemala, where the hill she stands on is dotted with animals, including a fat armadillo; as a crude little figure carved out of wood, the rays around her formed out of yellow toothpicks. I even have her likeness hand-painted on a T-shirt by a Casa María worker, holding a soup ladle and a white Styrofoam cup. Nuestra Señora del Caldo, I call her. Our Lady of the Soup. Glimpses of these images each day as I move from task to task serve to remind me to be grateful for the gift of roses in midwinter and to pray for the protection of us all.

Passover

MIRIAM SAGAN

Jews must be everywhere
Even in La Puebla, New Mexico
Where we pass Good Friday pilgrims
Wearing Walkmans
Dusty along the highway.
It's Shabbos, the two sets of candles
Adorn the tables
Set with sea shells
Seder means: the order
In which things happen
Egypt means: narrows
For plagues we dip our fingers in the wine
Hail kills your tomato plants
You quarrel
With a neighbor about a wall
A friend is unexpectedly in jail
Baby cries in the emergency room
Homeless men sleep in the arroyo
Stumble across Paseo to the liquor store
So drink four cups of wine
It's only the second time this year
Jews must get drunk
And lie down with our shoes off
On comfortable couches
The children are playing in the dusk
My daughter feeds a large white horse
A bunch of golden apples
Desert smells like the sea

Of sand and wind and something else
Clean, and scoured
Miriam's Well
Springs within
Green oasis that must
Reappear within our hearts
Voices singing slightly off-key
This source of water
Follows us
Despite our exile, wandering.

The Sons of La Malinche

OCTAVIO PAZ

Our hermeticism is baffling or even offensive to strangers, and it has created the legend of the Mexican as an inscrutable being. Our suspicions keep us at a distance. Our courtesy may be attractive but our reserve is chilling, and the stranger is always disconcerted by the unforeseen violence that lacerates us, by the solemn or convulsive splendor of our fiestas, by our cult of death. The impression we create is much like that created by Orientals. They too—the Chinese, the Hindus, the Arabs—are hermetic and indecipherable. They too carry about with them, in rags, a still-living past. There is a Mexican mystery just as there is a yellow mystery or a black. The details of the image formed of us often vary with the spectator, but it is always an ambiguous if not contradictory image: we are insecure, and our responses, like our silences, are unexpected and unpredictable. Treachery, loyalty, crime and love hide out in the depths of our glance. We attract and repel.

It is not difficult to understand the origins of this attitude toward us. The European considers Mexico to be a country on the margin of universal history, and everything that is distant from the center of his society strikes him as strange and impenetrable. The peasant—remote, conservative, somewhat archaic in his ways of dressing and speaking, fond of expressing himself in traditional modes and formulas—has always had a certain fascination for the urban man. In every country he represents the most ancient and secret element of society. For everyone but himself he embodies the occult, the hidden, that which surrenders itself only with great difficulty: a buried treasure, a seed that sprouts in the bowels of the earth, an ancient wisdom hiding among the folds of the land.

Woman is another being who lives apart and is therefore an enigmatic figure. It would be better to say that she is the Enigma. She attracts and repels like men of an alien race or nationality. She is an image of both fecundity and death. In almost every culture the goddesses of creation are also goddesses of destruction. Woman is a living symbol of the strangeness of the universe and its radical heterogeneity. As such, does she hide life within herself, or death? What does she think? Or does she think? Does she truly have feelings? Is she the same as we are? Sadism begins as a revenge against feminine hermeticism or as a desperate attempt to obtain a response from a body we fear is insensible. As Luis Cernuda has said, "Desire is a question that has no answer." Despite woman's full, rounded nakedness, there is always something on guard in her:

Eve and Aphrodite concentrate the mystery of the world's heart.

Rubén Darío, like all the other great poets, considered woman to be not only an instrument of knowledge but also knowledge itself. It is a knowledge we will never possess, the sum of our definitive ignorance: the supreme mystery.

In our daily language there is a group of words that are prohibited, secret, without clear meanings. We confide the expression of our most brutal or subtle emotions and reactions to their magical ambiguities. They are evil words, and we utter them in a loud voice only when we are not in control of ourselves. In a confused way they reflect our intimacy: the explosions of our vitality light them up and the depressions of our spirit darken them. They constitute a sacred language like those of children, poetry and sects. Each letter and syllable has a double life, at once luminous and obscure, that reveals and hides us. They are words that say nothing and say everything. Adolescents, when they want to appear like men, speak them in a hoarse voice. Women also repeat them, sometimes to demonstrate their freedom of spirit, sometimes to prove the truth of their feelings. But these words are definitive and categorical, despite their ambiguities and the ease with which their meanings change. They are the bad words, the only living language in a world of anemic vocables. They are poetry within the reach of everyone.

Each country has its own. In ours, with their brief, aggressive, electric syllables, resembling the flash given off by a knife when it strikes a hard opaque body, we condense all our appetites, all our hatreds and enthusiasms, all the longings that rage unexpressed in the depths of our being. The word is our sign and seal. By means of it we recognize each other among strangers, and we use it every time the real conditions of our being rise to our lips. To know it, to use it, to throw it in the air like a toy or to make it quiver like a sharp weapon, is a way of affirming that we are Mexican.

All of our anxious tensions express themselves in a phrase we use when anger, joy or enthusiasm cause us to exalt our condition as Mexicans: "*¡Viva México, hijos de la chingada!*" This phrase is a true battle cry, charged with a peculiar electricity; it is a challenge and an affirmation, a shot fired against an imaginary enemy, and an explosion in the air. Once again, with a certain pathetic and plastic fatality, we are presented with the image of a skyrocket that climbs into the sky, bursts in a shower of sparks and then falls in darkness. Or with the image of that howl that ends all our songs and possesses the same ambiguous resonance: an angry joy, a destructive affirmation ripping open the breast and consuming itself.

When we shout this cry on the fifteenth of September, the anniversary of our independence, we affirm ourselves in front of, against and in spite of the "others." Who are the "others"? They are the *hijos de la chingada*: strangers, bad Mexicans, our enemies, our rivals. In any case, the "others," that is, all those who are not as we are. And these "others" are not defined except as the sons of a mother as vague and indeterminate as themselves.

Who is the *Chingada?* Above all, she is the Mother. Not a Mother of flesh and blood but a mythical figure. The *Chingada* is one of the Mexican representations of Maternity, like *La Llorona* or the "long-suffering Mexican mother" we celebrate on the tenth of May.[1] The

---

[1] The "Weeping Woman," who wanders through the streets late at night, weeping and crying out. This belief, still current in some parts of Mexico, derives from pre-Conquest times, when "La Llorona" was the earth-goddess Cihuacóatl. The 10th of May is Mother's Day.—*Tr.*

Chingada is the mother who has suffered—metaphorically or actually—the corrosive and defaming action implicit in the verb that gives her her name. It would be worthwhile to examine that verb.

Darío Rubio, in his *Anarquía del lenguaje en la América Española*, examines the origins of *chingar* and enumerates the meanings given it by almost all Spanish-American people. It probably comes from the Aztecs: *chingaste* (lees, residue, sediment) is *xinachtli* (garden seed) or *xinaxtli* (fermented maguey juice). The word and its derivatives are used in most of America and parts of Spain in association with drinks, alcoholic or otherwise. In Guatemala and El Salvador *chingaste* means the residue or dregs that remain in a glass. In Oaxaca coffee lees are called *chingaditos*. Throughout Mexico alcohol is called *chínguere*—or, significantly, *piquete*.[2] In Chile, Peru and Ecuador a *chingana* is a tavern. In Spain *chingar* means to drink a great deal, to get drunk. In Cuba a *chinguirito* is a shot of alcohol.

Chingar also implies the idea of failure. In Chile and Argentina a petard *se chinga* when it fails to explode, and businesses that fail, fiestas that are rained out, actions that are not completed, also *se chingan*. In Colombia *chingarse* means to be disappointed. In Argentina a torn dress is a *vestido chingado*. Almost everywhere *chingarse* means to be made a fool of, to be involved in a fiasco. In some parts of South America *chingar* means to molest, to censure, to ridicule. It is always an aggressive verb, as can be seen in these further meanings: to dock an animal, to incite or prod a fighting-cock, to make merry, to crack a whip, to endanger, to neglect, to frustrate.

In Mexico the word has innumerable meanings. It is a magical word: a change of tone, a change of inflection, is enough to change its meaning. It has as many shadings as it has intonations, as many meanings as it has emotions. One may be a *chingón*, a *gran chingón* (in business, in politics, in crime or with women), or a *chingaquedito* (silent, deceptive, fashioning plots in the shadows, advancing cautiously and then striking with a club), or a *chingoncito*. But in this plurality of meanings the ultimate meaning always contains the idea of aggression, whether it is the simple act of molesting, pricking or censuring, or the violent act of wounding or killing. The verb denotes violence, an emergence from oneself to penetrate another by

[2]Literally, a bite, prick or sting; a picket or stake.—*Tr.*

force. It also means to injure, to lacerate, to violate—bodies, souls, objects—and to destroy. When something breaks, we say: *"Se chingó."* When someone behaves rashly, in defiance of the rules, we say: *"Hizo una chingadera."*

The idea of breaking, of ripping open, appears in a great many of these expressions. The word has sexual connotations but it is not a synonym for the sexual act: one may *chingar* a woman without actually possessing her. And when it does allude to the sexual act, violation or deception gives it a particular shading. The man who commits it never does so with the consent of the *chingada*. *Chingar*, then, is to do violence to another. The verb is masculine, active, cruel: it stings, wounds, gashes, stains. And it provokes a bitter, resentful satisfaction.

The person who suffers this action is passive, inert and open, in contrast to the active, aggressive and closed person who inflicts it. The *chingón* is the *macho*, the male; he rips open the *chingada*, the female, who is pure passivity, defenseless against the exterior world. The relationship between them is violent, and it is determined by the cynical power of the first and the impotence of the second. The idea of violence rules darkly over all the meanings of the word, and the dialectic of the "closed" and the "open" thus fulfills itself with an almost ferocious precision.

The magic power of the word is intensified by the fact that it is prohibited. No one uses it casually in public. Only an excess of anger or a delirious enthusiasm justifies its use. It is a word that can only be heard among men or during the big fiestas. When we shout it out, we break a veil of silence, modesty or hypocrisy. We reveal ourselves as we really are. The forbidden words boil up in us, just as our emotions boil up. When they finally burst out, they do so harshly, brutally, in the form of a shout, a challenge, an offense. They are projectiles or knives. They cause wounds.

The Spaniards also abuse their strongest expressions; indeed, the Mexican is singularly nice in comparison. But while the Spaniards enjoy using blasphemy and scatology, we specialize in cruelty and sadism. The Spaniard is simple: he insults God because he believes in Him. Blasphemy, as Machado wrote, is a prayer in reverse. The pleasure that many Spaniards, including some of their greatest poets, derive from allusions to body wastes, and from mix-

ing excrement with sacred matters, is reminiscent of children playing with mud. In addition to resentment, there is that delight in con-
trasts which produced the Baroque style and the drama of great
Spanish painting. Only a Spaniard can speak with authority about
Onan and Don Juan. In Mexican expressions, on the contrary, we
cannot find the Spanish duality that is symbolized by the opposition of the real and the ideal, the mystics and the picaresque he-
roes, the funereal Quevedo and the scatological Quevedo. What
we find is the dichotomy between the closed and the open. The
verb *chingar* signifies the triumph of the closed, the male, the powerful, over the open.

If we take into account all of its various meanings, the word
defines a great part of our life and qualifies our relationships
with our friends and compatriots. To the Mexican there are
only two possibilities in life: either he inflicts the actions im-
plied by *chingar* on others, or else he suffers them himself at the
hands of others. This conception of social life as combat fatally
divides society into the strong and the weak. The strong—the
hard, unscrupulous *chingones*—surround themselves with eager
followers. This servility toward the strong, especially among
the *políticos* (that is, the professionals of public business), is one
of the more deplorable consequences of the situation. Another,
no less degrading, is the devotion to personalities rather than
to principles. Our politicians frequently mix public business
with private. It does not matter. Their wealth or their influence
in government allows them to maintain a flock of supporters
whom the people call, most appositely, *lambiscones* (from the
word *lamer*: "to lick").

The verb *chingar*—malign and agile and playful, like a caged animal—creates many expressions that turn our world into a jungle:
there are tigers in business, eagles in the schools and the army, lions
among our friends. A bribe is called a "bite." The bureaucrats gnaw
their "bones" (public employment). And in a world of *chingones*, of
difficult relationships, ruled by violence and suspicion—a world in
which no one opens out or surrenders himself—ideas and accom-
plishments count for little. The only thing of value is manliness, personal strength, a capacity for imposing oneself on others.

The word also has another, more restricted meaning. When we

say, *"Vete a la chingada,"*[3] we send a person to a distant place. Distant, vague and indeterminate. To the country of broken and worn-out things. A gray country, immense and empty, that is not located anywhere. It is not only because of simple phonetic association that we compare it with China, for China is also immense and remote. The *chingada*, because of constant usage, contradictory meanings and the friction of angry or enthusiastic lips, wastes away, loses its contents and disappears. It is a hollow word. It says nothing. It is Nothingness itself.

After this digression, it is possible to answer the question, "What is the *Chingada?*" The *Chingada* is the Mother forcibly opened, violated or deceived. The *hijo de la Chingada* is the offspring of violation, abduction or deceit. If we compare this expression with the Spanish *hijo de puta* (son of a whore), the difference is immediately obvious. To the Spaniard, dishonor consists in being the son of a woman who voluntarily surrenders herself: a prostitute. To the Mexican it consists in being the fruit of a violation.

Manuel Cabrera points out that the Spanish attitude reflects a moral and historical conception of original sin, while that of the Mexican, deeper and more genuine, transcends both ethics and anecdotes. In effect, every woman—even when she gives herself willingly—is torn open by the man, is the *Chingada*. In a certain sense all of us, by the simple fact of being born of woman, are *hijos de la Chingada*, sons of Eve. But the singularity of the Mexican resides, I believe, in his violent, sarcastic humiliation of the Mother and his no less violent affirmation of the Father. A woman friend of mine (women are more aware of the strangeness of this situation) has made me see that this admiration for the Father—who is a symbol of the closed, the aggressive—expresses itself very clearly in a saying we use when we want to demonstrate our superiority: "I am your father." The question of origins, then, is the central secret of our anxiety and anguish. It is worth studying the significance of this fact.

We are alone. Solitude, the source of anxiety, begins on the day we are deprived of maternal protection and fall into a strange and hostile world. We have fallen, and this fall—this knowledge that

[3]Somewhat stronger than "Go to Hell."—*Tr.*

we have fallen—makes us guilty. Of what? Of a nameless wrong: that of having been born. These feelings are common to all men and there is nothing specifically Mexican in them. Therefore it is not necessary to repeat a description that has been given many times before. What *is* necessary is to isolate certain traits and emotions that cast a particular light on the universal condition of man.

In all civilizations, God the Father becomes an ambivalent figure once he has dethroned the feminine deities. On the one hand, the Father embodies the generative power, the origin of life, whether he be Jehovah, God the Creator, or Zeus, king of creation, ruler of the cosmos. On the other hand, he is the first principle, the One, from whom all is born and to whom all must return. But he is also the lord of the lightning bolt and the whip; he is the tyrant, the ogre who devours life. This aspect—angry Jehovah, God of wrath, or Saturn, or Zeus the violator of women—is the one that appears almost exclusively in Mexican representations of manly power. The *macho* represents the masculine pole of life. The phrase "I am your father" has no paternal flavor and is not said in order to protect or to guide another, but rather to impose one's superiority, that is, to humiliate. Its real meaning is no different from that of the verb *chingar* and its derivatives. The *macho* is the *gran chingón.* One word sums up the aggressiveness, insensitivity, invulnerability and other attributes of the *macho:* power. It is force without the discipline of any notion of order: arbitrary power, the will without reins and without a set course.

Unpredictability adds another element to the character of the *macho.* He is a humorist. His jokes are huge and individual, and they always end in absurdity. The anecdote about the man who "cured" the headache of a drinking companion by emptying his pistol into his head is well known. True or not, the incident reveals the inexorable rigor with which the logic of the absurd is introduced into life. The *macho* commits *chingaderas,* that is, unforeseen acts that produce confusion, horror and destruction. He opens the world; in doing so, he rips and tears it, and this violence provokes a great, sinister laugh. And in its own way, it is just: it re-establishes the equilibrium and puts things in their places, by reducing them to dust, to misery, to nothingness. The humor of the *macho* is an act of revenge.

A psychologist would say that resentment is the basis of his character. It would not be difficult to perceive certain homosexual inclinations also, such as the use and abuse of the pistol, a phallic symbol which discharges death rather than life, and the fondness for exclusively masculine guilds. But whatever may be the origin of these attitudes, the fact is that the essential attribute of the *macho*— power—almost always reveals itself as a capacity for wounding, humiliating, annihilating. Nothing is more natural, therefore, than his indifference toward the offspring he engenders. He is not the founder of a people; he is not a patriarch who exercises *patria potestas;* he is not a king or a judge or the chieftain of a clan. He is power isolated in its own potency, without relationship or compromise with the outside world. He is pure incommunication, a solitude that devours itself and everything it touches. He does not pertain to our world; he is not from our city; he does not live in our neighborhood. He comes from far away: he is always far away. He is the Stranger. It is impossible not to notice the resemblance between the figure of the *macho* and that of the Spanish conquistador. This is the model—more mythical than real—that determines the images the Mexican people form of men in power: caciques, feudal lords, hacienda owners, politicians, generals, captains of industry. They are all *machos, chingones.*

The *macho* has no heroic or divine counterpart. Hidalgo, the "father of the fatherland" as it is customary to call him in the ritual gibberish of the Republic, is a defenseless old man, more an incarnation of the people's helplessness against force than an image of the wrath and power of an awe-inspiring father. Among the numerous patron saints of the Mexicans there is none who resembles the great masculine divinities. Finally, there is no special veneration for God the Father in the Trinity. He is a dim figure at best. On the other hand, there is profound devotion to Christ as the Son of God, as the youthful God, above all as the victimized Redeemer. The village churches have a great many images of Jesus—on the cross, or covered with thorns and wounds—in which the insolent realism of the Spaniards is mingled with the tragic symbolism of the Indians. On the one hand, the wounds are flowers, pledges of resurrection; on the other, they are a reiteration that life is the sorrowful mask of death.

The fervor of the cult of God the Son would seem to be explained, at first glance, as an inheritance from the pre-Hispanic religions. When the Spaniards arrived, almost all of the great masculine divinities—with the exception of the rain-god Tláloc, a child and an old man at the same time, and a deity of greater antiquity—were sons of gods, like Xipe, god of the young corn, and Huitzilopochtli, the "Warrior of the South." Perhaps it is not idle to recall that the birth of Huitzilopochtli offers more than one analogy with that of Christ: he too was conceived without carnal contact; the divine messenger was likewise a bird (that dropped a feather into the lap of the earth-goddess Coatlicue); and finally, the infant Huitzilopochtli also had to escape the persecution of a mythical Herod. Nevertheless, it would be a mistake to use these analogies to explain that devotion to Christ, just as it would be to attribute that devotion to a mere survival of the cult of the sons of gods. The Mexican venerates a bleeding and humiliated Christ, a Christ who has been beaten by the soldiers and condemned by the judges, because he sees in him a transfigured image of his own identity. And this brings to mind Cuauhtémoc, the young Aztec emperor who was dethroned, tortured and murdered by Cortés.

Cuauhtémoc means "Falling Eagle." The Mexican chieftain rose to power at the beginning of the siege of México-Tenochtitlán, when the Aztecs had been abandoned by their gods, their vassals and their allies. Even his relationship with a woman fits the archetype of the young hero, at one and the same time the lover and the son of the goddess. Thus López Velarde wrote that Cuauhtémoc went out to meet Cortés—that is, to the final sacrifice—"separated from the curved breast of the Empress." He is a warrior but he is also a child. The exception is that the heroic cycle does not end with his death: the fallen hero awaits resurrection. It is not surprising that for the majority of Mexicans Cuauhtémoc should be the "young grandfather," the origin of Mexico: the hero's tomb is the cradle of the people. This is the dialectic of myth, and Cuauhtémoc is more a myth than a historical figure. Another element enters here, an analogy that makes this history a true poem in search of fulfillment: the location of Cuauhtémoc's tomb is not known. The mystery of his burial place is one of our obsessions. To discover it would mean nothing less than to return to our origins, to reunite ourselves with our ancestry, to break out of our solitude. It would be a resurrection.

If we ask about the third figure of the triad, the Mother, we hear a double answer. It is no secret to anyone that Mexican Catholicism is centered about the cult of the Virgin of Guadalupe. In the first place, she is an Indian Virgin; in the second place, the scene of her appearance to the Indian Juan Diego was a hill that formerly contained a sanctuary dedicated to Tonantzin, "Our Mother," the Aztec goddess of fertility. We know that the Conquest coincided with the apogee of the cult of two masculine divinities: Quetzalcóatl, the self-sacrificing god, and Huitzilopochtli, the young warrior-god. The defeat of these gods—which is what the Conquest meant to the Indian world, because it was the end of a cosmic cycle and the inauguration of a new divine kingdom—caused the faithful to return to the ancient feminine deities. This phenomenon of a return to the maternal womb, so well known to the psychologist, is without doubt one of the determining causes of the swift popularity of the cult of the Virgin. The Indian goddesses were goddesses of fecundity, linked to the cosmic rhythms, the vegetative processes and agrarian rites. The Catholic Virgin is also the Mother (some Indian pilgrims still call her Guadalupe-Tonantzin), but her principal attribute is not to watch over the fertility of the earth but to provide refuge for the unfortunate. The situation has changed: the worshipers do not try to make sure of their harvests but to find a mother's lap. The Virgin is the consolation of the poor, the shield of the weak, the help of the oppressed. In sum, she is the Mother of orphans. All men are born disinherited and their true condition is orphanhood, but this is particularly true among the Indians and the poor in Mexico. The cult of the Virgin reflects not only the general condition of man but also a concrete historical situation, in both the spiritual and material realms. In addition, the Virgin—the universal Mother—is also the intermediary, the messenger, between disinherited man and the unknown, inscrutable power: the Strange.

In contrast to Guadalupe, who is the Virgin Mother, the *Chingada* is the violated Mother. Neither in her nor in the Virgin do we find traces of the darker attributes of the great goddesses: the lasciviousness of Amaterasu and Aphrodite, the cruelty of Artemis and

Astarte, the sinister magic of Circe or the bloodlust of Kali. Both of them are passive figures. Guadalupe is pure receptivity, and the benefits she bestows are of the same order: she consoles, quiets, dries tears, calms passions. The *Chingada* is even more passive. Her passivity is abject: she does not resist violence, but is an inert heap of bones, blood and dust. Her taint is constitutional and resides, as we said earlier, in her sex. This passivity, open to the outside world, causes her to lose her identity: she is the *Chingada*. She loses her name; she is no one; she disappears into nothingness; she *is* Nothingness. And yet she is the cruel incarnation of the feminine condition.

Tlazolteotl

FRANCISCO X.
ALARCÓN

Goddess of Love
Goddess of Death
Eater of Filth
Mother of All Seasons:

Mother of the Rivers
cleanse him
with waters flowing
from the Fountain of Youth

Mother of the Hummingbirds
dry off his last tears
kiss each aching bone
dress him in morning flowers

Mother of the Mountains
caress him with murmurs
take him into your bosom
the dream of your deepest canyons

Mother of the Night
weep with us
light his path with the glow
of stars along the Milky Way

Mother of the Sea
embrace his ashes
turn him into bright red coral
amidst schools of laughing fish

Mother of All Season
Eater of Filth
Goddess of Death
Goddess of Love

Tlazolteotl!

"Don't Go Away, I'm Going to Bring You Something"

ELENA PONIATOWSKA

Translated by Deanna Heikkinen

*F*irst there is the smell, a smell that strikes the chest, reaches the heart and wounds it. Entering the nose, at that very instant, it makes its way, cutting like a knife, slicing the flesh; the blood begins to flow and rises through the throat.

—Come, come through here.

The jailer says it as if he were opening the doors to a palace. And he is. They call this jail the black palace of Lucumberri for a reason. From the highest ceilings, to the immense green metal walls, it has a regal bearing, especially when compared to the neighboring slums, those cardboard shacks level with the ground that gropingly look for something to lean against, an abandoned wall, a mountain of garbage that has finally become earth, an excavation site for the foundation of a building that was never constructed.

—Which ward do you want to go to first?

Seen from the sky, the jail is a star fallen onto the earth, a hellish star whose five points open so that the cells can line up; the rays of vigilance multiply out from the polygon and powerful beacons blind the prisoners.

—Do you want to go to F ward? It is where the fags are, laughs the jailer, who wears a cap, military uniform, glasses, a gold tooth, and insignias on his shoulders and his sleeves.

The wards correspond to the letters of the alphabet, the vowels and the consonants. The A, the E, the B, the F. F has been isolated. There are no cells there. What for? The prisoners all sleep together in long large rooms, their skinny beds lined up like in orphanages and nun's convents. There isn't even a curtain to protect their privacy. In spite of the fact that F has no doors, Luis Buñuel[1] stops as if to ask permission before entering. With shyness.

I stopped by for don Luis at eight o'clock in the morning. "Yes, yes, come early, I always get up at six." "Of course," said Jeanne, his wife, "it doesn't matter since he goes to bed at eight at night." He was already on the street waiting for me, a cigarette in his hand. From a distance I saw his black-and-white-tweed silhouette, his suit, all tweed, even the pants. He smiled his smile of separated teeth. I like men with spaces between their teeth.

Sunday is an empty day in Mexico. The people stay home. We reached the jail quickly even though I drove with special care. I wasn't about to have a wreck with Luis Buñuel at my side.

—I brought cigarettes, three packs, it seems to me that Mutis smokes.

—He reads even more. He reread all of Proust's works in jail.

—All of Proust? That's like reading all of Pérez Galdos! says Buñuel.

On Sundays the sidewalks in front of the jail become a fair. People bring baskets of tacos to sell, Coca-Colas, cakes and sweets. Among the booths, one with rosaries and holy cards, a full-length statue of San Martín de Porres with his broom, at one end, prayer leaflets are piled up. I pick up a leaflet off the ground that says in large print: "I renounce the world, I renounce the flesh, I renounce the Devil." Devil written with capitals. 496 Our Fathers, 958 Hail Marys, 379 Credos.

—The accounting of the Church, notes don Luis, who has lit a second cigarette.

We don't stop to buy anything.

Captain Sánchez has orders from the penal director, a little old man that I thought a very good person and answered to the name Martín de Campo, to receive don Luis with due respect. Alvaro Mutis has organized the "tour" of the fortress. We first go to the psychiatric ward which is the pride of the jail. They have all kinds of devices, among other things one for electric shock treatment. The walls of the ward are so white they seem to scatter chalk in the

---

[1] The Spaniard Luis Buñuel is one of the most noted filmmakers of the twentieth century, along with Ingmar Bergman and Federico Fellini.

air that burns when you breathe. "It is a first-rate hospital," assures Captain Sánchez, whose gold tooth shows when he smiles.

—We have a Spaniard here, he tells don Luis, who has not stopped lighting one cigarette after another.

—Oh really?

The Spaniard turns out to be a skinny man, a white sheet like tissue paper who pronounces "c" like "th" and rustles as if he were being folded. He treats Captain Sánchez with deference, almost as if paying court, and don Luis like a compatriot. He tells him that he was in the war in Spain, in Turuel, that he worked at the Workers' Hospital which was seized by the republicans under the orders of Dr. Juan Planelles. But he doesn't tell him why he is in Lecumberri. Later Sánchez will reveal to us that he killed his wife. Out of jealousy.

—Afterwards he lost his marbles. He doesn't cause any major problems here, we're talking about a calm man; since he is a doctor and knows a lot, he treats those that end up in the psychiatric ward.

Upon leaving, we run into the "population," as Captain Sánchez calls them; men that circulate to the right and return from the left, they pass through the polygon from one ward to the other walking hurriedly, as if they had much to do. We greet a man among them who is taller than the rest, dressed in navy blue, his army cap on just so. Sánchez becomes excited:

—You must see his cell.

We walk toward the green metal cell. The prisoner opens it with pride. A tangle of cables and plugs hang from the ceiling. A crowd of televisions and radios, domestic appliances; blenders, mixers, irons, and dryers fill the metal shelves that look like a child's Erector Set.

—He's our electrician, Sánchez says proudly.

—How nice!

We say good-bye, congratulate him, and again say good-bye.

—Do you know who you just met? asks Sánchez with even more enthusiasm.

—Who? asks don Luis mechanically.

—Ramón Mercader, the one that killed Trotsky, a famous case, haven't you heard of it?

Don Luis, who already is very bug-eyed, looks like his eyes are going to pop out of his head.

—Jacques Mornard or Ramón Mercader?

—His real name is Ramón. He took the other name you just said. . . . Oh, look, there comes Siqueiros with the bag of stuff!

David Alfaro Siqueiros is carrying a plastic bag with the provisions that his wife, Angélica Arenal, brings every day. We go from one surprise to the next, from one emotion to another, most of all when Siqueiros speaks to us, pointing to his cell:

—I have my studio in the next one. Do you want to see the portrait I'm painting in memory of Alfonso Reyes for the Colegio Nacional?

In the center of the green metal walls, on a lectern, don Alfonso smiles playfully. He looks like a satyr with his white curly hair and his inciting smile.

—A very good portrait, Siqueiros, a very good portrait.

—Coming from you, Maestro, it is a compliment that fills me with satisfaction.

At the back of the cell-studio, Angélica has placed the bag on the table and removes the paintbrushes, the palette, the turpentine, the linseed oil, the tubes of oil paints.

—Would you like to eat with us?, she asks mundanely.

—No thank you, Buñel says hastily. We are visiting the prison and the tour hasn't ended yet.

Food is discussed a lot in prisons and in hospitals.

We have one encounter yet to make. It is afforded by Siqueiros.

—Look, that person walking over there is Fatso Lepe.

—Who?

—Fatso Lepe, the father of Ana Berta Lepe, the actress, the one who killed her lover. You don't know what a riot it creates when Ana Berta comes to visit her father. All the prisoners whistle, yell, howl. Even though she wears dark glasses and a silk scarf on her head, they recognize her by her walk.

—Is she a good daughter?

—Besides being a good lay she is a very good daughter (Siqueiros allows himself to say).

Siqueiros is a wonderful conversationalist. He goes on to tell about the screaming. He says that every time a new prisoner enters the jail, the others howl, yell from behind the bars: "The lioness just gave birth!"

After wishing Siqueiros *bon appétit,* we finally go to F, an open ward. Every time we pass from one ward to another, the guards come to attention to salute Captain Sánchez. Every time the gigantic gates open and close, the double chains that hold the rails closed resonate. It is a reminder.

—Enter, enter, Ramona tells us with an enveloping gesture.

In reality he is the major, his name is Ramón, but everyone calls him "Ramona." He tells us that this morning they were forced to take the makeup off their faces, to take off their frilly blouses, their brassieres, their skirts, their pumps, and to put on prison uniforms.

—Here we can go around dressed as we please, Ramona informs us. One individual who didn't want to take off his makeup was put in solitary confinement.

—What is that?

—The punishment cell.

—Where is it?

—Right there. That is solitary.

We walk toward a metal cage painted green. From the looks of things, everything here is green, but not the green of hope.

—Where is the person being punished? asks Buñuel.

—In there, he must be squatting down, yell to him so that he gets up.

Buñuel calls:

—Friend.

Since no one answers he calls out again.

—Friend.

The man must have heard something in his voice, because he responds. He shows his bloody face through the bars of the diminutive opening.

—What happened to you, friend?

—They washed my face with a brick.

Buñuel passes him a pack of cigarettes.

You have to obey, my friend, otherwise look at the consequences.

Don Luis speaks Mexican. If he could he would get into the

solitary cell in place of the prisoner. Standing in front of the cell he inquires:

—When are they going to let him out?

—When visiting hours are over.

—What time is that?

—At five in the afternoon, Ramona informs him.

Captain Sánchez offers:

—If you want, out of consideration for you, we will take him out right now.

—Take him out, Buñuel orders, showing the spaces between his teeth.

Men are sponges full of blood, flesh, rags. This one that comes out of the punishment cell is a loose sack on the verge of fainting. Captain Sánchez explains:

—That one always has a bad time of it because he never wants to do chores. Chores are the prisoners' work. In the morning, they must throw bucketfuls of water on the floors to wash them, scrub the ward floors, and keep the jail clean. Those are their chores.

We move through the large barrack to the rear, under the gaze of the prisoners. On the headboard of each iron cot is a Virgin of Guadalupe, some other saint, or the photograph of a woman. His mother? Captain Sánchez explains: "It is them dressed as women." At the back of the ward an impressive altar awaits us. In green, white, and red lights hangs a life-size picture of the Virgin of Guadalupe, as big as the one at the basilica under the hill in Tepeyac. An abundance of red satin falls from the ceiling to the floor. Even Versailles falls short of such luxury with such generous amounts of fabric. At the feet of the Virgin a multitude of votive candles remind one of the scene from the film *Macario* by Gabriel Figueroa and Emilio Fernández. To one side hang plaques, offerings, altarpieces, with stories written in Palmer handwriting with spelling mistakes, the "miracles," gifts of gratitude, the marvels that certify the celestial character of the Virgin and of her well-timed intervention.

—Has she gotten freedom for many?

—Not that, but she has saved many from dying here.

Ramona removes the military cap and makes the sign of the cross. Captain Sánchez also takes off his cap and holds it to his chest.

—She has performed many miracles for us, insists Ramona.

—She has prevented several crimes here, confirms captain Sánchez, she saved Cuco's life when the Three Cains from Tepeyac had already gotten hold of him.

—From Tepeyac? The home of the Virgin of Guadalupe?

—Yes, that is what those killers call themselves, can you believe it, Mr. Buñuel?

We contemplate the miracle maker, whose eyes appear to blink in the candlelight.

I suppose that not dying here inside is miracle enough. I am at the point of falling to my knees. I barely hear Ramona explain:

—She made four appearances before filling Juan Diego's apron with roses.

The jail now smells of boiled meat and Captain Sánchez explains what "the ranch" is, the food that we are about to eat, cooked over a slow fire in gigantic pots.

—Why don't you stay to see how well the Mexican prisoners eat? That's why the rabbits commit crimes again and again. They never eat as well out there as they do here inside. What's more, they return hungry.

—The rabbits?

—That's what we call repeat offenders. What do you say? Will you stay?

Don Luis doesn't know how to say no: he would die of shame before not accepting.

—You'll excuse me if I don't join you, says Captain Sánchez, but today is Sunday and the only day of the week that I eat with my family. You know what they say, the jailer is just as confined as the prisoner. Yes, eat, you must eat in A because it is the best ward.

—Let's go to A.

Under the merciless sun we sit with our plates, which are divided into compartments like in the army. The rice is here, the greens here, the meat here, the soup here, the beans here. As I claim to love broth, a quick and smiling rabbit brings me a full soup bowl.

On the plate, the pewter spoon runs aground on an obstruction the size of the Rock of Gibraltar (I say that although I don't have the slightest idea what the Rock of Gibraltar is like).

Don Luis comes over.

—What is that?

—It is a bone, says the rabbit that is serving us. Let me have it for just a minute, I'll be right back. You go ahead and eat peacefully.

He politely puts his thumb and his index finger into the broth and takes out a respectable-sized bone. The bowl is left almost empty.

—Can I serve you some more?

—No thank you.

—Okay, I'll be right back, I won't be long at all! he says happily, the white bone between his fingers.

Standing in front of the rails, he insists, with a big smile:

—Don't go away, I'm going to bring you something.

The bread is delicious. Don Luis dunks his into the broth. We talk about the bread, about how good it is, about how there isn't bread like this on the outside; we insist on the advantages to make those who listen to us think that they are all right, that everything is bad outside, that this time of bread, just like the bread, is nourishing, crusty, protected, warmed by the sun. Mutis looks the other way. Then don Luis goes on to ask his Buñuelesque questions; he asks if there are rats, how many and what their names are, what kind they are, how many rats could there be? If there are rat paw prints, and they tell him yes, in the loose dirt in the patio where the prisoners play soccer you can see little rat feet clearly outlined on the ground, ask the jailers to show them to you. Later they tell him no, you hardly ever hear birds because there aren't any trees, but you can hear airplanes a lot, there are many many planes around here, you see we are close to the airport. I think, what a nightmare to be a prisoner and to hear flying, the humming of aerial motors, of any motor that comes into sight, and to see the metal wings and the red lights on the ends of the wings at night. One prisoner knows the cartography of the sky by heart: the takeoff and the landing of the planes, the interval between them. That is how he spends his time. They should hire him at the control tower.

The question mark in don Luis's eyes never disappears. He hears like the deaf, with his eyes. He listens to questions and he

asks questions between each puff on his cigarette, one of the last
that are left because he has given all the rest away.

—Too bad I didn't bring more. If I had known . . .

—Next time.

Don Luis doesn't answer.

As we are about to leave, I hear the voice of someone almost
out of breath:

—Miss, miss . . .

It's the rabbit who served the soup.

—Look what I have . . .

He reaches us and puts something star-shaped in my hand.

—What is that? asks don Luis with suspicion.

—It's our little Mother . . . I made it.

—What do you mean you made it?

—Yes, with the bone. Have you already forgotten about the
bone?

An ivory Chinese carving from the Ming dynasty could not
have caused greater amazement. In the palm of my hand I hold the
Virgin of Guadalupe in her starry robe, her feet on the moon, a halo
of well-defined points around her body, her downcast eyes, her thin
brows, and her brown complexion. Stunned with emotion I ask:

—But who is it?

—Our little brownie, she is the Mother of all Mexicans, she is
your Mother, blondie, the Mother of all of us.

—How wonderful!

—The Empress of America! The rabbit shows his red gums.

—But how did you make it?

—It just took a little time.

—You are a master! You haven't left out a single detail, look,
you even carved the little angel at her feet.

The rabbit doesn't stop smiling. I have a little dove in my
hands, a round dove. I had never thought of the Virgin's roundness,
of her fluid shoulders, a little bulky, of her embracing arms. This
Virgin is round. She fills out her dress, her breast lifts it, at the elbows the fabric folds, it is frayed at the hem. I always thought that
every part of the Virgin of Guadalupe had to be painted with
curlicued spirals of leaves and stems on her gown, gold stars on her

navy-blue robe, but it turns out that under all that stiff clothing beats a heart. This little dove throbs, her knee pushes forward and the step she takes hollows out her skirt. I imagine her thighs, her womb, the strength of her left leg.

—Incredible! You are a master, I repeat.

Don Luis becomes absorbed in thought. He raises the sculpture to his eyes, he examines it, he smiles almost, as delighted as the rabbit himself.

—You should show this to Siqueiros.

Don Luis's fervor has no limits. It was his fervor that made him conceive The Hague, San Simón el Estilista, Nazarín, Viridiana, Silvia Pinal with Christ's beard and other sacrileges. This fervor compelled him to tell me on another occasion that as an adolescent he would masturbate in front of the sculpture of the Virgin in her grotto at the altar at Lourdes in the garden of the school, which scandalized many readers. Now, in his strong drumming Calanda hands he holds the patron of New Spain, the Queen of the Heavens who favored Mexico above all other nations. *Non fecit taliter omni nationi,* the accomplice of Father Hidalgo and all the flag-bearing revolutionaries, the comfort of the mortals.

—Her pose is that of the Immaculate Conception, don Luis reflects, and he blows smoke from his last cigarette of the day in her face.

The Virgin shields herself behind lowered eyelids. She feels nothing, she says nothing. We say good-bye. I hug the rabbit. I ask his name. Andrés Martínez. I tell him that I will come some Sunday, not the next one but the following, or maybe the last one of the month, it all depends. No, don Luis will not return. He is going on a trip. The Atlantic, yes. Maybe next year. The rabbit advises that Mutis suffers badly from depression. He shouldn't be forgotten. Most likely they will release him soon. Really? It all depends. You must come. Of course, once you know the way it is much easier to return to the black palace of Lecumberri.

We pull out and a fine rain begins to fall on the windshield, the kind that doesn't usually bless Mexico, because here everything is violent and when it rains it pours. Maybe because we have just seen the Spaniard in the psychiatric ward, don Luis talks of the civil war and of how an anarchist from Aragon gave the order in the plaza to practice free love. No one knew what he was talking about, imagine in Calanda. It occurred to one person who did know what he was talking about to carry out the order; the woman on the street frightened him with her screams. Later, from the balcony of his house in Calanda, the governor of Aragon, yes, Mantecón, who later came to Mexico, the one we all know, told them not to bother with love because war was more important.

Don Luis doesn't seem to notice that he doesn't have any more cigarettes and goes on to tell me about Edward James, the one with the marvelous garden in Xilitla, the Englishman that they say is the son of the king. He wanted to give the republicans a bomber. Of course he had the money. He had already bought all of Dalí's paintings from that year, 1938. Instead he attempted to organize an exposition of the masterpieces from the Prado throughout the rest of Europe, under the auspices of the International Tribunal of The Hague. Álvarez del Vayo refused.

The Virgin of Guadalupe travels on my lap and performs the miracle of prolonging the journey by making all the stoplights red. This prompts don Luis to tell me how some anarchist workers formed a firing squad; they put a large, tall Sacred Heart Virgin in a truck and executed her at the side of the road between Madrid and Toledo. There isn't a more blasphemous people than the Spanish, he says. They carry this irreverence in their blood. The Mexicans' "fuck you" is tame compared to the language the Spanish use. They have made an art of blasphemy. Buñuel smiles his saintly profane smile of separated teeth in his almost shaved head. I ask him to tell me some other curses.

—Here inside and with the Virgin of Guadalupe?

On the windshield, the rain has become ever finer. When don Luis gets out of the VW it is no longer raining. I see him through the glass standing on the sidewalk. He smiles. I can't see his teeth. Above all else, I look at his beautiful solid ascetic head. Around his face, the Virgin of Guadalupe has created a triple-layered rainbow from the water droplets. Watercolors emanate from it in pale hues, but nevertheless I can discern: green, white, and red.

Notes on the Contributors

FRANCISCO X. ALARCÓN, Chicano poet and educator, has published nine collections of poetry, most recently *No Golden Gate for Us* and *Snake Poems: An Aztec Invocation*, and has been the recipient of several awards, including The American Book Award 1993, the 1993 PEN Oakland Josephine Miles Award, and the 1994 Chicano Literary Prize. He teaches at the University of California at Davis.

LUIS ALFARO is a gay Chicano who was born and raised in the Pico-Union district of downtown Los Angeles. He is a resident artist/director at the Mark Taper Forum theater and an instructor in the Writer's Program of UCLA Extension. He works primarily in poetry, performance, playwriting, and journalism, and curates numerous literary and performance programs throughout Los Angeles.

GLORIA ANZALDÚA is the author of *La Frontera/Borderlands: The New Mestiza*, a collection of memoirs, essays, poetry, and folklore, and the author of two children's books. Along with Cherríe Moraga, she is the coeditor of the anthology *This Bridge Called My Back: Writings by Radical Women of Color* (recipient of the Before Columbus Foundation's American Book Award), and the editor of *Haciendo Caras/Making Face, Making Soul: Creative and Critical Perspectives by Feminists of Color*.

RONNIE BURK is the author of two chapbooks of surrealist poetry, *En El Jardin de los Nopales*, and *Father of Reason, Daughter of Doubt*. His poetry has appeared in recent issues of *Caliban, Cafe Review, Exquisite Corpse, Ignite, Night, Mesenchabe*, and *Verbal Abuse*.

Writer, diplomat, and feminist ROSARIO CASTELLANOS was emerging as one of Mexico's major literary figures before her untimely death in 1974. Her poetry, short fiction, essays, and a three-act play, *The Eternal*

Feminine, are brought together in *The Rosario Castellanos Reader.* Translator Maureen Ahern is coeditor of *Homenaje a Rosario Castellanos* and a professor of Spanish at the Ohio State University.

DENISE CHÁVEZ is a native of Las Cruces, New Mexico. She is the author of *Face of an Angel* (winner of the 1995 American Book Award), and the one-woman show, *Women in the State of Grace.* Chávez is a Visiting Professor of Creative Writing at the New Mexico State University in Las Cruces, as well as Artistic Director for the Border Book Festival, a regional book fair based in southern New Mexico and serving the border corridor. Chávez is at work on her second novel, *Loving Pedro Infante.*

SANDRA CISNEROS is the author of three works of fiction, *The House on Mango Street, Woman Hollering Creek and Other Stories,* and *Hairs/Pelitos,* a children's book. Her books of poetry include *Bad Boys, My Wicked Wicked Ways,* and *Loose Woman.* She is the recipient of the Before Columbus Foundation's American Book Award, a Lannan Foundation Literary Award, the PEN Center West Award for the best fiction of 1991, and the Quality Paperback Book Club New Voices Award, in addition to a MacArthur Foundation Fellowship. She is at work on a novel, *Caramelo.*

Born in Mexico City in 1943, FELIPE EHRENBERG trained first as a printer then as a visual and graphic artist, though he is perhaps best known as a book artist and the cofounder of the Beau Geste Press. Ehrenberg has held over sixty one-person shows and has participated in nearly two hundred major groups shows around the world. A selected anthology of his newspaper columns, *Broken Glasses and the Eye That Looks at Them,* was published by Mexico's Consejo Nacional para la Cultura y las Artes.

CLARISSA PINKOLA ESTÉS, PH.D., a practicing Católica, was consecrated to Our Lady at age seven and is a lifetime devotee. She is an activist, award-winning poet, Jungian psychoanalyst, and the author of *Women Who Run with the Wolves.* Dr. Estés heads La Sociedad de Nuestra Señora Guadalupe, a spritual and human rights educational organization. Her forthcoming books are *The Dangerous Old Woman* and *La Pasionara,* both from Alfred A. Knopf.

ROSARIO FERRÉ was born in 1938 in Ponce, Puerto Rico. She is the author of *Papeles de Pandora, Sitio a Eros, Fábulas de la garza desangrada, Maldito Amor, Sweet Diamond Dust, The Youngest Doll,* and *The House on the Lagoon,* which was nominated for the National Book Award in 1995.

FRANCISCO GOLDMAN'S first novel, *The Long Night of White Chickens*, won the Sue Kaufman Prize for First Fiction from the American Academy of Arts and Letters and was a PEN/Faulkner finalist. His new novel, *The Ordinary Seaman*, will be published in 1997. Goldman covered Central America throughout the 1980s as a contributing editor for *Harper's* and other publications.

Born and raised in Mexico City, interdisciplinary artist/writer GUIL-LERMO GÓMEZ-PEÑA came to the United States in 1978. Since then he has been exploring cross-cultural issues and North-South relations through performance, bilingual poetry, journalism, video, radio, and installation art. A 1991 recipient of a MacArthur Fellowship, he has contributed to the national radio magazines *Crossroads* (1987–1990) and *Latino USA*, and is a contributing editor at *High Performance* and *The Drama Review*. He is the author of *Warrior for Gringostroika*, a collection of essays and performance texts, and *The New World Border*.

F. GONZALEZ-CRUSSI is a professor of pathology at Northwestern University Medical School, and head of Laboratories at the Children's Memorial Hospital in Chicago. Born in Mexico City, he received a medical degree from the National Autonomous University of Mexico (1961) and obtained post-graduate training in the United States. He pursued a career in academic medicine in Canada and the United States, and turned to writing as a means of examining this experience. His books include *Notes of an Anatomist*, *The Five Senses*, *On the Nature of Things Erotic*, *The Day of the Dead*, and *Suspended Animation*.

NANCY MAIRS is the author of a spiritual autobiography, *Ordinary Time*; a memoir, *Remembering the Bone House: An Erotics of Place and Space*; two collections of essays, *Plaintext* and *Carnal Acts*; and a volume of poetry, *In All the Rooms of the Yellow House*. Her most recent book is *Voice Lessons: On Becoming a (Woman) Writer*.

RUBÉN MARTÍNEZ is the author of *The Other Side: Notes from the New L.A., Mexico City and Beyond*. A poet, journalist, and performer, he is an editor at Pacific News Service. He is currently working on his second book, a journey into the heart of Mexico's cultural and political crisis.

PAT MORA has written three books of poetry, numerous children's books, and a book of nonfiction, *Nepantla: Essays from the Land in the Middle*.

CHERRÍE MORAGA is a poet, playwright, editor, and essayist. A founding editor of Kitchen Table: Women of Color Press, she is the coeditor (with Gloria Anzaldúa) of *This Bridge Called My Back: Writings by Radical Women of Color* and other anthologies. Moraga has been the recipient of fellowships from the National Endowment for the Arts and the Fund for New American Plays. She has taught at the University of California at Berkeley for several years.

Recipient of the 1982 Neustadt Prize for Literature, Mexican poet and essayist OCTAVIO PAZ is one of the world's foremost writers. He served as a Mexican diplomat in France and Japan, and as Mexican Ambassador to India before resigning from the diplomatic service in protest of the Tlatelolco massacre in 1968. *The Labyrinth of Solitude: Life and Thought in Mexico* is his best-known work.

Novelist, essayist, and journalist, ELENA PONIATOWSKA was the first woman to win Mexico's prestigious National Journalism Award. Her works include the novella *Dear Diego;* an account of the Mexican student revolts of 1968, *La Noche de Tlatelolco;* the novels *Husta No Verte, Jesus Mio,* and the bestselling *La Flor de Lis;* and a novel on the life of Tina Modotti, *Tinissima.*

MARGARET RANDALL is a writer, photographer, and political activist who lived in Mexico for eight years in the 1960s. Among her most recent titles are *Sandino's Daughters Revisited; Our Voices, Our Lives: Stories of Women from Central America and the Caribbean; The Price You Pay: The Hidden Cost of Women's Relationship to Money;* and *Hunger's Table,* a new collection of her poetry.

JEANETTE RODRIGUEZ is an assistant professor at the Institute for Theological Studies at Seattle University. She holds a Ph.D. from the Graduate Theological Union.

LUIS J. RODRÍGUEZ is the author of *Always Running: La Vida Loca, Gang Days in L.A.* and the recipient of a Lannan Foundation Fellowship. He is a founder of the organization Youth Struggling for Survival in Chicago and an elder-teacher in a number of multicultural men's retreats organized by the Mosaic Foundation. He is the director of Tia Lucha Press, a publisher of cross-cultural, society-engaged poetry.

RICHARD RODRIGUEZ is the author of *Hunger of Memory.* He works as an editor at The Pacific News Service in San Francisco and is a contributing editor for *Harper's* and the Sunday "Opinion" section of the *Los Angeles Times* and a regular contributor to the *MacNeil/Lehrer NewsHour*.

MIRIAM SAGAN'S poetry collections include *Aegean Doorway; Acequia Madre: Through the Mother Ditch; True Body; Pocahontas Discovers America;* and *The Art of Love: New and Selected Poems*. She is the author of a novel, *Coastal Lives,* and two books for children.

LUISAH TEISH, author of *Carnival of the Spirit: Seasonal Celebrations and Rites of Passage* and *Jambalaya: The Natural Woman's Book of Personal Charms and Practical Rituals,* is a storyteller, actress, dancer-choreographer, teacher, writer, spiritual advisor, and ritual leader. Born in New Orleans, Teish is a priestess of Oshun in the Yoruba Lucumi (African tradition). A feminist activist, Teish's essays on women have been collected in several anthologies, including *Take Back the Night,* and *Homegirls*.

LILIANA VALENZUELA was born in Mexico City in 1960 and moved to Texas fifteen years ago. A poet, writer, and literary translator, she was awarded the Chicano Literary Prize from the University of California at Irvine, for her fiction. Valenzuela's poetry and stories have appeared in various anthologies and journals, including *Entre Guadalupe y Malinche: A Tejana Anthology of Literature and Art*.

Permissions

About the Editor

ANA CASTILLO is the author of the novels *The Mixquiahuala Letters*, *Sapogonia*, and *So Far from God*; a collection of poetry, *My Father Was a Toltec and Selected Poems 1973–1988*; a collection of short stories, *Loverboys*; and *Massacre of the Dreamers: Essays on Xicanisma*, among other works. She has received an American Book Award, a Carl Sandburg Award, a Mountains and Plains Booksellers Award, and fellowships from the National Endowment for the Arts in fiction and poetry. Castillo lives in Chicago with her son, Marcel.